FOUNDATIONS

New Testament

A 260-DAY BIBLE READING PLAN FOR *Teen Girls*

Kandi Gallaty

LIFEWAY PRESS®
BRENTWOOD, TENNESSEE

**EDITORIAL TEAM,
STUDENT MINISTRY PUBLISHING**

Ben Trueblood
Director, Student Ministry

John Paul Basham
*Manager, Student Ministry
Publishing*

Karen Daniel
Editorial Team Leader

Kate Michaelsen
Content Specialist

Amanda Mejias
Content Editor

Amy Lyon
Graphic Designer

Published by Lifeway Press®
© 2020 Replicate Ministries
Reprinted Jan. 2023

ISBN 978-1-0877-4058-4
Item 005831314

Dewey decimal classification: 225.07
Subject headings: BIBLE. N.T.—STUDY
AND TEACHING / DISCIPLESHIP /
CHRISTIAN LIFE

Unless otherwise noted, all Scripture
quotations are taken from the Christian
Standard Bible®, Copyright © 2017
by Holman Bible Publishers. Used by
permission. Christian Standard Bible® and
CSB® are federally registered trademarks
of Holman Bible Publishers.

To order additional copies of this resource,
write to Lifeway Church Resources
Customer Service; 200 Powell Place, Suite
100, Brentwood, TN 37027; order online
at www.lifeway.com; fax 615.251.5933;
phone toll free 800.458.2772; or email
orderentry@lifeway.com.

Printed in the United States of America.

Student Ministry Publishing
Lifeway Church Resources
200 Powell Place, Suite 100
Brentwood, TN 37027

Contents

KANDI GALLATY has been investing in the lives of women for over a decade. She believes there are three major sources to draw from when investing in the lives of others: God's Word, God's work in one's life, and God's Spirit. She's passionate about cultivating a biblical worldview from the truths of Scripture and about teaching women how to steward the life experiences and lessons God has allowed in their lives. Together, Kandi and Robby lead Replicate Ministries. Kandi loves being a pastor's wife and serving alongside her husband at Long Hollow Baptist Church. Kandi and Robby are the proud and thankful parents of two boys, Rig and Ryder. Kandi is the author of *Disciple Her: Using the Word, Work, and Wonder of God to Invest in Women* (B&H, 2019) and the coauthor with Robby of *Foundations: A 260-Day Bible Reading Plan for Busy Believers* (Lifeway, 2015).

I am thrilled to be able to offer a Foundations Bible reading plan specifically for teen girls! The Lord has so much to say to you and teach you. I am beyond excited to share this resource with you to assist you in spending time with God as you read your Bible. I truly believe there is no greater discipline that will affect your life like the reading and applying of God's Word.

When considering spiritual disciplines, Bible engagement rises to the top. Many, if not all other disciplines flow from the time we spend in the Scriptures. The earlier we can learn and implement this, the more impact it will have on our lives. It will endure through the years, and enhance our journey as we follow after Christ.

As you read through this plan, you will be encouraged to journal what you HEAR from the Lord. Writing helps you to remember and retain what you have read and more importantly it allows you to focus in on a few things that God is showing you. The goal is to apply what you hear to your life today. James 1:22 tells us "But be doers of the word and not hearers only, deceiving yourselves." You will not be transformed into the image of Christ by information alone. You will be transformed by learning and applying what you read to your life.

I encourage you to pray before you read each day. Psalm 119:18-19 are two verses I have prayed for years before I read and journal.

"Open my eyes so that I may contemplate wondrous things from your instruction. II am a resident alien on earth; do not hide your commands from me."

Keep in mind, as you are reading, that a light bulb doesn't have to go off each and every day. Approach the Bible with the mindset that yes God will speak to you, but you are also learning about God. You are learning who He is, what He has done, and how He works in and through mankind.

The Word will always speak. It is living and active which means it is doing something. It is not stale or stagnant. It is the very breath of God to you! The time you spend with God will never be wasted but will accomplish the purpose God intends.

I pray for you as you begin this plan to develop a love and a passion for the Word that increases each and every year. I pray that as you learn God's Word that it will form the basis of all your thoughts and decisions. I pray that your relationship with your heavenly Father will grow and you will know you are loved beyond what you can even imagine. I pray that the Lord will bless you and keep you and make his face to shine upon you and be gracious to you, and may He lift up His countenance and give you peace (Num. 6:24-26).

I would love to pray for you as you begin this journey.

Lord,
I pray for each sweet girl who picks up this plan and reads through your Word. May this journey be rich with Your blessings and powerful with Your truths. I ask that You speak through Your Spirit and reveal to her what You want her to hear each time she opens the Bible. Guide her on this journey and may she be forever changed because of it.

Blessings and love to you,

How Do I Log a HEAR Journal Entry? The HEAR journal helps you read the Bible in a way that can change your life. No longer will you focus on checking off boxes on your daily reading schedule; instead, you'll be reading in order to understand and respond to God's Word.

HEAR stands for highlight, explain, apply, and respond. It's all about creating an atmosphere where you can hear God speak. God can speak to us anywhere: on the bus, between classes, in our bedrooms, or waiting to pick up our little brothers from practice. But we have to be listening. If you can commit to finding a consistent time to read Scripture and focus on what God has to say, you'll be ready to hear from Him.

Here's how it works. Say you're about to start 2 Timothy. Before reading the day's text, pause to sincerely ask God to speak to you. It may seem trite, but it's absolutely imperative that we seek God's guidance in order to understand His Word (see 1 Cor. 2:12-14). Every time we open our Bibles, we should pray the simple prayer David prayed:

Open my eyes so that I may contemplate wondrous things from your instruction [Word] (Ps. 119:18).

After praying for the Holy Spirit's guidance, open your book or journal and in the upper left-hand corner write the letter H. This will remind you to read with a purpose. As you read, one or two verses may speak to you. After reading the passage of Scripture, highlight each verse that speaks to you by copying it under the letter H. Record the following.

- The name of the book
- The passage of Scripture
- The chapter and verse numbers that especially speak to you
- A title to describe the passage

Next, write the letter E. Here, you'll explain what the text means. By asking some simple questions, with the help of God's Spirit, you can understand the meaning of a passage or verse. Here are a few questions to keep in mind.

- Why was this text written?
- To whom was it originally written?
- How does this text fit with the verses before and after it?
- Why did the Holy Spirit include this passage in the book?
- What does the Holy Spirit intend to communicate through this text?

At this point you're beginning the process of discovering the specific, personal word God has for you from His Word. You're engaging with the text and wrestling with its meaning—reading the Bible the way it was meant to be read.

After writing a short summary of what you think the text means, next write the letter A. Beneath it, write apply. This application is the heart of the process. Everything you've done so far culminates under this heading. Again, answer a series of questions to uncover how these verses affect your life personally, questions like:

- What does this text teach me about God?
- What does this passage mean today?
- What would the application of this passage look like in my life?
- Does the text identify an action or attitude to avoid or embrace?
- What is God saying to me?

Challenge yourself to write between two and five sentences about how the text applies to your life. These questions are important—they bring the words to life. The Bible is a living, breathing book, meant to be woven into our day-to-day lives. This section will show you the way.

Finally, below the first three entries, write the letter R, for respond. Your response to the passage may take on many forms. You might describe how you'll be different because of what you learned. You might write a prayer to God, the name of a person to pray for, or a friend who needs to hear the gospel.

You can see an example of a HEAR entry on page 270. Notice that all of the words in the HEAR formula are action words: highlight, explain, apply, and respond. God doesn't want us to sit back and wait for Him to drop truth into our laps. He wants us to actively pursue Him. Jesus said:

> *Keep asking, and it will be given to you. Keep searching, and you will find. Keep knocking, and the door will be opened to you (Matt. 7:7).*

Think of the miracle of the Bible. Over centuries, God supernaturally led multitudes of people to write down the exact words of God. He led them to recognize that these words were divine, different from anything else that has ever been written. God's people brought these sixty-six books together and preserved them, an act almost as miraculous as its writing. Finally, God gave His people, starting with Gutenberg and his printing press, the technological knowledge to copy and transmit the Bible so that all people could have it. All because God has something to say to you.

SAMPLE HEAR ENTRY

READ: Philippians 4:10-13
DATE: 12/22/20
TITLE: The Secret of Contentment

HIGHLIGHT

"I am able to do all things through Him who strengthens me" (Phil. 4:13).

EXPLAIN

Paul was telling the church at Philippi that he had discovered the secret of contentment. No matter the situation in Paul's life, he realized that Christ was all he needed, and Christ was the One who strengthened him to persevere through difficult times.

APPLY

In my life I will experience many ups and downs. My contentment isn't found in circumstances. Rather, it's based on my relationship with Jesus Christ. Only Jesus gives me the strength I need to be content in every circumstance of life.

RESPOND

Lord Jesus, please help me as I strive to be content in You. Through Your strength I can make it through any situation I must face.

Memorizing the Word

The Bible isn't only meant to be read—it's meant to be remembered. Each week provides three options to help you memorize Scripture. Options 1 and 2 come from Psalms and Proverbs, while option 3 is a one-year plan to memorize Jesus' Sermon on the Mount. Choose one of the three options or mix them up however you like.

There are lots of ways to memorize Scripture, but my method is simple. All you need are a pack of index cards and a committed desire to memorize God's Word. It's easy. Write the verse reference on one side of the card and the text of the verse on the other. Focus on memorizing five verses at a time and carry your pack of Scripture cards with you.

Whenever you have a few minutes during the day, pull out your pack of Scripture cards and review them. Read the reference first, then the verse. Recite the verse over and over until you get a feel for the flow of the passage. When you think you've got it, turn over the card to the reference side to test your memory.

It's important to recite the reference when you start and when you finish so that you always know where a verse originates when you need it. This is crucial. When I was a new believer, sometimes I would quote Scripture while witnessing to someone, only to have the person ask me, "Where did you get that?" I could only answer, "Um… somewhere in the Bible." As you can imagine, that's not a convincing answer for a non-believer. By memorizing the references, you'll speak with authority and gain the respect of your listeners when you quote Scripture.

After you master five verses, take on five more. Review all the verses you've learned at least once a week. Soon you'll have a stack of index cards in your hand—and in your head. As your pack grows, you'll experience Scripture's powerful effects in your life.

Hand Lettering Practice

Practice your hand lettering skills by tracing the letters below and the Bible verse on the next page. Incorporate this practice as you'd like throughout this devotion.

Aa Bb Cc Dd Ee Ff Gg Hh Ii

Jj Kk Ll Mm Nn Oo Pp Qq Rr

Ss Tt Uu Vv Ww Xx Yy Zz

May the words of my mouth and the meditation of my heart be acceptable to you, Lord, my rock and my Redeemer.

Psalm 19:14

Check In

WEEK 1

- ☐ Luke 1
- ☐ Luke 2
- ☐ Luke 3
- ☐ Luke 4
- ☐ Luke 5

MEMORY VERSES

OPTION 1: Psalm 1:1-2
OPTION 2: Proverbs 1:7
OPTION 3: Matthew 5:1-2

WEEK 3

- ☐ Luke 11
- ☐ Luke 12
- ☐ Luke 13
- ☐ Luke 14
- ☐ Luke 15

MEMORY VERSES

OPTION 1: Psalm 1:5-6
OPTION 2: Proverbs 3:5-6
OPTION 3: Matthew 5:5-6

WEEK 2

- ☐ Luke 6
- ☐ Luke 7
- ☐ Luke 8
- ☐ Luke 9
- ☐ Luke 10

MEMORY VERSES

OPTION 1: Psalm 1:3-4
OPTION 2: Proverbs 2:6-7
OPTION 3: Matthew 5:3-4

WEEK 4

- ☐ Luke 16
- ☐ Luke 17
- ☐ Luke 18
- ☐ Luke 19
- ☐ Luke 20

MEMORY VERSES

OPTION 1: Psalm 3:3-4
OPTION 2: Proverbs 3:9-10
OPTION 3: Matthew 5:7-8

SCAN THIS QR CODE TO ACCESS A FUN SURPRISE!

MEMORY VERSE OPTIONS: Psalm 1:1-2; Proverbs 1:7; Matthew 5:1-2

DAY 1 | LUKE 1

HIGHLIGHT the verses that speak to you. *Luke 1*

Write out the name of the book: ~~Luke the gospel according to~~

Which chapter and verse numbers stand out to you? *46-55 & 67-75*
because they are praising

EXPLAIN what this passage means.

To whom was it originally written? Why? *Theophilus to give him hope*

How does it fit with the verses before and after it?

What is the Holy Spirit intending to communicate through this text?
to trust God

APPLY what God is saying in these verses to your life.

What does this mean today? *things of this earth are nothing*
compared to god

What is God saying to you personally? *No reason to worry cuz*
God can do all things

How can you apply this message to your life?
Trust in god more

RESPOND to what you've read.

In what ways does this passage call you to action? *the miricals & praise*

How will you be different because of what you've learned? *I will be joyful*
and trust in god

Write out a prayer to God in response to what you read today:
thankyou God for all you do and please help
me to put more trust in you cuz you can do all things. Amen

What Else Should I Know? In the Old Testament, God repeatedly promised that He would send a Savior to redeem His people from their sin. But 400 years passed between the Old and New Testaments when God was silent. He made no promises; He offered no new hope. Thankfully, God didn't remain silent forever. In Luke 1, we see God sent His Son, Jesus, whose name means "Deliverer" or "Savior." He came to save God's people from their bondage to sin. But for Jesus, that didn't mean saving just God's people, the Israelites. As Luke will show us, it meant offering His gift of salvation to anyone and everyone who would believe in Him as "the way of peace" (1:79). This is the gospel, the good news with which the New Testament begins.

QUESTION: Do you ever feel like God is silent in your life? Looking at these passages, how can you always know He is working? *Sometimes I forget to pray*
and feel like gods not there until I
reach out again.

DAY 2 | LUKE 2

> God has limitless, unconditional, equal love for all people.

H The angies say this:
"Glory to God in the highest heaven, and on earth peace to thoes whom his favor rest." Luke 2:14

E It is showing the birth of Jesus

A I want to be as joyfull as evryone in the story, I want to show the joy that comes from the Lord

R I will be joyful and loving.

What Else Should I Know? From the beginning of Jesus' story, we learn that God's Son wouldn't fit people's expectations of the Messiah, the great Deliverer of the Jews. In fact, we quickly realize that the invitation to know Jesus extends to everyone, regardless of class, education, race, or position. God has limitless, unconditional, equal love for all people. We're called to have the same mindset as we obey His call to share the gospel.

PRAY: Write down the names of two people who need to hear the gospel. Pray and ask Jesus to give you courage to share the good news with them this week.

DAY 3 | LUKE 3

What Else Should I Know? John's ministry fulfilled the prophet Isaiah's prophecy about one who would "prepare the way for the Lord" (v. 4) and help bring God's salvation into focus. The message John preached wasn't a pleasant one, but it was critical and life-changing. He called people to repentance, to turn from their sin toward the right living God prescribed in the Old Testament law. Because of his bold call to repentance, people wondered whether John was the Messiah, but he quickly corrected them by drawing attention to Jesus.

The climactic moment of John's ministry came when he baptized Jesus. Unlike all the other baptisms John performed, this one set Jesus apart as God's chosen Son, the One whom He had sent to save the world from its sins. This chapter ends with Jesus' genealogy, which Luke traced through David all the way back to Adam in order to highlight Jesus' authority to carry out God's mission of salvation.

REPENTANCE

DAY 4 | LUKE 4

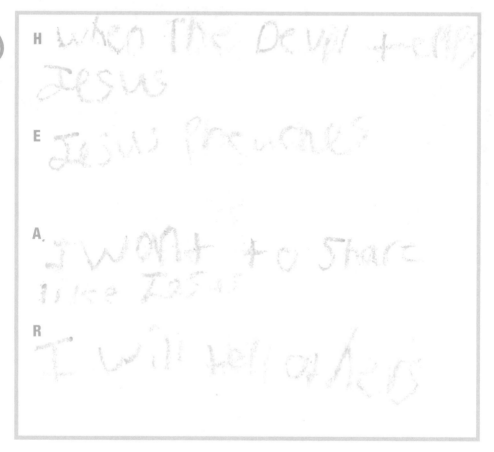

H When The Devil tempt Jesus

E Jesus Preaches

A I want to share like Jesus

R I will tell others

What Else Should I Know? After validating Jesus' identity and establishing His authority as the Son of God, Luke began chapter 4 with Satan's temptation of Jesus in the desert. Before Jesus' earthly ministry even began, Satan called into question Jesus' divine nature and tried to convince Him to turn against His Heavenly Father. But because Jesus was "full of the Holy Spirit" (v. 1), the devil didn't stand a chance. Jesus' responses to Satan remind us that we have the power we need to withstand Satan's temptations when we obey the Word of God and depend on God to give us the strength we need.

Still "in the power of the Spirit" (v. 14), Jesus returned to Galilee from the desert and officially began His ministry of salvation. The quoted text from Isaiah 61 establishes key responsibilities God gave His Messiah, ones Jesus intended to fulfill. Although not everyone appreciated Jesus' message of hope and ministry of healing, He was fully committed to His mission.

? QUESTION: How can you live in the power of the Spirit today?

DAY 5 | LUKE 5

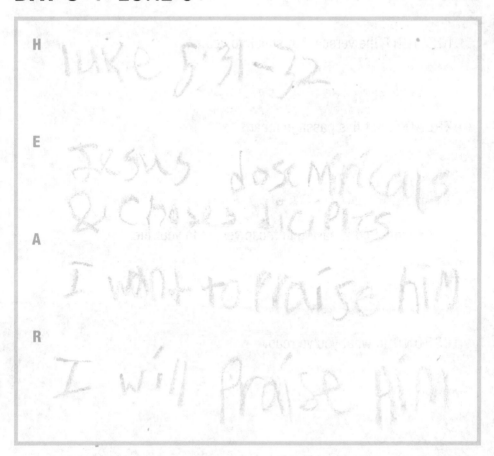

H Luke 5:31-32

E Jesus dose miracals & choses diciples

A I want to praise him

R I will Praise Him

What Else Should I Know? Early in His ministry Jesus called disciples to join Him. This was a huge request: These men would have to give up their lives and jobs and become fully devoted followers who would learn from Him, travel with Him, and eventually continue His ministry by spreading the gospel throughout the world. It might even cost them their lives. But the disciples "left everything, and followed him" (v. 11).

Toward the end of Luke 5, Jesus made a critical statement about the goal of His ministry on earth: "It is not those who are healthy who need a doctor, but those who are sick. I have not come to call the righteous, but sinners to repentance" (vv. 31-32). Through the miracles recorded in this chapter, we learn that Jesus has the power to forgive sins. All of His miraculous acts points to His more important—and much more costly—miracle to offer a way for people who are dead in their sins to find new life in God. And Jesus' encounter with the tax collector, Levi (vv. 27-32), reminds us that Jesus' grace has no limits. No one has sinned so greatly or wandered so far that God's love and forgiveness can't reach him or her.

QUESTION: What do you need to surrender today to completely follow Jesus?

MEMORY VERSE OPTIONS: Psalm 1:3-4; Proverbs 2:6-7; Matthew 5:3-4

DAY 6 | LUKE 6

HIGHLIGHT the verses that speak to you.

Write out the name of the book:

Which chapter and verse numbers stand out to you?

EXPLAIN what this passage means.

To whom was it originally written? Why?

How does it fit with the verses before and after it?

What is the Holy Spirit intending to communicate through this text?

APPLY what God is saying in these verses to your life.

What does this mean today?

What is God saying to you personally?

How can you apply this message to your life?

RESPOND to what you've read.

In what ways does this passage call you to action?

How will you be different because of what you've learned?

Write out a prayer to God in response to what you read today:

What Else Should I Know? While the Pharisees elevated this law as most important, Jesus, the lawmaker Himself, taught that to love and care for others is true obedience to God. When Jesus healed the lame man's hand, He set Himself apart from the religious leaders in a conflict that would escalate until it ended at the cross.

From that scene Luke shifted to the calling and teaching of Jesus' disciples. The teachings recorded in verses 20-49 reveal the countercultural way of life to which Jesus calls His disciples. Jesus' teachings highlight the character of a disciple, chief of which is love. Among the marks of a disciple's love is the ability to love enemies and to extend forgiveness and generosity. This standard to which Jesus calls His followers is made possible only through His love for us. To love others as we've been loved sets us apart from the world.

CHALLENGE: Look for ways to love and serve those around you today.

DAY 7 | LUKE 7

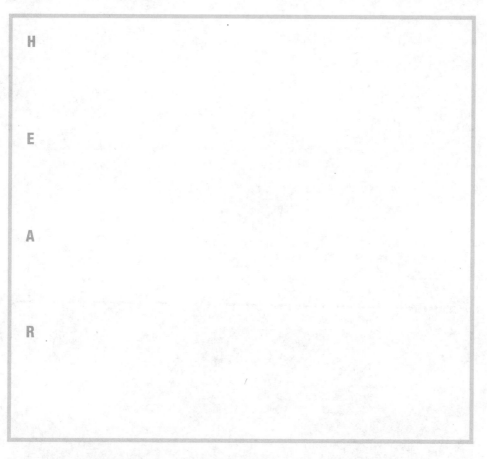

H

E

A

R

What Else Should I Know? One of the major themes of Luke's Gospel is that Jesus came to save all people from their sins, not just the Jews. The centurion at the center of the first story was a Gentile, not of Jewish ethnicity. Jesus affirmed this man's faith and healed his servant, despite his ethnic heritage.

In the next encounter a desperate widow received one of Jesus' greatest miracles. Widows were easy to overlook in Jesus' day, but Jesus saw the woman's grief and raised her son from the dead, a power reserved for God alone. It's no wonder people began to question who Jesus really was (see vv. 18-35). He had the authority of God's promised Messiah, but He didn't look or act anything like the militaristic ruler people expected. That contrast would deepen as His ministry continued.

DEFINE: Look up the definition of salvation. Write it out in your own words.

DAY 8 | LUKE 8

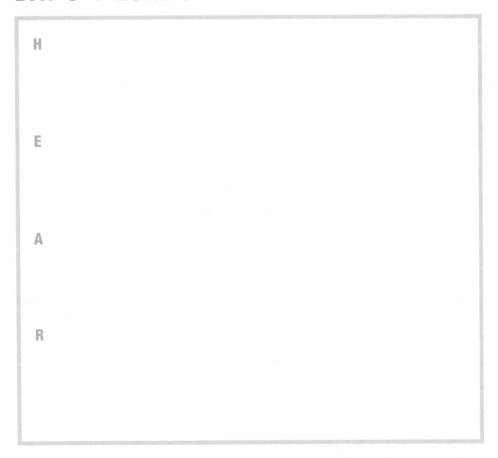

H

E

A

R

What Else Should I Know? Because Luke's Gospel highlights the fact that Jesus' grace and forgiveness are available to all people, it repeatedly features women as the recipients of Jesus' teaching and healing. This positive attention to women would have been countercultural in the first century.

As if to prove why God's Word is worthy of being listened to and obeyed, Luke included three miracles that show the power of Jesus' words over both the physical world (wind and waves and the human body) and the spiritual world (demons). In each of these miracles, Jesus intervened to save people in need, showing again His mercy and love. We're reminded that the only appropriate response to Jesus' love and power is to place our faith in Him: "Your faith has saved you. Go in peace" (v. 48).

? **QUESTION:** What does it look like to trust in Jesus?

DAY 9 | LUKE 9

H

E

A

R

What Else Should I Know? Luke 9 is a key passage of Scripture for understanding what it means to be a disciple of Jesus. The teachings and miracles in this chapter provide instruction and demonstrate Jesus' ministry in action. Through Jesus' conversations with His disciples in this chapter, we learn about His true identity and mission as the Son of God, the Messiah, who would die and be resurrected as the atonement for sin. Jesus' transfiguration with Moses and Elijah validated God's approval of His Son and the mission He was living out.

As Jesus' disciples, we're challenged to live a life of self-denial that focuses on selflessly serving others. That's a challenge we can take on wherever we are: at school, at work, on the practice field, or at church. Jesus didn't idealize discipleship; instead, He taught that following Him requires placing the needs of others—both physical and spiritual—ahead of our own.

DEFINE: Look up the definition of disciple. Write it out in your own words.

DAY 10 | LUKE 10

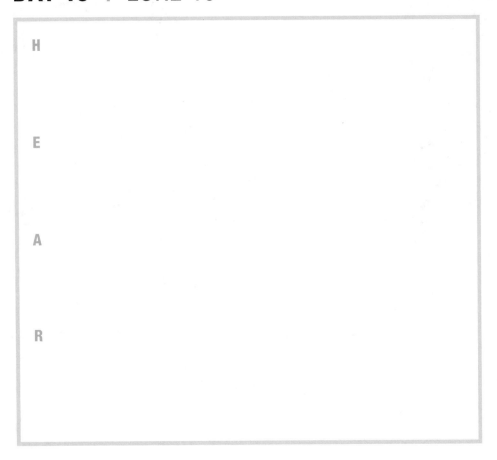

H

E

A

R

What Else Should I Know? After Jesus commissioned the twelve disciples in Luke 9, Luke began to place greater emphasis on what discipleship and life on mission involve: meet people's needs and preach the gospel. The way people respond to the gospel is never in the disciples' control, and many people will reject them, just as He was rejected. The point, however, is that the disciples are obeying Jesus' command by preaching the gospel and giving people an opportunity to believe.

 **QUESTION:** Where has God placed you to be on mission?

MEMORY VERSE OPTIONS: Psalm 1:5-6; Proverbs 3:5-6; Matthew 5:5-6

DAY 11 | LUKE 11

HIGHLIGHT the verses that speak to you.

Write out the name of the book:

Which chapter and verse numbers stand out to you?

EXPLAIN what this passage means.

To whom was it originally written? Why?

How does it fit with the verses before and after it?

What is the Holy Spirit intending to communicate through this text?

APPLY what God is saying in these verses to your life.

What does this mean today?

What is God saying to you personally?

How can you apply this message to your life?

RESPOND to what you've read.

In what ways does this passage call you to action?

How will you be different because of what you've learned?

Write out a prayer to God in response to what you read today:

What Else Should I Know? At the start of Luke 11, Jesus' disciples asked Him how to pray. He responded with an example that is known as the Lord's Prayer. Jesus teaches that prayer should include acknowledgment and praise of who God is (Father), requests for Him to continue working in our world (be holy and bring the kingdom), and petitions for Him to meet our daily needs (sustain us, forgive our sins, give us power to resist temptation).

The remainder of Luke 11 returns to a common theme: opposition to Jesus and His teaching. The crowds, along with the scribes and the Pharisees, doubted Jesus and questioned His authority: was it from God or from Satan? Again, the scribes and Pharisees missed the point of Jesus' teachings, clinging to dead religion instead of the living God who stood before them. A relationship with God begins with believing Jesus is who He says—the Messiah, to whom the entire Old Testament pointed.

 CHALLENGE: Use the Lord's prayer as a guide as you pray every day this week.

DAY 12 | LUKE 12

H

E

A

R

What Else Should I Know? Throughout His earthly ministry Jesus taught His followers truths to live by. Among the practical teachings in Luke 12, Jesus encouraged His followers to avoid hypocrisy by revering God and by boldly confessing Jesus before others. He also told a parable to warn them about greed and worry. The life of a daughter of God should be marked by trust in Him as the ultimate Provider and Protector. Throughout Scripture, God proves time and again that He takes care of His children.

Jesus also reminds us that this world isn't our home, so temporary things shouldn't lead to fear or worry. The things that stress us out—all our everyday anxieties—are nothing compared to the eternity that awaits. The temporary nature of this world is the point of Jesus' parable on expectantly awaiting the Master's return. For disciples of Jesus, our task in this world is to anticipate and prepare for eternity. Our emphasis in the meantime should be on obeying Christ and sharing the gospel.

 DEFINE: Look up the definition of obedience. Write it out in your own words.

DAY 13 | LUKE 13

H

E

A

R

What Else Should I Know? Luke 13 focuses on two important themes of Jesus' ministry: God's judgment and the coming kingdom. When people questioned Jesus about a murderous act by Pilate, He used it as an opportunity to call them to repentance. Everyone will die, and no one can escape God's judgment. This is why repentance is such an important part of the gospel. People who repent of their sins (confess them to God and do a 180-turn away from them) escape God's punishment and receive the gift of eternal life in His presence. The parable in verses 6-9 reminds us that God is patient with sinners, but a day will come when Jesus will return and the opportunity to repent will end.

And although entrance into the kingdom is through a narrow door, meaning it's limited to people who believe in Jesus and repent of their sins, it's a door anyone can enter. No one is beyond the reach of God's kingdom and the reach of Jesus' saving grace.

QUESTION: Knowing that this world is not your home and eternity is real, how should your life look different than a non-believer?

DAY 14 | LUKE 14

H

E

A

R

What Else Should I Know? Through these parables in Luke 14, we learn that God values and honors a humble spirit that seeks to put others ahead of ourselves. Jesus had grieved over Jerusalem at the close of Luke 13 because He knew the leaders of God's people, the Jews, had turned from Him and would ultimately be responsible for His death. Their lack of humility and elevated sense of self-importance had blinded them to Jesus' identity as their Messiah. Jesus, on the other hand, modeled the humble spirit God values. He was a humble servant to the end, culminating at the cross, where the Son of God died for us. Jesus is our model for a life of humble service in the kingdom of God.

Luke also teaches that in order to be obedient to Jesus' call to discipleship, we must prioritize Him and His mission above everything else—even above life itself. Jesus made the ultimate sacrifice to restore humanity's broken relationship with God; we must make personal sacrifices if we want to be His disciples.

DEFINE: Look up the definition of parable. Write it out in your own words.

DAY 15 | LUKE 15

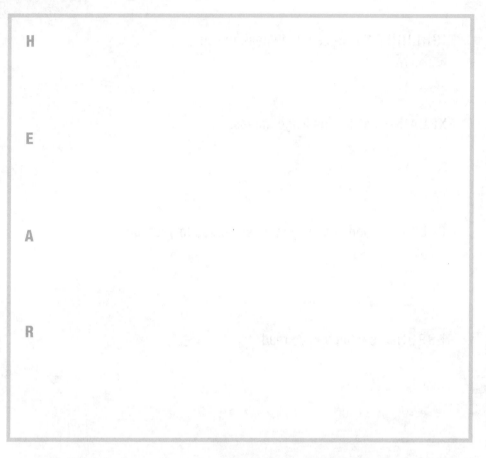

H

E

A

R

What Else Should I Know? In the three parables of chapter 15, often referred as the lost parables, Luke describes the joy that comes when sinners repent. The parables in Luke 15 are a response to how the religious leaders judged Jesus for associating with those kinds of people—"tax collectors and sinners" (v. 1). These parables remind us that all people matter to God and that their salvation should matter to us, too. In fact, God loves sinners so much that He actively goes in search of them to bring them back to Himself, just as the shepherd and the woman searched for their lost possessions.

As the parable of the prodigal son demonstrates, no sin is so great that it can keep us out of reach of God's loving grace. The joy and celebration at the end of each parable illustrate that all of heaven rejoices when people turn to God through faith in Jesus. And once we experience salvation, everything changes—the way we live our lives each day, and the way we view the things of this world.

 CHALLENGE: Tell someone about Jesus today.

W
E
E
K

4

DAY 16 | LUKE 16

HIGHLIGHT the verses that speak to you.

Write out the name of the book:

Which chapter and verse numbers stand out to you?

EXPLAIN what this passage means.

To whom was it originally written? Why?

How does it fit with the verses before and after it?

What is the Holy Spirit intending to communicate through this text?

APPLY what God is saying in these verses to your life.

What does this mean today?

What is God saying to you personally?

How can you apply this message to your life?

RESPOND to what you've read.

In what ways does this passage call you to action?

How will you be different because of what you've learned?

Write out a prayer to God in response to what you read today:

What Else Should I Know? Jesus' parables continue in Luke 16 with a series on money. In the kingdom of God, money can serve a good purpose when used properly. Jesus used the parable of the "unrighteous manager" to make the point that His disciples can make wise choices that maximize their money for the kingdom of God. As Jesus noted, "You cannot serve both God and money" (v. 13), so disciples must put their money to good use in serving God.

Money can often blind a person to what matters most—a right relationship with God. This truth is at the heart of the second parable, an indictment of the Pharisees, who were so focused on themselves that they failed to see Jesus as the fulfillment of Old Testament prophecy. We must be careful that we don't let greed keep us from knowing Jesus and serving Him.

DEFINE: Look up the definition of stewardship. Write it out in your own words.

DAY 17 | LUKE 17

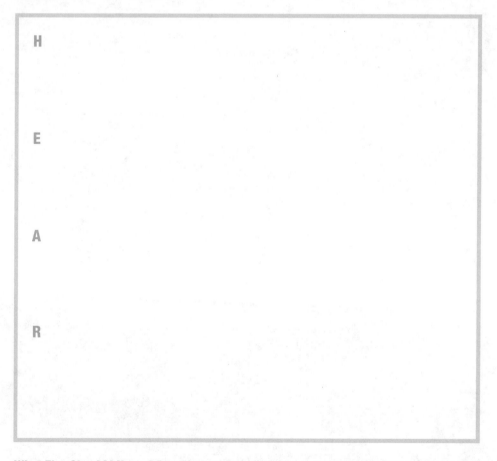

H

E

A

R

What Else Should I Know? Because our job as disciples is to help people see their sin and need for forgiveness, it's important that our hearts are motivated by love and not judgment (see vv. 1-4). Jesus' disciples asked for greater faith to believe He could turn even the darkest heart toward Him, but Jesus reminded them that as His followers, they already had that faith; they just needed to apply it.

The teachings in chapter 17 focus on the not-yet aspect of the kingdom, most notably Jesus' second coming. Although no one can know when Jesus will return, one fact is certain: He's coming back. When He does, He will find people who have surrendered their lives to Him and people who haven't. In the meantime, we should be busy telling people about Him

 CHALLENGE: Share with someone your story of how Jesus changed you. Who were you before and after Christ?

DAY 18 | LUKE 18

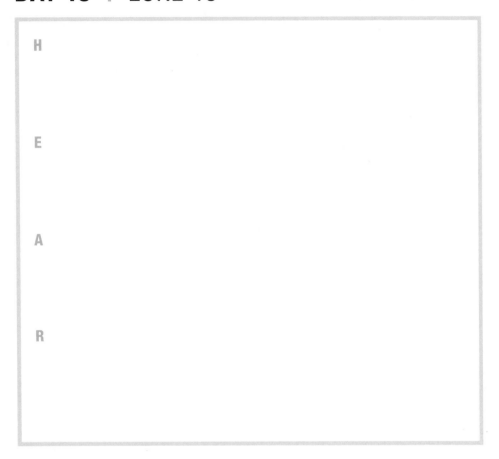

H

E

A

R

What Else Should I Know? As Luke noted in verse 1 of chapter 18, Jesus wanted His disciples to persist in prayer and not give up while they waited for His return and the culmination of God's kingdom. The parable about the Pharisee and the tax collector emphasizes the need for humility in prayer. When we are persistent and humble in prayer, we communicate our total dependence on God and a desire to unite with Him. Prayer is one of the greatest gifts God gives His children, and we should be eternally grateful for it.

The stories that follow in this chapter illustrate that salvation comes to those who are humble enough to recognize their need for Jesus and who are willing to follow Him at any cost. Jesus' prediction of His death (vv. 31-34) reminds readers of the great lengths Jesus went to in order to make salvation possible. The sacrifice God expects from His children pales in comparison to the price Jesus paid to redeem us.

CHALLENGE: Write down the names of five people you can pray for. Commit to praying for them all week.

DAY 19 | LUKE 19

H

E

A

R

JESUS
CHANGES
Everything

What Else Should I Know? Like those we've seen before, Zacchaeus is an unlikely person for Jesus to associate with. Yet when he met Jesus, Zacchaeus changed instantly. His life became defined by generosity rather than greed, by humility rather than self-gratification. Zacchaeus's salvation prompted Jesus to remind the people of His mission: "to seek and to save the lost" (v. 10).

In verse 28, the focus shifts to Passion Week and Jesus' final teachings. Both the triumphal entry and the clearing of the temple show the stark contrast between the Messiah people expected and the actual Messiah embodied in Jesus. Although the people expected a strong political leader who would restore Israel to prominence and power, Jesus came in humility to restore all human hearts to God.

DAY 20 | LUKE 20

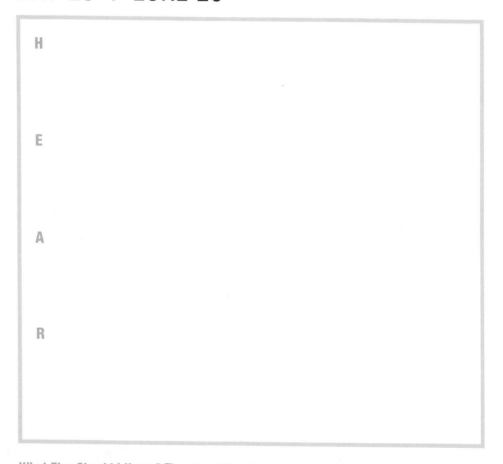

H

E

A

R

What Else Should I Know? Throughout His ministry, Jesus acted and spoke with an authority reserved for God alone. The Jewish leaders wanted to know where this authority came from. Though Jesus didn't directly answer that question, He told a parable that presented Him as the Son of God and the religious leaders as people who rejected and killed the Son. The religious leaders next questioned Jesus over governmental authority, but again their trap didn't work. Followers of God have an obligation to their governments, which operate within the world He governs.

The religious leaders' third question concerned the resurrection of the dead. Again Jesus answered their question in a way that maintained the truth and authority of God's kingdom without belittling the questioner or succumbing to the trap. Jesus took the opportunity to remind listeners of the Messiah's identity as the divine Son of David, God incarnate. Jesus was that promised Messiah, the Son of God.

DEFINE: Look up the definition of sovereignty. Write it out in your own words.

Check In

WEEK 5

- ☐ Luke 21
- ☐ Luke 22
- ☐ Luke 23
- ☐ Luke 24
- ☐ Acts 1

MEMORY VERSES

OPTION 1: Psalm 8:4-5
OPTION 2: Proverbs 3:11-12
OPTION 3: Matthew 5:9-10

WEEK 6

- ☐ Acts 2
- ☐ Acts 3
- ☐ Acts 4
- ☐ Acts 5
- ☐ Acts 6

MEMORY VERSES

OPTION 1: Psalm 9:9-10
OPTION 2: Proverbs 3:33-34
OPTION 3: Matthew 5:11-12

WEEK 7

- ☐ Acts 7
- ☐ Acts 8
- ☐ Acts 9
- ☐ Acts 10
- ☐ Acts 11

MEMORY VERSES

OPTION 1: Psalm 13:5-6
OPTION 2: Proverbs 4:23
OPTION 3: Matthew 5:13-14

WEEK 8

- ☐ Acts 12
- ☐ Acts 13
- ☐ Acts 14
- ☐ James 1
- ☐ James 2

MEMORY VERSES

OPTION 1: Psalm 16:11
OPTION 2: Proverbs 5:20-21
OPTION 3: Matthew 5:15-16

SCAN THIS QR CODE TO ACCESS A FUN SURPRISE!

Circle the verse you want to memorize this week.

MEMORY VERSE OPTIONS: Psalm 8:4-5; Proverbs 3:11-12; Matthew 5:9-10

DAY 21 | LUKE 21

HIGHLIGHT the verses that speak to you.

Write out the name of the book:

Which chapter and verse numbers stand out to you?

EXPLAIN what this passage means.

To whom was it originally written? Why?

How does it fit with the verses before and after it?

What is the Holy Spirit intending to communicate through this text?

APPLY what God is saying in these verses to your life.

What does this mean today?

What is God saying to you personally?

How can you apply this message to your life?

RESPOND to what you've read.

In what ways does this passage call you to action?

How will you be different because of what you've learned?

Write out a prayer to God in response to what you read today:

What Else Should I Know? At the end of Luke 20, Jesus gave warnings to the religious leaders. One criticism was that they "devour widows' houses" (v. 47), they took advantage of widows in their impoverished state. In direct contrast in chapter 21, Jesus commended a widow who gave all she had to the temple offering. Although her offering was small, her faith and obedience were great. Jesus used an unlikely example to highlight how much God values our generosity and sacrifices.

In this chapter, Jesus included warnings about what His followers could expect between His resurrection and His second coming. However, Jesus called His followers to persevere in faith because God had sealed them for eternity, and they had the promise of His return. Thankfully, we too can cling to the hope of Jesus' return as we live for Him today.

 QUESTION: How can you be a part of helping the poor and needy in your community?

Fun Fact:

Jesus' prophecy about the temple (vv. 5-9) was fulfilled in AD 70, when the Roman army burned it to the ground.

DAY 22 | LUKE 22

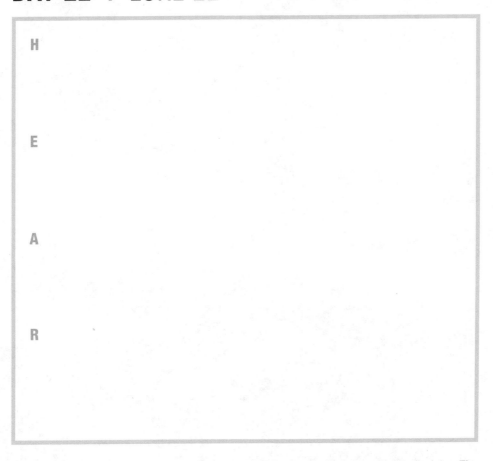

H

E

A

R

What Else Should I Know? In Luke 22, Jesus held the Passover dinner with His disciples. The Passover meal had been part of Jewish tradition since the exodus: God had commanded the Israelite households to sacrifice a lamb and cover their doorposts with its blood so that He would pass over their houses when He struck the firstborn sons of Egypt with a plague (see Ex. 11–12). Jesus' celebration of the Passover brought it new meaning. Jesus was the Passover Lamb, the ultimate sacrifice God sent once and for all to pay the price for people's sins. During this meal with His disciples, Jesus predicted Judas's betrayal and Peter's denial. He knew His arrest and crucifixion would bring serious trials for His followers, but He again called them to humility and self-sacrifice, traits that would be put to the test in the days to come.

The powerful scene in the garden marks the climactic moment of Luke's Gospel. In Luke 9:51, Luke wrote that Jesus "determined to journey to Jerusalem," knowing what awaited Him there. As He prayed in the garden, He fully surrendered to God's plan. Shortly thereafter, Jesus was arrested, Peter denied knowing Him, and His trial began.

QUESTION: As you study the last days of Jesus, what do you see that was very important to Him?

DAY 23 | LUKE 23

H

E

A

R

What Else Should I Know? From the beginning of his Gospel, Luke was committed to presenting evidence that Jesus was the Messiah, the Son of God. The details he included in his record of Jesus' trial and crucifixion further support this focus. Even though Jesus was innocent, Pilate gave in to the crowd's demands and agreed to have Jesus crucified in exchange for the murderer Barabbas. Including Barabbas in the crucifixion account provides a dramatic picture of the gospel. Guilty in our sin, we deserve death, but because of the death of Jesus in our place, we've been set free.

The remainder of the chapter describes Jesus' death on the cross and burial in a tomb. Luke recorded three statements by Jesus on the cross, each of which affirmed His identity as the Son of God and united Him with His heavenly Father (see vv. 34,43,46). Jesus willingly gave up His own life for the sins of the world. After He died, His body was placed in a tomb, marking what seemed to be the end of His life.

? **QUESTION:** How does reading about the death of Jesus make you want to live differently for Him?

DAY 24 | LUKE 24

H

E

A

R

What Else Should I Know? The Gospel of Luke records the account of Jesus' resurrection and the women's faithful obedience in relaying the angels' message to the rest of the disciples. Luke also included details about Jesus' post-resurrection appearances, which proved His resurrection and provided Him the opportunity to give final orders to His disciples before ascending to heaven.

Jesus' time on earth ended with a commission to His disciples. He left them with a charge to minister and proclaim the gospel on His behalf. As Jesus' disciples today, we know Him because others have been faithful to carry His gospel around the world, and we pick up where those disciples left off as Jesus' faithful ambassadors.

? **QUESTION:** Jesus defeated sin and death by His resurrection. How does His life give you victory over your sin?

DAY 25 | ACTS 1

H

E

A

R

What Else Should I Know? The Book of Acts, which Luke wrote as a second volume to his Gospel, documents the growth of the early church during the first three decades after Jesus' ascension. Throughout those years, Christianity, which was first extended to the Jewish people, became predominantly Gentile.

Acts 1 set the stage for the coming of the Holy Spirit (described in Acts 2) by moving readers from Jesus' post-resurrection appearances to the disciples prayerfully waiting in the upper room. As Jesus prepared to leave, He gave the disciples a new perspective on the kingdom of God by establishing a worldwide vision for this mission. The church, under the Holy Spirit's guidance and power, was to take the gospel to the ends of the earth, a task that Christ expects us to continue today by starting where we are in our own lives. That mission could start anywhere—at school, home, practice, or with the next person you meet. Where are you going to start?

DAY 26 | ACTS 2

HIGHLIGHT the verses that speak to you.

Write out the name of the book:

Which chapter and verse numbers stand out to you?

EXPLAIN what this passage means.

To whom was it originally written? Why?

How does it fit with the verses before and after it?

What is the Holy Spirit intending to communicate through this text?

APPLY what God is saying in these verses to your life.

What does this mean today?

What is God saying to you personally?

How can you apply this message to your life?

RESPOND to what you've read.

In what ways does this passage call you to action?

How will you be different because of what you've learned?

Write out a prayer to God in response to what you read today:

What Else Should I Know? As Jesus promised, God empowered the disciples with the Holy Spirit. Prior to the Pentecost event in Acts 2, God had given the Spirit's power to certain individuals for particular purposes and periods of time. With Pentecost, however, the Spirit's power became an indwelling part of every Christian. Jesus commissioned His followers to witness about His saving power to the corners of the earth, and they (and we) would become dependent on the Spirit's power to accomplish this task. The signs that accompanied the coming of the Holy Spirit revealed God's power and presence in His people, as well as the universality of the gospel message.

Chapter 2 concludes with a picture of the early church in action. People united, giving generously, sharing with those in need, modeling the gospel in action, worshiping, partaking of the Lord's Supper, and serving through various ministries—a model the church continues to follow today.

? **QUESTION:** After reading about the early church, how can your life model their practices?

DAY 27 | ACTS 3

H

E

A

R

What Else Should I Know? From the first healing mentioned in Acts, we learn several important characteristics of the early church's ministry.

1. The disciples healed in the name of Jesus Christ. The primary purpose of their healing was to point people to Jesus and to give the disciples an audience for preaching the gospel.
2. The miraculous healing evoked a response of "awe and astonishment" (v. 10). The miracle earned the disciples the ear of the crowd.
3. The healing was followed with the gospel.

Just as He did in the first century, God continues to empower His people to meet spiritual and physical needs so that His name will be glorified and people will be drawn to Him.

QUESTION: He is the same God who used Peter to heal the blind beggar. Do you believe in God's healing today? Why or why not?

DAY 28 | ACTS 4

H

E

A

R

What Else Should I Know? In Acts 4 we see the first evidence of the persecution of Christians, when Peter and John were arrested for teaching people about Jesus. This result shouldn't be surprising; Jesus had prophesied that His followers would be hated because of Him (see Matt. 10:22,24:9; Mark 13:13; Luke 21:17). When pressed about the miraculous healing they had done, Peter and John responded by pointing the religious leaders to Jesus and the power of His name. Every follower of Jesus today should echo their response: "We are unable to stop speaking about what we have seen and heard" (Acts 4:20).

Verses 32-37 end this chapter by highlighting the unity of the early church. The believers shared their possessions to meet physical needs. Luke gave special attention to Barnabas, who exemplified this spirit of generosity and would become a key figure in the growth of the early church. Unity, generosity, and boldness are three traits of the early church that the body of Christ should seek to imitate today.

QUESTION: How can you be bold in sharing your faith today?

DAY 29 | ACTS 5

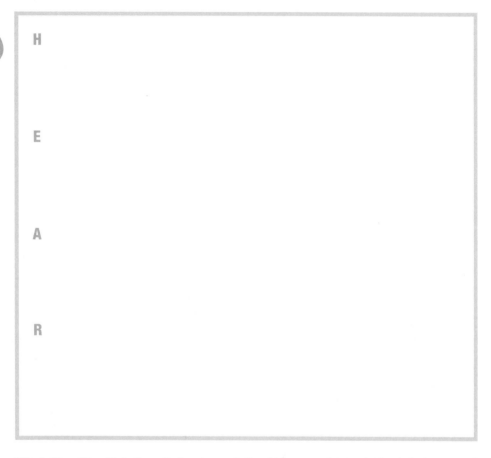

H

E

A

R

What Else Should I Know? Ananias and Sapphira were dishonest about their personal contribution and, as a result, experienced the harsh judgment of death. Their story reminds us that the church is made up of imperfect people. For this reason, it's vitally important we rely on the wisdom and guidance of the Holy Spirit. When believers deviate from the leading of the Spirit, we're tempted to imitate the actions of Ananias and Sapphira, who misled the disciples to enhance their own reputations.

Again Peter, John, and other apostles were jailed for sharing the gospel, but this time their release happened by miraculous means: An angel of the Lord delivered them from prison and instructed them to continue sharing the gospel in the temple courts, where they had been arrested. They obeyed, and the religious leaders who found them were so bewildered that again they didn't know how to handle the situation. The Pharisee Gamaliel stands out as the voice of reason in this encounter, acknowledging that a fight against God isn't a fight anyone can win. God used this Jewish religious leader to protect the lives of His apostles and to continue the advancement of the gospel.

 PRAY: Ask God to search you for any impure motives and desires. Let Him wash you clean.

DAY 30 | ACTS 6

A life following Jesus is never free of opposition.

H

E

A

R

What Else Should I Know? As the church continued to grow rapidly, noticeable growing pains began to surface. In chapter 6, Luke recounted that some widows in the Christian community in Jerusalem weren't receiving their daily distributions of food. This incident brought to the church's attention the need for better administration of service so that the apostles could focus on spreading the gospel. The church set apart seven men to carry out this new ministry.

As the gospel went forth, opposition against the church increased. Stephen, one of the seven men appointed to serve the widows, attracted the attention of the corrupt religious leaders because of his fearless proclamation of the word of Christ. His preaching led some unbelieving Grecian Jews to bring him before the Sanhedrin on false charges. When the gospel begins to change lives, we can expect people to oppose us. Living out Jesus' Great Commission doesn't exempt us from hardship and trouble—in fact, we can count on it. But like Stephen, God's Spirit gives us boldness and confidence to stand strong for Him.

MEMORY VERSE OPTIONS: Psalm 13:5-6; Proverbs 4:23; Matthew 5:13-14

WEEK 7

DAY 31 | ACTS 7

HIGHLIGHT the verses that speak to you.

Write out the name of the book:

Which chapter and verse numbers stand out to you?

EXPLAIN what this passage means.

To whom was it originally written? Why?

How does it fit with the verses before and after it?

What is the Holy Spirit intending to communicate through this text?

APPLY what God is saying in these verses to your life.

What does this mean today?

What is God saying to you personally?

How can you apply this message to your life?

RESPOND to what you've read.

In what ways does this passage call you to action?

How will you be different because of what you've learned?

Write out a prayer to God in response to what you read today:

What Else Should I Know? In Acts 7, Luke recorded Stephen's defense before the Sanhedrin—a powerful testimony of the gospel, traced throughout the Old Testament. Stephen opened with God's call of Abraham in Mesopotamia. He then highlighted Joseph and his brothers' experience in Egypt. Next, Stephen recounted the Israelites' slavery in Egypt and their journey to freedom through the desert under Moses' leadership. He reminded the crowd of the Israelites' rebellion and idol worship in the wilderness. After discussing the traveling tabernacle and the temple of Solomon, Stephen emphasized that God doesn't dwell in buildings, emphasizing the change brought about by the arrival of the Holy Spirit at Pentecost.

Stephen's defense, a powerful witness about Christ, resulted in his death by stoning, making him the first Christian martyr.

 QUESTION: How does reading about the boldness of Stephen inspire you to live differently today?

DAY 32 | ACTS 8

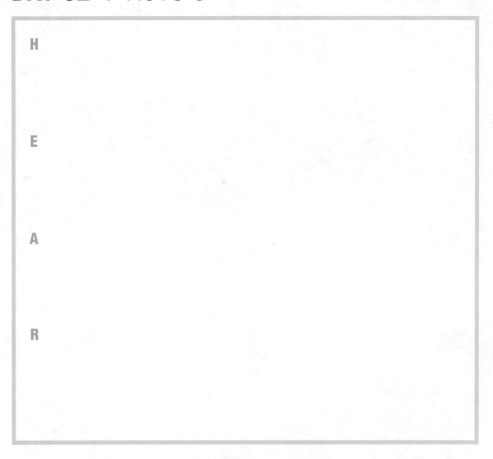

H

E

A

R

What Else Should I Know? Among the people Philip interacted with in Samaria was a former sorcerer. When Simon witnessed Philip's work among the people, he believed in Jesus and was baptized. However, Simon sought God's gifts and power for personal gain. Peter's rebuking serves as a good warning for all Christians. God gives His people good gifts, but we're to use them for His purposes and His glory rather than our own.

The chapter ends with Philip's witness to an Ethiopian eunuch. The Ethiopian man, who was curious about spiritual matters, was reading the Book of Isaiah when Philip met him. Philip quoted Isaiah 53:7-8 to illustrate that God's redemptive plan is woven throughout all Scripture. The man responded to Philip's message by believing and being baptized. Despite—or rather because of—the persecution in Jerusalem, the gospel was spreading, and the church was rapidly growing throughout the region.

 DEFINE: Look up the definition of redemption. Write it out in your own words.

DAY 33 | ACTS 9

> There is no one too far for the grace of God to meet.

H

E

A

R

What Else Should I Know? Acts 8 briefly alluded to Saul's acts of persecution against the early church, but Luke returned to Saul in chapter 9 where the Lord saved him on his journey to Damascus. God had big plans for Saul's life, and he sent Ananias to inform Saul of these plans. Saul's reputation was such that even Ananias, a faithful disciple of Jesus, was hesitant to even reach out to him, finding it hard to believe Saul could be God's "chosen instrument to take my name to Gentiles, kings, and Israelites" (v. 15). After meeting Ananias in Damascus, Saul regained his sight, was filled with the Holy Spirit, and was eventually baptized. Almost immediately Saul began proclaiming the gospel.

Few encounters in Scripture provide such a powerful picture of the immediate change Jesus brings to a person's life. If you're a Christian, then like Saul, you have a powerful testimony of being raised from spiritual death to eternal life through the good news of Christ. Don't ever take that story for granted. Acts 9 ends by shifting the focus back to Peter, who continued to perform miracles and preach the gospel in Jesus' name. The church continued to grow as many more people believed.

DAY 34 | ACTS 10

H

E

A

R

GOD SHOWS NO
favoritism.

What Else Should I Know? Through Peter's efforts people understood that the gospel of Jesus Christ applies to the whole world, not just the Jews. In large part this revelation took place as a result of Peter's interactions with Cornelius, a Roman centurion in Caesarea.

As Peter preached the gospel to the people at Cornelius's house, the Spirit descended on the hearers, and they were baptized. The lesson for Peter and for all Christians today is that in God's kingdom, people are more important than religious regulations or racial differences. All people matter to God, and He desires that all people hear His gospel and experience the salvation He offers through belief in His Son.

DAY 35 | ACTS 11

H

E

A

R

What Else Should I Know? In this passage, we see that it was hard for some Christians in Jerusalem to understand that people were being saved by belief in Jesus alone, without observing Jewish practices or customs. The Jews had lived for centuries as God's chosen people, but Jesus made it clear the gospel was for everyone, not just for the Jews. Peter's explanations of why he acted as he did at Cornelius's home made it clear he acted in obedience to God, and Peter's critics were convinced of the truth.

In Acts 11:19, Luke noted the expansive growth of Christianity among Gentile regions. The church in Antioch would become one of the most influential groups of Christians in the early church, so it's appropriate that they were the first to be called Christians, or Christ followers. Chapter 11 ends with a brief note about the generosity and love of the Antioch church. Their quick action to send money to other Christians in need shows how the unity of the early church strengthened as Christianity spread.

CHALLENGE: Write down one person at your school or in your neighborhood that you can begin to pray for today.

MEMORY VERSE OPTIONS: Psalm 16:11; Proverbs 5:20-21; Matthew 5:15-16

DAY 36 | ACTS 12

HIGHLIGHT the verses that speak to you.

Write out the name of the book:

Which chapter and verse numbers stand out to you?

EXPLAIN what this passage means.

To whom was it originally written? Why?

How does it fit with the verses before and after it?

What is the Holy Spirit intending to communicate through this text?

APPLY what God is saying in these verses to your life.

What does this mean today?

What is God saying to you personally?

How can you apply this message to your life?

RESPOND to what you've read.

In what ways does this passage call you to action?

How will you be different because of what you've learned?

Write out a prayer to God in response to what you read today:

What Else Should I Know? Persecution against the early church continued, even though Paul no longer led the charge. King Herod Agrippa I, the ruler of Judea, beheaded the apostle James, the brother of John, and imprisoned Peter. When Herod discovered Peter had escaped, he had Peter's guards executed and traveled to Caesarea, where he suffered a horrible death. In spite of oppression, the gospel continued to flourish. Additionally, Barnabas and Paul completed their relief mission at this time.

It's easy to overlook a small detail in verse 5. While Peter was in prison, the church "was praying fervently to God for him," likely for his safety and strength in the face of persecution. The events that followed reveal the power of their prayers, reminding us that prayer remains our most effective tool against any opposition or temptation we face, both in our personal lives and in the church. Prayer lets us commune with God and confess our reliance on Him in every arena of our lives.

 QUESTION: What can you say no to this week in order to spend more time talking to God?

WEEK 8

DAY 37 | ACTS 13

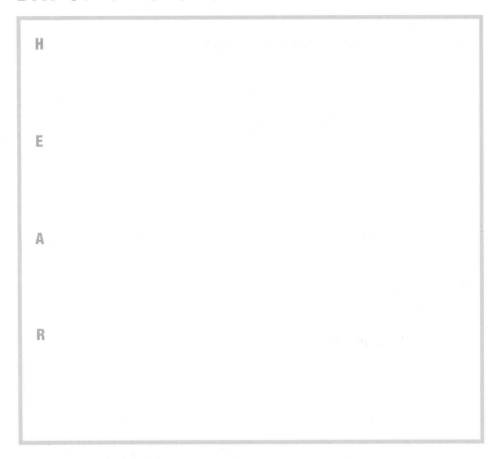

H

E

A

R

What Else Should I Know? Acts 13 begins the section of the Book of Acts that describes the first of Paul's three missionary journeys. (Paul was Saul's Greek name, which Luke used for the remainder of Acts.) Paul's first journey began when the church in Antioch commissioned and dispatched him and Barnabas, a model for missions the church continues to follow today. The Spirit's presence with Paul and the Roman leader's response of faith established the validity and intensity of this first missionary journey. Paul and Barnabas had a clear mission to spread the gospel, and they wholeheartedly focused on that mission.

The scene in Pisidian Antioch was the first of many that would become a pattern of Paul's missionary efforts. On arriving in a community, he first preached to the Jews in the synagogue. When they rejected the gospel, he turned his attention to the Gentiles, many of whom believed. In a scene similar to Jesus' ministry, the Jews grew jealous of the attention Paul and Barnabas received and expelled them from the city. Unfazed, the missionaries followed the Holy Spirit's leading and set their sights on the next town.

 QUESTION: What mission has God placed in your heart?

DAY 38 | ACTS 14

H

E

A

R

What Else Should I Know? Paul's healing of a crippled man led the crowds to assume Paul and Barnabas were gods. The missionaries could have accepted the praise and given in to their pride, but they quickly and adamantly spoke the truth about God and the ways He had revealed Himself in an effort to correct the misguided crowd. Soon a group of Jews again attacked them and threw them out of the city.

Paul's example reminds us that serving Christ brings with it both victories and difficulties. Sometimes people will reject you. At times you'll feel like an outcast. But regardless of what we encounter as we live for Christ, God expects us to be faithful in the tasks He has given us.

 QUESTION: Even in persecution, the church grew. How has suffering grown you closer to God?

DAY 39 | JAMES 1

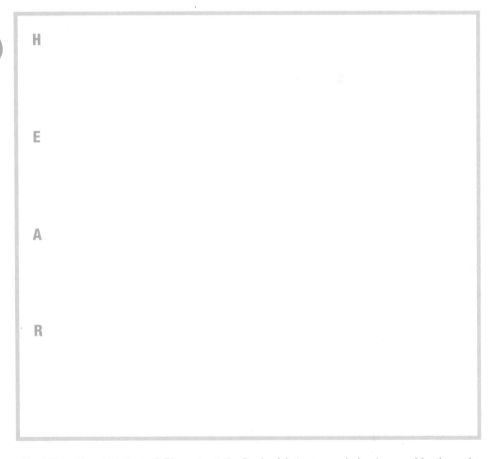

H

E

A

R

What Else Should I Know? Throughout the Book of Acts we read about several leaders who emerged as influential to the growth of the early church. One of those leaders was James, the brother of Jesus, whom Acts 12:17 identifies as a leader of the local church in Jerusalem. The Book of James is a practical book that addresses issues Christians deal with both inside and outside the church. Although James's letter was originally written for Christians who had scattered from Jerusalem as a result of the persecution described in Acts, his letter has a much broader appeal that continues to have practical implications for Christians today.

In chapter 1, James reminded his readers that God offers believers wisdom to cope with times of trials and testing. Though temptations are a normal, expected part of life, God never tempts anyone; temptations arise from our sin nature. God, on the other hand, graciously gives only good gifts to those He loves. James also emphasized the importance of preparing our hearts to receive, listen to, and obey the Word of God. By applying God's Word, we give evidence that our religion is genuine.

 CHALLENGE: Ask God for wisdom today, in faith.

DAY 40 | JAMES 2

H

E

A

R

JAMES' POINT IS CLEAR: OUR SAVING FAITH IN JESUS ALWAYS LEADS TO GOOD WORKS.

What Else Should I Know? James began chapter 2 with a more specific example of the genuine religion to which he had called readers at the close of chapter 1. Evidently, a problem among Christians in the early church was a tendency to show favoritism to those who had money. Without mincing words, James reminded his readers that Christian love should be blind to the prejudices and judgments of the world. You're to "love your neighbor as yourself" (v. 8), no matter who your neighbor is. James went so far as to call favoritism a sin and he urged readers to put into practice the mercy and love God showed through the cross.

The second half of James 2 turns to the broader issue of faith in action. As Christians, we're called to love others. It's how we put feet to our faith—as James pointed out, faith is dead without actions. To illustrate this point, James gave two Old Testament examples of people whose faith motivated them to act: Abraham and Rahab. Abraham's faith in God was so strong that he willingly placed his son Isaac on the altar of sacrifice (see Gen. 22), an action that showed God how much Abraham trusted Him. Rahab acted against her people when she hid Israelite spies (see Josh. 2) and, like Abraham, showed God that she trusted Him and His purposes.

Check In

WEEK 9

- ☐ James 3
- ☐ James 4
- ☐ James 5
- ☐ Acts 15
- ☐ Acts 16

MEMORY VERSES

OPTION 1: Psalm 18:2
OPTION 2: Proverbs 6:10-11
OPTION 3: Matthew 5:17-18

WEEK 11

- ☐ Galatians 6
- ☐ Acts 17
- ☐ Acts 18
- ☐ 1 Thessalonians 1
- ☐ 1 Thessalonians 2

MEMORY VERSES

OPTION 1: Psalm 23:1-2
OPTION 2: Proverbs 10:9
OPTION 3: Matthew 5:21-22

WEEK 10

- ☐ Galatians 1
- ☐ Galatians 2
- ☐ Galatians 3
- ☐ Galatians 4
- ☐ Galatians 5

MEMORY VERSES

OPTION 1: Psalm 19:14
OPTION 2: Proverbs 9:9-10
OPTION 3: Matthew 5:19-20

WEEK 12

- ☐ 1 Thessalonians 3
- ☐ 1 Thessalonians 4
- ☐ 1 Thessalonians 5
- ☐ 2 Thessalonians 1
- ☐ 2 Thessalonians 2

MEMORY VERSES

OPTION 1: Psalm 23:3-4
OPTION 2: Proverbs 10:27-28
OPTION 3: Matthew 5:23-24

SCAN THIS QR CODE TO ACCESS A FUN SURPRISE!

MEMORY VERSE OPTIONS: Psalm 18:2; Proverbs 6:10-11; Matthew 5:17-18

DAY 41 | JAMES 3

HIGHLIGHT the verses that speak to you.

Write out the name of the book:

Which chapter and verse numbers stand out to you?

EXPLAIN what this passage means.

To whom was it originally written? Why?

How does it fit with the verses before and after it?

What is the Holy Spirit intending to communicate through this text?

APPLY what God is saying in these verses to your life.

What does this mean today?

What is God saying to you personally?

How can you apply this message to your life?

RESPOND to what you've read.

In what ways does this passage call you to action?

How will you be different because of what you've learned?

Write out a prayer to God in response to what you read today:

What Else Should I Know? A running theme throughout James' letter is how faithful Christians should act. As people transformed by Jesus, we're to live and act differently from the rest of the world. In chapter 3, James specifically connected this mandate to speech, using three word pictures to illustrate the power of our words. Each illustration makes the point that although the tongue is a small part of our bodies, our words have great power, a power we must learn to control and exercise in a God-honoring way.

James warned against the dangers of a Christian with an uncontrolled tongue, but he also challenged believers to be consistent in their speech. James reminded readers that the words that come from our mouths clearly reflect our true identity. What we say reflects who we are.

? **QUESTION:** Think about the past week. In what ways have you used your tongue for good and for evil?

DAY 42 | JAMES 4

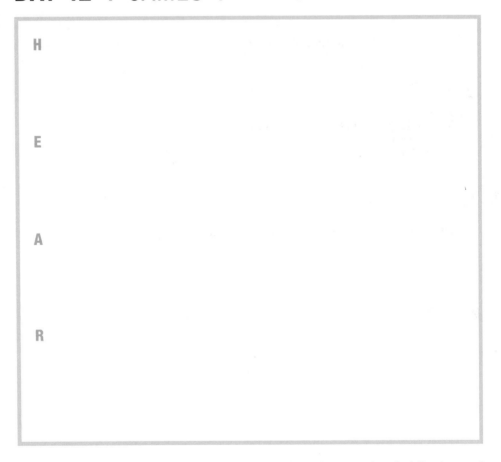

H

E

A

R

What Else Should I Know? In addition to speech, James also warned against the danger of unaddressed conflict, another struggle for Christians today. James had already reminded readers of the command to love their neighbors and had warned them against judging others. But this issue received James's strongest words of warning in his letter, demonstrating the severity of the issue and the danger of this sin.

James called on readers to submit and draw near to God through repentance and humility. When we do, God is ready and willing to give us the grace needed to correct our selfish attitudes that lead to conflicts.

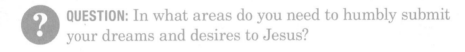

QUESTION: In what areas do you need to humbly submit your dreams and desires to Jesus?

DAY 43 | JAMES 5

H

E

A

R

What Else Should I Know? Before bringing his letter to a close, James addressed one more practical problem the early church faced. This problem again centered on money and wealth, but this time on the person who pursues worldly wealth at the expense of others. James reminded readers that earthly treasures have no lasting value in the kingdom of God, so to pursue and hoard them, especially at the expense of loving God and others well, is a worthless endeavor.

Verses 7-20 end James's letter by calling for believers to be patient through suffering as they await Jesus' return and to endure on the basis of God's nature. James mentioned the Old Testament prophets and Job as examples of people who lived with patient endurance.

For each of those individuals, God was faithful to His promises, so we can trust that He will be faithful to His promise to send Jesus back as well. In the meantime we're to maintain our faith in God and utilize the power of prayer He has given us.

THERE IS NOTHING THAT WILL SATISFY YOU THE WAY JESUS CAN.

DAY 44 | ACTS 15

H

E

A

R

What Else Should I Know? Paul and Barnabas met with the council in Jerusalem to clarify the role of Old Testament law in the life of new-covenant believers. Some Jewish Christians argued that Gentile believers should adhere to these practices and customs of the Jewish faith. However, Peter told the council that God had sent him to proclaim the gospel to Gentiles and had shown him that the traditional Jewish practices had been fulfilled in Jesus and were no longer necessary for faith. Peter declared that Jews were saved by grace and faith in Jesus through the Holy Spirit, just as Gentiles were.

Christians today should take a lesson from how the council debated and reached their conclusion. The message of the gospel and the unity of the church always remained at the forefront of the meeting, despite the differing and passionate opinions. You'll always have disagreements in life—even in the church. But even if we disagree, we should always look to the gospel as our guide.

 DEFINE: Look up the definition of unity. Write it out in your own words.

DAY 45 | ACTS 16

H

E

A

R

What Else Should I Know? While in Philippi, Paul and Silas encountered a slave girl possessed by a fortune-telling spirit. After days of being ridiculed by the spirit, Paul exorcised the demon in the name of Jesus. This angered the girls owners, and they had the missionaries thrown into prison. When an earthquake opened the jail's doors, the prisoners refused to escape. Instead, Paul and Silas shared Christ with the jailer, and he and his household became believers. Because of Paul's Roman citizenship the missionaries were freed and resumed their journey. This chapter continues to emphasize Jesus' saving grace for everyone. It's the basis for our faith and our source of strength—no matter what we face.

 PRAY: Spend some time listening to Jesus today. Let the Holy Spirit and His Word lead you.

DAY 46 | GALATIANS 1

HIGHLIGHT the verses that speak to you.

Write out the name of the book:

Which chapter and verse numbers stand out to you?

EXPLAIN what this passage means.

To whom was it originally written? Why?

How does it fit with the verses before and after it?

What is the Holy Spirit intending to communicate through this text?

APPLY what God is saying in these verses to your life.

What does this mean today?

What is God saying to you personally?

How can you apply this message to your life?

RESPOND to what you've read.

In what ways does this passage call you to action?

How will you be different because of what you've learned?

Write out a prayer to God in response to what you read today:

What Else Should I Know? The apostle Paul, whose conversion and ministry are recorded in the Book of Acts, wrote thirteen books of the New Testament. Many of these books were written to churches he had ministered to or helped establish on his missionary journeys. Galatians is a letter to churches in the region of Galatia, where Paul had ministered on his first trip (see Acts 14). Paul wrote this letter with a specific purpose and audience in mind: to correct the Galatians' faulty understanding of the gospel.

Many in Galatia falsely believed Gentiles had to be converted to Judaism in order to be Christians. However, as Paul argued in this letter, that belief opposes the heart of the true gospel, Jesus' gospel: our freedom from being bound to the law.

 QUESTION: Whose approval are you seeking? Why?

DAY 47 | GALATIANS 2

H

E

A

R

What Else Should I Know? At the close of Galatians 1 and the beginning of chapter 2, Paul used his own story and experiences to build the case that Jewish religious customs no longer bound Christian practice. Paul also referred to his confrontation with Peter (Cephas) when Peter confused some of the young Christians in Antioch by trying to please both the Gentiles and the Judaizers. This mixed message was confusing, if not dangerous, for the Gentiles to whom Peter ministered. Paul, on the other hand, argued that the law, apart from Jesus, can't save anyone. That's why Jesus had to come in the first place. The law highlighted humanity's brokenness and need of a Savior. To say that grace and faith in Jesus alone aren't sufficient for salvation is to say that "Christ died for nothing" (v. 21).

 DEFINE: Look up the definition of Judaizer. Write it out in your own words.

DAY 48 | GALATIANS 3

H

E

A

R

What Else Should I Know? Paul wanted his readers to clearly understand that the law and grace are both important to Christianity, but only one has the power to save: the grace extended to us through the death of Jesus. Paul emphasized that justification—being made right before God—comes by grace through faith in Christ, not by keeping the law.

When Christ came, He fulfilled the law; therefore, faith in Him is the only requirement to experience His saving grace. In verses 26-29, Paul reminded readers that salvation in Jesus unites all people—regardless of race, social status, or gender—as children of God and inheritors of His promises. As daughters of God, we live out our faith in Him by obeying His law.

JUSTIFICATION THROUGH *faith.*

DAY 49 | GALATIANS 4

H

E

A

R

What Else Should I Know? God has adopted believers as His children and has given them the Holy Spirit. Because we're no longer slaves to the world but heirs of God, we offend Him when we obey the law in an attempt to earn His love and grace. Verses 8-20 contain Paul's personal plea for the Galatians not to turn back to the law as the basis of their relationship with God. These verses reflect how deeply Paul cared for these brothers and sisters and how grave their mistake was. One obvious change Paul noticed in them was how they lost their sense of joy they once had as a result of their freedom in Christ.

? **QUESTION:** How does knowing you are a daughter of Christ change the way you view yourself?

DAY 50 | GALATIANS 5

H

E

A

R

What Else Should I Know? Throughout his letter to the Galatians, Paul emphasized that God's call to salvation in Christ is a call to freedom. The freedom of the gospel isn't license to sin but deliverance to serve others. The freedom we receive in Christ can make it tempting to abuse the grace of Jesus, but the heart truly changed by Jesus will reject such temptations.

The Holy Spirit's activity in Christians produces evidence—the fruit of the Spirit—that a person belongs to Christ. These virtues include "love, joy, peace, patience, kindness, goodness, faithfulness, gentleness, and self-control" (vv. 22-23). Each virtue enriches our relationships with God and others. To live them out the way Jesus modeled requires us to depend on the Spirit at work in us. The point Paul repeatedly made in Galatians was that true spiritual transformation comes only through the gospel.

PRAY: Jesus, would you produce in me the fruit of the Spirit?

DAY 51 | GALATIANS 6

HIGHLIGHT the verses that speak to you.

Write out the name of the book:

Which chapter and verse numbers stand out to you?

EXPLAIN what this passage means.

To whom was it originally written? Why?

How does it fit with the verses before and after it?

What is the Holy Spirit intending to communicate through this text?

APPLY what God is saying in these verses to your life.

What does this mean today?

What is God saying to you personally?

How can you apply this message to your life?

RESPOND to what you've read.

In what ways does this passage call you to action?

How will you be different because of what you've learned?

Write out a prayer to God in response to what you read today:

What Else Should I Know? Paul ended Galatians 5 with a reminder that believers in Jesus live by the Holy Spirit. The fruit of the Spirit is a present reality in every Christian's life. What follows in chapter 6 is one practical example of what the outworking of the Spirit looks like. Christians are to hold one another spiritually accountable in the face of sin. They're expected to walk together through the struggles and burdens of sin, supporting one another to endure in the fight against the enemy.

Furthermore, when we're tempted to think we've conquered sin and won the battle, the Spirit's continual conviction reminds us of our need for Jesus and the truth that He alone has won that battle for us. The humility that conviction brings enables us to sympathize with our brothers and sisters in Christ even more.

QUESTION: How have you allowed others to speak into your life and ask you hard questions?

DAY 52 | ACTS 17

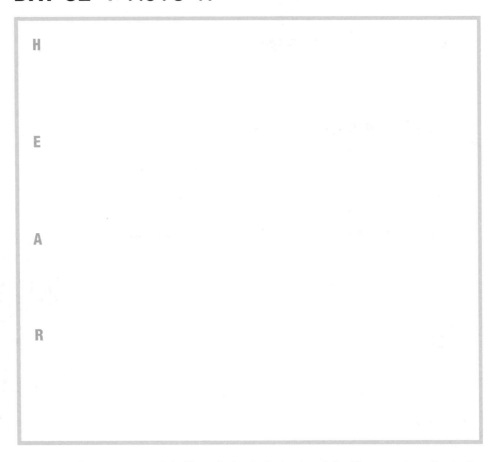

H

E

A

R

What Else Should I Know? In Thessalonica both Jews and Gentiles were receptive to the gospel. Not surprisingly, however, jealous Jews gathered a group of dissenters ("wicked men," v. 5), who started a riot in response. Unable to find Paul and Silas, the mob turned on the people who had welcomed the missionaries into the city. This reaction forced Paul and Silas to move on to Berea, where many more people accepted their message of Christ. Again Jews from Thessalonica caused trouble, so Paul left for Athens.

The account of Paul in Athens gives readers insight into the way Paul changed his approach to sharing the gospel based on his environment and audience. The message never changed, but Paul used their curiosity about spiritual matters to begin a conversation about the one true God. This is a good model for us today: The gospel message we share with others can't change, but, like Paul, we should meet people where they are and share it with them in a way they can understand.

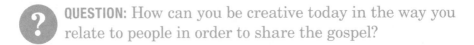

QUESTION: How can you be creative today in the way you relate to people in order to share the gospel?

DAY 53 | ACTS 18

H

E

A

R

What Else Should I Know? As his ministry continued, Paul's steadfast commitment to the gospel proved that God's hand was on him. Acts briefly breaks from Paul's travels to tell readers about a man named Apollos. Apollos was preaching about Jesus in Ephesus. He was well intentioned in his preaching, but his knowledge of Jesus' life and ministry was incomplete. He "knew only John's baptism" (v. 25), which means he understood John the Baptist's teaching about the coming Messiah but didn't yet know the person and work of Jesus Christ.

When Priscilla and Aquila heard his message, they took the opportunity to tell him the rest of the story: not only was Jesus the Messiah, but He had also died on the cross, risen from the dead, and brought the gift of the Holy Spirit for all who believed in Him. With a complete understanding of the gospel, Apollos continued to preach and teach. Sometimes we'll receive correction in our walk with the Lord. As long as that correction aligns with Scripture, we should humbly embrace it as Apollos did: with openness and humility.

 CHALLENGE: Share with a friend what you learned today in your reading.

DAY 54 | 1 THESSALONIANS 1

H

E

A

R

What Else Should I Know? During his time in Thessalonica, briefly mentioned in Acts 17, Paul formed a strong bond with the Christians there. The new believers had enthusiastically embraced the gospel and formed a church, but because of Paul's abrupt departure the believers were immature in the faith.

The Thessalonians' newfound faith was so strong that word of it had spread throughout the region and had become an example to others of turning from a life of sin and idolatry to a life of faith in Jesus. They were outstanding examples for other Christians, both near and far, specifically in their faith, love, and hope (see v. 3). Even in the face of "severe persecution" (v. 6), these people chose to believe the gospel message Paul preached.

DEFINE: Look up the definition of transformation. Write it out in your own words.

DAY 55 | 1 THESSALONIANS 2

H

E

A

R

What Else Should I Know? In chapter 2 Paul reminded the believers in Thessalonica about the purpose of his ministry while he lived among them. Verses 1-12 focus on the time he and his missionary team spent with the Thessalonians and the degree to which they loved these new believers. This passage provides one of the clearest examples of discipleship in all Scripture as Paul models for us how to nurture new believers in Christ.

Verses 13-16 highlight the Thessalonians' response to the gospel. Paul's reminders of their shared history encouraged them to stand strong in their faith and not to abandon it or grow frustrated as they waited for Jesus' return. Verses 17-20 show us Paul's love for these believers and his intense desire to return to them.

PRAY: Jesus, will You help me to reflect You today in my actions, thoughts and words? May people see You in me.

W
E
E
K

12

DAY 56 | 1 THESSALONIANS 3

HIGHLIGHT the verses that speak to you.

Write out the name of the book:

Which chapter and verse numbers stand out to you?

EXPLAIN what this passage means.

To whom was it originally written? Why?

How does it fit with the verses before and after it?

What is the Holy Spirit intending to communicate through this text?

APPLY what God is saying in these verses to your life.

What does this mean today?

What is God saying to you personally?

How can you apply this message to your life?

RESPOND to what you've read.

In what ways does this passage call you to action?

How will you be different because of what you've learned?

Write out a prayer to God in response to what you read today:

What Else Should I Know? Paul sent Timothy to check on the young church and report back to him about the strength of their faith and their commitment to the gospel. Timothy's report to Paul about the church's faith and love was overwhelmingly positive, and it became a source of hope for Paul and his missionary companions, who were being persecuted intensely for their faith.

The prayer in verses 11-13 provides a glimpse into Paul's heart for this church. Paul specifically asked God to "cause you to increase and overflow with love for one another and for everyone" (v. 12) and to "make your hearts blameless in holiness" (v. 13) before God. The most important ways we live out our faith in Christ today are by loving and serving God and others. We should lift up these same prayers to God for ourselves and our church on a daily basis.

DEFINE: Look up the definition of sanctification. Write it out in your own words.

DAY 57 | 1 THESSALONIANS 4

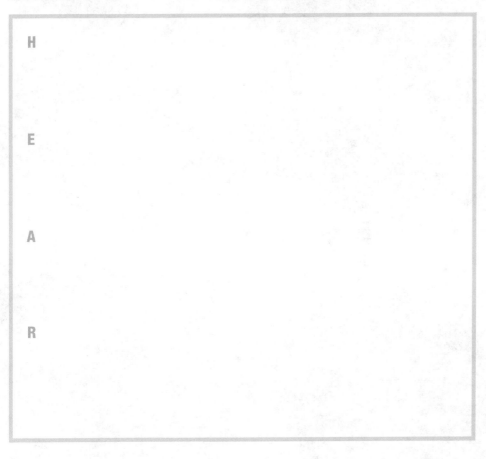

H

E

A

R

What Else Should I Know? Paul began this section by urging the Thessalonians to continue in their devotion to the Lord. Everything they did was to be driven by the overarching goal of pleasing God in their daily lives. Specifically, Paul urged them to work on their sanctification in two key areas: sexual purity (vv. 3-8) and brotherly love (vv. 9-12). Much like Christians today, the Thessalonians lived in a world where immorality was the norm and sexual purity was countercultural. Being set apart as God's children meant pursuing holiness in this area of life, no matter what the world said differently.

Paul's instructions at the close of chapter 4 and the beginning of chapter 5 also included teaching about Jesus' second coming. The Thessalonians had clung to Paul's promise of Jesus' return, but assuming He was coming back soon, they were growing impatient. Understandably in the face of persecution, they wanted to be reunited with Jesus sooner rather than later. Paul encouraged them to believe Jesus was coming back because He promised He would.

 PRAY: Take ten minutes and ask God if there are areas in your life that are not pleasing to Him. Bring that before Him.

DAY 58 | 1 THESSALONIANS 5

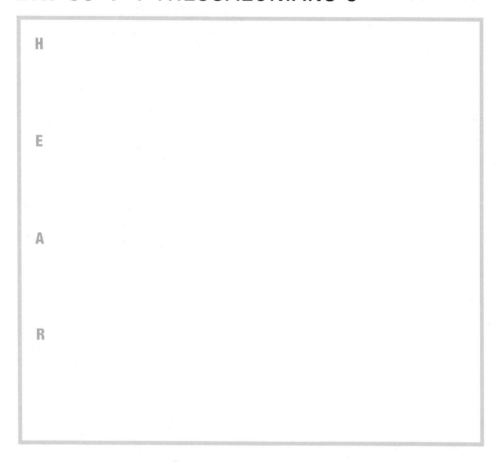

H

E

A

R

What Else Should I Know? We all have questions about Jesus' return, as the Thessalonians did, but it's important to remember that Jesus' return is to be a source of hope, comfort, and motivation for our present walk with Christ. While we wait for Jesus to return, we're to be united with other believers in the church who strive for Christlikeness along with us.

Paul closed chapter 5 with a series of instructions for our lives in and out of church that are incredibly relevant to the present day. In church, Paul encouraged the believers to respect their teachers and leaders, pursue peace in the body of Christ, practice accountability and patience, and serve people in need. In our personal lives, we are to practice joy and gratitude, and pray continually.

 PRAY: Circle which one is the hardest for you to practice. Then, ask God to give you what you need to do better in that area.

Pursuing peace   *Practice accountability*

Patience to Serve People in Need   *Pray Continually*

DAY 59 | 2 THESSALONIANS 1

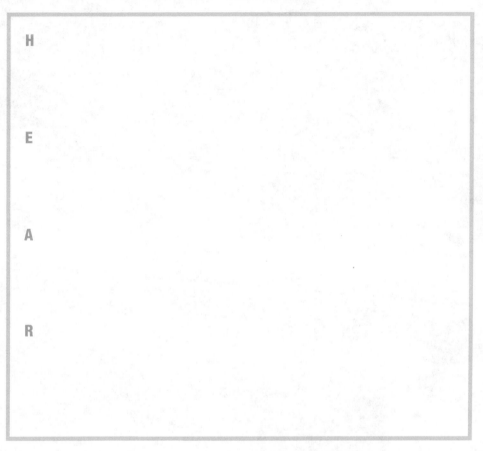

H

E

A

R

What Else Should I Know? Shortly after Paul had written his first letter to the group of new believers in Thessalonica, he received a report about specific issues confronting them, prompting him to send them a follow-up letter. Before correcting the false teaching these believers were being exposed to, Paul affirmed their strong faith and continued spiritual growth, as he typically encouraged other churches where he ministered. Because of the strength of their faith, Paul knew the Thessalonians would be able to endure the persecution they faced. Paul encouraged them to persevere, being confident in Jesus' return and their future with Him in eternity.

Suffering is all but guaranteed for believers who live out their faith in our broken, sinful world, but Paul's words to this young church remind us that the God-honoring way to respond to suffering is with our eyes fixed on eternity. When we live in anticipation of Jesus' return, the temporary trials of this world are easier to endure, and our faith points people to Jesus.

 QUESTION: How should you respond in the face of suffering?

DAY 60 | 2 THESSALONIANS 2

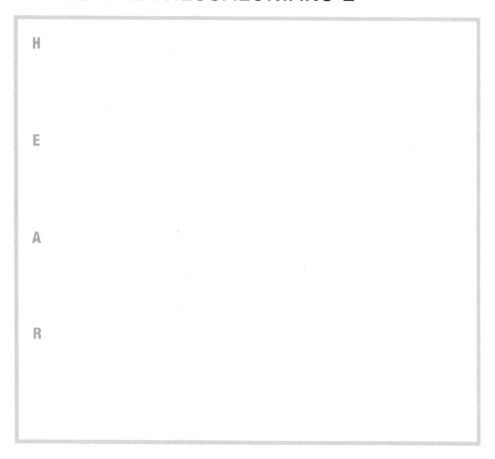

H

E

A

R

What Else Should I Know? Paul had taught this church about Jesus' promise to return one day, but after Paul left, someone had led them to believe that God's great day of judgment had already happened; therefore, Jesus was coming back any day. As a result, some people quit working and became lazy as they waited for Jesus. Jesus never specified when He would return, so Paul didn't either. Instead, the clear command of Jesus was to live diligently for Him in the meantime, taking advantage of the time to tell people about Him and build His kingdom (see Matt. 25; Mark 13).

While we continue to wait for Jesus' return, we must remember that God is sovereignly in control of the world's events, including the end times, and He continues to delay His coming in order to draw as many people as possible to Him. Our mission is to help in that effort while we wait.

 QUESTION: As you wait on the return of Christ, how can you wait well?

Check In

WEEK 13

- ☐ 2 Thessalonians 3
- ☐ Acts 19
- ☐ 1 Corinthians 1
- ☐ 1 Corinthians 2
- ☐ 1 Corinthians 3

MEMORY VERSES

OPTION 1: Psalm 23:5-6
OPTION 2: Proverbs 11:24-25
OPTION 3: Matthew 5:25-26

WEEK 15

- ☐ 1 Corinthians 9
- ☐ 1 Corinthians 10
- ☐ 1 Corinthians 11
- ☐ 1 Corinthians 12
- ☐ 1 Corinthians 13

MEMORY VERSES

OPTION 1: Psalm 25:4-5
OPTION 2: Proverbs 13:2-3
OPTION 3: Matthew 5:29-30

WEEK 14

- ☐ 1 Corinthians 4
- ☐ 1 Corinthians 5
- ☐ 1 Corinthians 6
- ☐ 1 Corinthians 7
- ☐ 1 Corinthians 8

MEMORY VERSES

OPTION 1: Psalm 24:3-4
OPTION 2: Proverbs 12:2-3
OPTION 3: Matthew 5:27-28

WEEK 16

- ☐ 1 Corinthians 14
- ☐ 1 Corinthians 15
- ☐ 1 Corinthians 16
- ☐ 2 Corinthians 1
- ☐ 2 Corinthians 2

MEMORY VERSES

OPTION 1: Psalm 26:2-3
OPTION 2: Proverbs 13:13-14
OPTION 3: Matthew 5:31-32

SCAN THIS QR CODE TO ACCESS A FUN SURPRISE!

WEEK 13

DAY 61 | 2 THESSALONIANS 3

HIGHLIGHT the verses that speak to you.

Write out the name of the book:

Which chapter and verse numbers stand out to you?

EXPLAIN what this passage means.

To whom was it originally written? Why?

How does it fit with the verses before and after it?

What is the Holy Spirit intending to communicate through this text?

APPLY what God is saying in these verses to your life.

What does this mean today?

What is God saying to you personally?

How can you apply this message to your life?

RESPOND to what you've read.

In what ways does this passage call you to action?

How will you be different because of what you've learned?

Write out a prayer to God in response to what you read today:

What Else Should I Know? Each chapter of 2 Thessalonians emphasizes God's sovereignty in different situations. In chapter 3, Paul asked for prayer for his ministry efforts, specifically for the rapid spread of the gospel and for his deliverance from persecution. He prayed the same for them and pointed to God's justice, both now and in the future, which enables believers to feel safe despite troubling circumstances.

Paul encouraged the Thessalonians to hold one another accountable and to encourage one another in their pursuit of Jesus. This letter reminds us that we can endure together because God has proved His faithfulness to us through the life, death, and resurrection of Jesus.

 QUESTION: Have you chosen idleness over obedience this week?

DAY 62 | ACTS 19

Jesus' power is greater than any stronghold.

H

E

A

R

What Else Should I Know? Acts 19:4-7 gives readers one of the most complete accounts of Paul's church-planting efforts. He recruited disciples of Apollos who, like Apollos, had a solid foundation in the teachings of John the Baptist but lacked some of the details about the gospel and the presence and work of the Holy Spirit. Paul taught these men what they lacked, baptized them into the faith, and then used them to form the foundation of the church in Ephesus.

To remain true to the gospel, Paul witnessed of the only true God by revealing the foolishness of worshiping idols. Likewise, we should always stand against values that run contrary to the truth of the Scriptures. Speaking out may spark conflict or draw criticism, but only when we're willing to risk our pride and reputations will we be able to influence our world with the truth of the gospel.

How's your memory verse and Bible reading coming along?

DAY 63 | 1 CORINTHIANS 1

H

E

A

R

What Else Should I Know? During Paul's time in Ephesus, he received a troubling report about the state of the church in Corinth, so he wrote a letter to the congregation. One of the main issues facing this church was a lack of unity. Many teachers, some of whom presented different messages, visited the churches in the New Testament. As a result, various factions that favored one Christian leader over another threatened the unity of the church and undermined its effectiveness.

Paul's solution was the gospel. He reminded the Corinthians that the church is a community that should be centered on Jesus and His message. Division, no matter the cause, is destructive to the body of Christ because it distracts people from the gospel, the singular truth that should draw people in and motivate them toward spiritual growth.

 CHALLENGE: Make a list of all the things you are grateful for in your life. Praise the Lord for His goodness to you.

DAY 64 | 1 CORINTHIANS 2

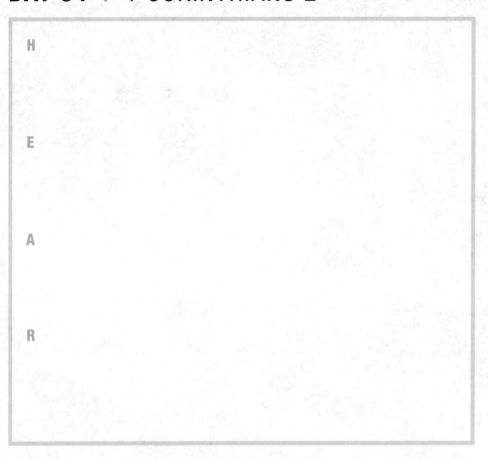

H

E

A

R

What Else Should I Know? As we saw yesterday, the Corinthian church was fractured by loyalties to different teachers who had risen among the congregation. To restore the church's unity, Paul pointed them back to the message of Christ. Paul's emphasis on the Spirit was an attempt to bring them back into unity around the source of all wisdom and the only One whose ministry changes lives.

People without Christ don't have the Spirit to help them understand God's truth; therefore, they don't receive what comes from God's Spirit. However, those indwelled by the Spirit of the Lord have the mind of Christ. Although no human being can know everything about God, our understanding of Him and His purposes always has room to expand. God will give us the spiritual insight we need to understand more about Him through the Holy Spirit's activity in our lives.

? **QUESTION:** How will you live differently this week knowing you have the Holy Spirit?

DAY 65 | 1 CORINTHIANS 3

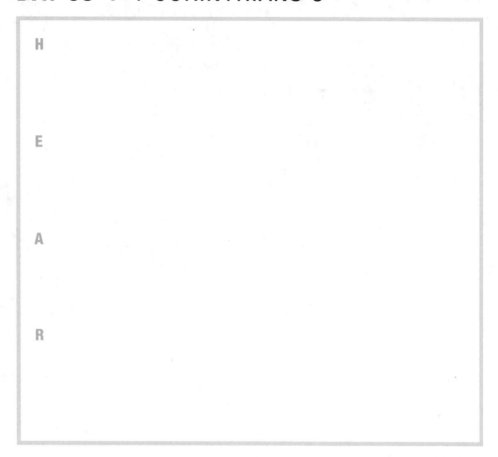

H

E

A

R

What Else Should I Know? In chapter 3, Paul returned to the issue that prompted his letter: divisions in the Corinthian church. The lack of unity in the church proved to Paul that these Christians were still infants in their spiritual maturity. This is why he focused much of his letter on instructing and reminding them how to live and mature as followers of Christ in the church.

The Corinthians' weakness highlighted the need for spiritual leaders in the church. Paul taught that church leaders serve God and, as a result, are accountable first and foremost to Him. He referred to himself and his fellow ministers as servants, using several metaphors to illustrate this concept. Paul's teaching here emphasizes the important role of church leaders to point people to Jesus and His gospel. These verses also remind us of the enduring significance and relevance of God's church in the world and how important it is to treat it with the respect and honor it deserves.

 DEFINE: Look up the definition of servant. Write it out in your own words.

MEMORY VERSE OPTIONS: Psalm 24:3-4; Proverbs 12:2-3; Matthew 5:27-28

DAY 66 | 1 CORINTHIANS 4

HIGHLIGHT the verses that speak to you.

Write out the name of the book:

Which chapter and verse numbers stand out to you?

EXPLAIN what this passage means.

To whom was it originally written? Why?

How does it fit with the verses before and after it?

What is the Holy Spirit intending to communicate through this text?

APPLY what God is saying in these verses to your life.

What does this mean today?

What is God saying to you personally?

How can you apply this message to your life?

RESPOND to what you've read.

In what ways does this passage call you to action?

How will you be different because of what you've learned?

Write out a prayer to God in response to what you read today:

What Else Should I Know? Because the Corinthians were divided by loyalties to different spiritual leaders in their church, Paul reminded them that Christian leaders are first and foremost servants of Christ. He insisted that being an effective Christian leader includes humbly enduring suffering for the faith, whether physically or through criticism.

Paul sought to present the Corinthians with a servant image of leadership, one that followed Jesus' example. Viewing spiritual leaders as servants of Christ removes the potential for division, because the gospel unites us. Leadership is a call to serve humbly, not to strut proudly. Above all, spiritual leaders must prove faithful. Paul claimed that all leaders should be evaluated only by how faithful they are to Christ, not by their own eloquence or wisdom.

Paul's teaching in 1 Corinthians 4 reminds us that all believers, not just leaders, are servants of Christ and should give our entire lives to serving Him.

QUESTION: What does it mean to be a student of the ministry of God?

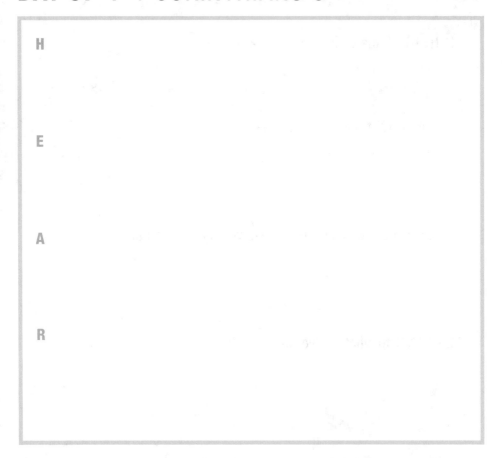

H

E

A

R

What Else Should I Know? Because of the lack of solid leadership in the Corinthian church, the church faced a number of issues that weren't being properly dealt with. The body of believers desperately needed spiritual growth and godly leadership. Paul said he was stunned by an incident of immorality in the church involving a man's inappropriate sexual misconduct with his stepmother. Apparently, the church turned a blind eye toward this behavior. The appropriate response, according to Paul, should have been one of deep grief. The church's role in the matter was not only to express displeasure with the man's behavior but also to actively seek to change his behavior.

Paul used the illustration of yeast in bread to describe the danger of allowing immoral behavior to continue in the church. If left unaddressed, sin spreads throughout the entire Christian community, just as yeast spreads throughout an entire batch of dough. This image reminds readers how severe sin is and the great lengths we should go in order to hold one another accountable.

 PRAY: What sin are you hiding from God? Pray and surrender it right now. He sees you and loves you.

DAY 68 | 1 CORINTHIANS 5

H

E

A

R

What Else Should I Know? The Corinthian church members needed to embrace Christian ethics completely and to reject any immoral conduct in their fellowship. At issue was one believer suing another believer in a secular court rather than in church. Paul argued taking an issue to court showed that the goal of the dispute was rooted in malicious greed rather than a desire for righteous justice or the edification of the parties. Paul feared that involving secular courts in such arguments distracted people from the gospel message and portrayed the church as a divisive group of people instead of the unified body of Christ.

Verses 9-11 remind readers that in Christ everything about a person's identity changes, and we become people set apart from the rest of the world. Paul closed this chapter with a reminder that Christian freedom isn't a license to do anything we want but rather the ability to embrace Christian morality as God intended. With salvation a person's body becomes a temple of the Holy Spirit. When we reflect on Christ's work of forgiveness and reconciliation in our lives, we are reminded of our need to repent of our sins and rely on His grace.

QUESTION: What are some ways you should honor the Lord with your body?

DAY 69 | 1 CORINTHIANS 7

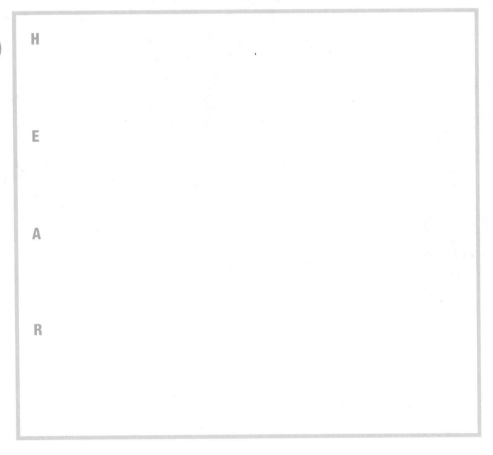

H

E

A

R

What Else Should I Know? The Corinthians had a question concerning marriage and sexuality. Having addressed sexual immorality in chapters 5–6, Paul addressed a related question in chapter 7 about whether it was good for a Christian to be married. He first stated the importance of sex within marriage, as God ordained it, and the danger of temptation when spouses aren't united sexually. In verses 8-9, Paul spoke to unmarried people like him, reminding them of God's call to abstinence. Verses 10-16 highlight the importance of avoiding divorce when no justifiable reason exists.

The remainder of chapter 7 supports Paul's belief that every person should faithfully live for God, regardless of the relational status He has given him or her for each given season. Paul used the image of slavery to remind readers that they're first and foremost slaves of Christ, not slaves of people. This fact means regardless of relational circumstances, we're to fully give ourselves to Jesus and the advancement of His gospel.

PRAY: Jesus, I pray you would allow me to fix my eyes on you—not on a relationship. Would you satisfy my heart? Be with my future spouse. Keep Him pure.

DAY 70 | 1 CORINTHIANS 8

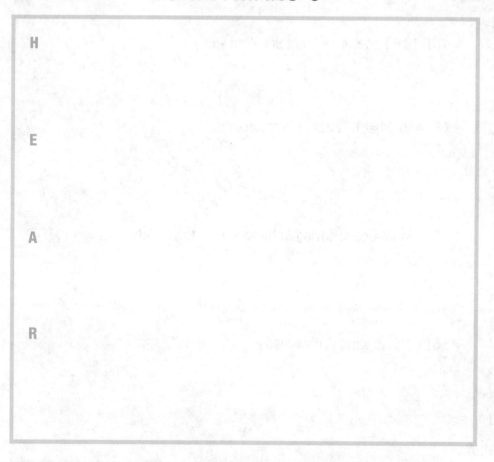

H

E

A

R

What Else Should I Know? Paul's instructions in this chapter answer the second question raised by the Corinthians: whether they could eat food that came from animals previously sacrificed to idols. Paul first reminded the Corinthians that because of their love for God, they knew the world's idols were worthless. This meant in theory, eating the meat from sacrifices wouldn't harm them or constitute a sin.

The greater issue Paul wanted them to consider, however, was the way that action would look to new or immature Christians who had previously practiced idol worship. When exercising Christian freedom, we must take into account the faith of the people around us. If our actions could potentially cause other believers to question their faith or revert to habitual sins, exercising our freedom isn't worth the cost.

? **QUESTION:** How can you practice your freedom in a way that honors God and builds up others?

W
E
E
K

15

DAY 71 | 1 CORINTHIANS 9

HIGHLIGHT the verses that speak to you.

Write out the name of the book:

Which chapter and verse numbers stand out to you?

EXPLAIN what this passage means.

To whom was it originally written? Why?

How does it fit with the verses before and after it?

What is the Holy Spirit intending to communicate through this text?

APPLY what God is saying in these verses to your life.

What does this mean today?

What is God saying to you personally?

How can you apply this message to your life?

RESPOND to what you've read.

In what ways does this passage call you to action?

How will you be different because of what you've learned?

Write out a prayer to God in response to what you read today:

What Else Should I Know? The city of Corinth was known for its immorality and perversion, while many of the Corinthian Christians were impressed with their own knowledge and spirituality. This pride led to insensitivity and inappropriateness in their relationships with other Christians.

In chapter 9 Paul used himself as an example of the principle he taught in chapter 8: mature believers should avoid behavior that can cause less mature believers to sin. Throughout this passage Paul talked about his rights as an apostle, such as the right to eat certain foods or accept financial support. However, Paul didn't take advantage of rights like these for fear they would draw people away from Christ. He didn't want any of his actions to hinder his sharing the gospel. Instead, everything he did was intentionally designed to point people to Christ and receive the heavenly reward that awaited him.

Paul regularly emphasized his goal of reaching people for Christ and leading them to more focused discipleship. For him, that mission outweighed every other consideration. Paul's deep passion for sharing the gospel at all costs is evident in this passage.

 QUESTION: What lengths are you willing to go in order to reach people?

DAY 72 | 1 CORINTHIANS 10

H

E

A

R

What Else Should I Know? To help his readers better understand Christian freedom, Paul returned in 1 Corinthians 10 to the issue of food that had been offered to idols. Paul urged mature Christians to embrace the responsibility of seeking what was good for other believers over exercising their freedom in Christ to engage in certain activities. Paul recounted several occasions when groups of Israelites faced God's judgment because they gave in to sin by practicing idolatry, committing sexual immorality, testing the Lord, and grumbling against Him. Each of those sins led to grave consequences that should warn the Corinthians—and us—not to abuse Christian freedom.

With freedom in Christ comes great responsibility. As new creations in Christ, we need to choose actions that further God's kingdom and mission. When we abandon our will and control, we allow someone else to rule and lead our lives. Following Christ gives us a desire to change our ways and make the gospel known. As Paul wrote, the driving force behind everything a Christian does should be living "for the glory of God" (v. 31).

 QUESTION: What idols in your life have stolen your devotion to Jesus?

DAY 73 | 1 CORINTHIANS 11

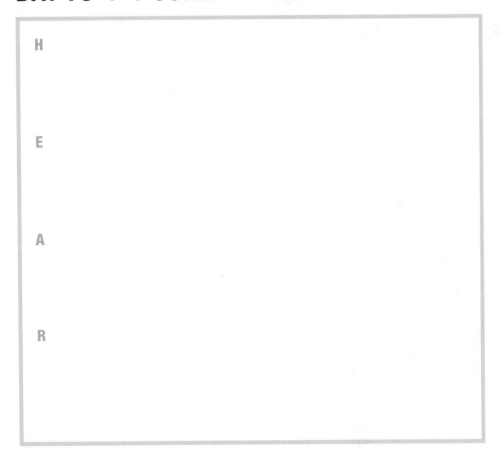

H

E

A

R

What Else Should I Know? In this chapter Paul turned to the matter of proper conduct in worship. Paul began with the participation of Christian women in worship. The issue of head coverings pointed to the disunity between Jewish and Greek customs, both of which were coming together in the church. These instructions were Paul's attempt to unify the church so that such matters didn't distract from worship or cause further conflict. He reminded the Corinthians that every Christian is primarily subject to the authority of Christ, the Head of the church.

Paul also provided instructions on the Lord's Supper, highlighting the irreverent approach some Corinthians took toward that practice. The Lord's Supper wasn't to be a time to indulge or feast but a time to reflect on and rejoice together over Jesus' sacrifice. The key problem at the root of the issues Paul addressed in this chapter was selfish behavior that was inconsistent with the holy lives Christians are called to lead.

 PRAY: Jesus, help me to be unified to other believers. Would You meet me in the areas I have become distracted?

DAY 74 | 1 CORINTHIANS 12

H

E

A

R

What Else Should I Know? Among the many problems the Corinthian church faced, one thorny issue centered on the nature and purpose of spiritual gifts. Some church members viewed the type of gift a believer possessed as a measuring stick for that believer's level of spirituality. They considered some gifts to be more important than others.

In response to this misconception, Paul set out a basic rule for considering all spiritual gifts: all Christians share the common confession of faith that Jesus is Lord. On this foundation Paul affirmed the value of all spiritual gifts and declared that each gift comes from one and the same source—the Holy Spirit. God gives every believer his or her gifts and determines the way they're to be used for His purposes. Paul used the analogy of a body to highlight the importance of every spiritual gift.

 QUESTION: What gifts has God given you? How are you using them for the church?

DAY 75 | 1 CORINTHIANS 13

H

E

A

R

What Else Should I Know? In the previous chapter Paul argued that every spiritual gift is necessary for the health of the church. In chapter 13 he revealed the "even better way" (12:31) spiritual gifts should be put into practice. All gifts, no matter what purpose they serve in the church, must be governed by Christlike love. Without love as their motive, spiritual gifts are empty shells. The love Paul had in mind isn't something believers must produce on their own but a gift God gives to them through His indwelling Holy Spirit.

Church members are to demonstrate that we're the body of Christ on earth by loving one another in this manner. In verses 8-13 Paul went on to highlight the permanent nature of the Holy Spirit's love. All spiritual gifts will eventually fade because the day will come when Jesus returns and those gifts are no longer needed to further His kingdom on earth. When that day comes, love alone will remain.

 PRAY: Jesus, help us to love the way you love. Expand our hearts and open our eyes to see people and to love well.

MEMORY VERSE OPTIONS: Psalm 26:2-3; Proverbs 13:13-14; Matthew 5:31-32

DAY 76 | 1 CORINTHIANS 14

HIGHLIGHT the verses that speak to you.

Write out the name of the book:

Which chapter and verse numbers stand out to you?

EXPLAIN what this passage means.

To whom was it originally written? Why?

How does it fit with the verses before and after it?

What is the Holy Spirit intending to communicate through this text?

APPLY what God is saying in these verses to your life.

What does this mean today?

What is God saying to you personally?

How can you apply this message to your life?

RESPOND to what you've read.

In what ways does this passage call you to action?

How will you be different because of what you've learned?

Write out a prayer to God in response to what you read today:

What Else Should I Know? First Corinthians 14 brings Paul's instructions on corporate worship to a close by warning against the abuse of certain spiritual gifts, specifically prophecy and speaking in tongues. Here, Paul argued that more important than exercising spiritual gifts in corporate worship was clearly communicating the gospel. While spiritual gifts are given first and foremost to serve the church, it's always important to keep in mind ways those gifts can be used to encourage unbelievers and point them to Jesus. Every gift can fulfill this purpose when practiced the way it's meant to be practiced.

When the church gathers for worship, the purpose should always be to exalt God and strengthen all who are present. That becomes possible when worship is peaceful and reverent, an environment in which people are waiting to hear from Him.

QUESTION: How can spiritual gifts be used in both positive and negative ways?

DAY 77 | 1 CORINTHIANS 15

H

E

A

R

What Else Should I Know? Some church members were questioning the resurrection, not because they doubted Jesus' resurrection but because they failed to understand how Jesus' resurrection guaranteed that God would raise all believers. Every Christ-follower's story ends with bodily resurrection and eternal communion with Christ. Our glorious future reminds us that we're not to live only for the present day, though because our actions have eternal consequences, each day's choices are important. The future hope of being with Christ and being made new shapes every aspect of our Christian life. We live for His purposes in the present because everything we do for Christ matters eternally.

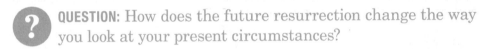

QUESTION: How does the future resurrection change the way you look at your present circumstances?

DAY 78 | 1 CORINTHIANS 16

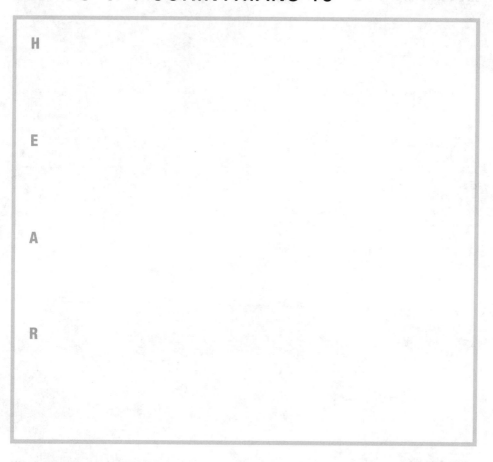

H

E

A

R

What Else Should I Know? Paul encouraged the Corinthians to set aside money from their earnings to give as a gift to their suffering brothers and sisters. Practicing generosity is a clear way for the church to excel in the Lord's work and ensure that our labor isn't in vain.

This letter closes, as many of Paul's letters do, with a series of personal requests. Paul intended to return to Corinth and spend time with the believers there. He asked that in the meantime they accept Timothy on Paul's behalf and welcome him into their community.

Along with the final greetings, Paul left the Corinthians with a clear set of marching orders to carry out until his return. This instruction, summarizing everything Paul wrote in the letter, is a worthy goal for disciples of Christ today: "Be alert, stand firm in the faith, be courageous, be strong. Do everything in love" (1 Cor. 16:13-14).

 QUESTION: How can you practice generosity toward others?

DAY 79 | 2 CORINTHIANS 1

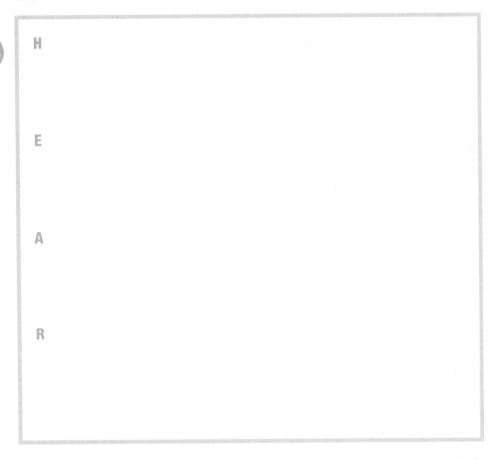

H

E

A

R

What Else Should I Know? In chapter 1 we witness the vital connection between Paul's commitment to Christ and his commitment to Christ's church. Paul reminded the Corinthians that God is a God of comfort. The apostle described the suffering he had experienced and sought to comfort them in their suffering for the gospel as well. Although God has warned that serving Him brings suffering, He also equips His servants to comfort one another through suffering with the promises that they don't suffer in vain and that eternal peace awaits.

We serve a God who keeps His promises—a truth shown throughout the entirety of Scripture. We know God will keep His promises to us because He has proved Himself trustworthy through the life, death, and resurrection of Jesus Christ, who is the same yesterday, today, and for eternity (see Heb. 13:8). Because God keeps His promises, we can confidently wait for Him to fulfill them all.

CHALLENGE: Who around you is hurting? Comfort them today. Reach out and encourage them.

DAY 80 | 2 CORINTHIANS 2

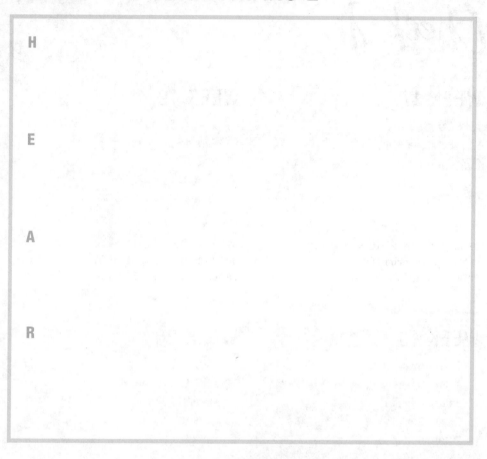

H

E

A

R

What Else Should I Know? Paul wrote 2 Corinthians to defend his ministry, which false teachers were calling into question, and to provide further spiritual guidance for the young church. That guidance begins in verses 5-11 with a call for the church to extend forgiveness to someone among them who had sinned but later repented. Paul said it was time for the church to forgive him and put the incident behind them so that Satan wouldn't gain leverage over the congregation.

The remainder of chapter 2 begins Paul's defense of his ministry decisions that were being questioned. He described the reason for an unplanned trip to Macedonia, reminding his readers that God was the One who charted the course of His missionary journeys. Paul understood that God was at work spreading His gospel message, and sometimes that reality meant Paul's plans had to change.

 CHALLENGE: Who in your life do you need to ask for forgiveness from today? Who do you need to forgive?

Check In

AS YOU BEGIN A NEW MONTH OF READING, TAKE A MINUTE AND PRAY ABOUT ALL GOD HAS IN STORE FOR YOU.

WEEK 17

- [ ] 2 Corinthians 3
- [ ] 2 Corinthians 4
- [ ] 2 Corinthians 5
- [ ] 2 Corinthians 6
- [ ] 2 Corinthians 7

MEMORY VERSES

OPTION 1: Psalm 27:10
OPTION 2: Proverbs 14:2-3
OPTION 3: Matthew 5:33-35

WEEK 19

- [ ] 2 Corinthians 13
- [ ] Mark 1
- [ ] Mark 2
- [ ] Mark 3
- [ ] Mark 4

MEMORY VERSES

OPTION 1: Psalm 32:1
OPTION 2: Proverbs 14:26-27
OPTION 3: Matthew 5:38-39

WEEK 18

- [ ] 2 Corinthians 8
- [ ] 2 Corinthians 9
- [ ] 2 Corinthians 10
- [ ] 2 Corinthians 11
- [ ] 2 Corinthians 12

MEMORY VERSES

OPTION 1: Psalm 30:5
OPTION 2: Proverbs 14:12
OPTION 3: Matthew 5:36-37

WEEK 20

- [ ] Mark 5
- [ ] Mark 6
- [ ] Mark 7
- [ ] Mark 8
- [ ] Mark 9

MEMORY VERSES

OPTION 1: Psalm 33:4-5
OPTION 2: Proverbs 14:34
OPTION 3: Matthew 5:40-42

SCAN THIS QR CODE TO ACCESS A FUN SURPRISE!

MEMORY VERSE OPTIONS: Psalm 27:10; Proverbs 14:2-3; Matthew 5:33-35

W
E
E
K

17

DAY 81 | 2 CORINTHIANS 3

HIGHLIGHT the verses that speak to you.

Write out the name of the book:

Which chapter and verse numbers stand out to you?

EXPLAIN what this passage means.

To whom was it originally written? Why?

How does it fit with the verses before and after it?

What is the Holy Spirit intending to communicate through this text?

APPLY what God is saying in these verses to your life.

What does this mean today?

What is God saying to you personally?

How can you apply this message to your life?

RESPOND to what you've read.

In what ways does this passage call you to action?

How will you be different because of what you've learned?

Write out a prayer to God in response to what you read today:

What Else Should I Know? While false teachers among the Corinthians wrote their own letters of recommendation to try to validate their authority as ministers, Paul reminded the Corinthians that *they* were his letter; their changed lives and commitment to the gospel validated Paul's ministry efforts. Paul's method of discipleship mirrors the way Jesus designed gospel ministry to work and the way He modeled it for us. Disciples go out and make disciple-makers, who make more disciple-makers.

Paul wanted the Corinthian believers to understand that the ministry he did—the same ministry to which they were called—was guided by the work of the Holy Spirit in their lives. Paul wanted his readers to be confident in the work to which God called them and to remember that they didn't labor alone—a message that still rings true for us today.

QUESTION: How have you experienced discipleship in your own life?

DAY 82 | 2 CORINTHIANS 4

H

E

A

R

What Else Should I Know? Paul highlighted all the suffering he had endured, contending that his suffering proved that ministry success rested in God's power, not in human accomplishments.

To help his readers understand, Paul used the image of jars of clay, in which people in his day stored their most valuable possessions. In the gospel of Jesus Christ, God has given His people the greatest treasure in the universe. But believing in this treasure doesn't make us impervious to pain. Instead, we hold this treasure in lives of clay. Just as people of the time had to shatter the clay jar to reveal the treasure, God at times must break His people for the gospel to shine forth. When a person is broken, Jesus shines through. God uses our experiences of brokenness to bring glory to Himself and to mold us into His image.

If you feel unworthy, unloved, or like you've fallen short, let that be a promise to you today. You are loved—and God is not through with you.

 QUESTION: Though you are a weak and fragile jar of clay, how can you let Jesus shine through the cracks of your brokenness?

DAY 83 | 2 CORINTHIANS 5

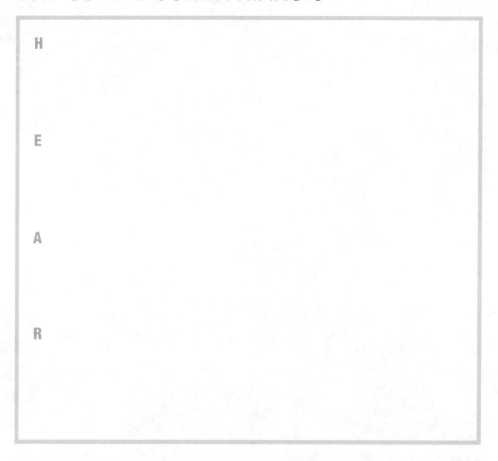

H

E

A

R

What Else Should I Know? Because of the hardships Christians endure in living for the gospel, as Paul described in chapter 4, it's important that we learn to set our eyes on eternity. Suffering because of Christ prepares us for eternity because it challenges us to serve God faithfully and to live each day for our future with Him. Although eternity holds the promise of hope for Christians, it brings the promise of judgment and condemnation for those who don't know Jesus. For this reason Paul also emphasized the importance of the ministry of reconciliation, both with God and with others. Paul's motivation for seeking reconciliation with others was God's love.

As we grow to understand our identity in Christ, we'll embrace the great task with which God has blessed us in Christ: to be His ambassadors of Christ's message of reconciliation. Reconciliation is a radical idea—and it starts with Christ's love.

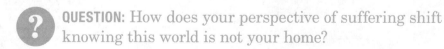

? **QUESTION:** How does your perspective of suffering shift knowing this world is not your home?

DAY 84 | 2 CORINTHIANS 6

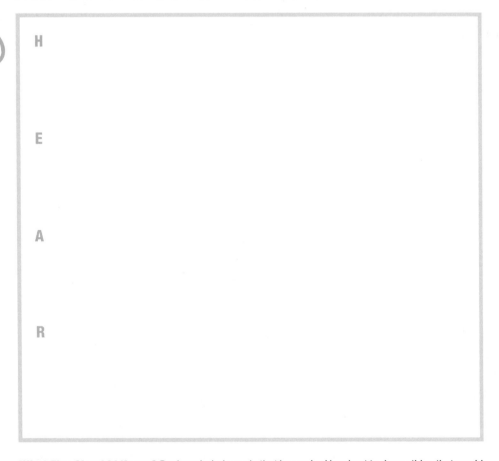

H

E

A

R

What Else Should I Know? Paul reminded people that he worked hard not to do anything that would cause others to stumble into sin. What follows is a catalog of experiences he faced through which he was able to remain a faithfully committed servant of God. The list includes everything from general hardship, beatings, hunger, and dishonor to purity, kindness, and great rejoicing. No matter the situation, Paul served Jesus by guiding people to Him and helping them grow in their faith. He challenged the Corinthian believers to do the same, beginning with their love for and affirmation of Paul.

Paul followed this encouragement with a word of caution against becoming "partners with those who do not believe" (v. 14). Paul didn't mean they shouldn't associate with unbelievers (he often encouraged just the opposite) but that a Christian's loyalty should always be first and foremost to Jesus. Relationships that hinder our primary relationship with Jesus are to be avoided.

DEFINE: Look up the definition of resurrection. Write it out in your own words.

DAY 85 | 2 CORINTHIANS 7

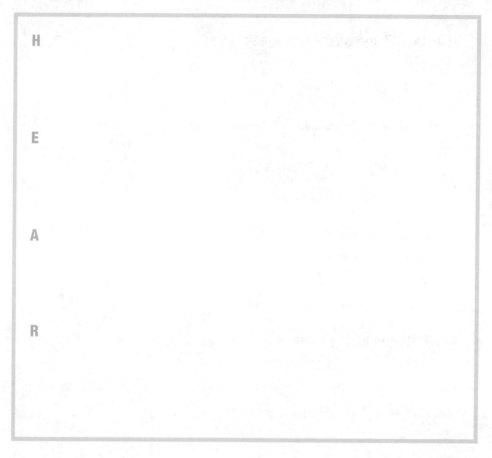

H

E

A

R

What Else Should I Know? Second Corinthians 7 provides additional insight into Paul's interaction with the church in Corinth. Having received a report from Titus about the church, Paul rejoiced that their once-strained relationship was improving. His goal throughout his long-distance relationship with Corinth was to maintain love and intimacy.

This affirmation gave Paul the opportunity to talk about godly sorrow versus worldly sorrow. He noted that not until sin is exposed and grieved over can a person truly turn away from it and turn back to God, which is the meaning of repentance. This understanding of sorrow makes it a necessary, albeit unpleasant, part of spiritual growth. In contrast, worldly sorrow refers to something like the grief that comes from being caught in sin, not grief over the sin itself. Though coming face-to-face with one's sins is never pleasant, God offers great hope and restoration to those who turn to Him in repentance. This is the example the Corinthians set for us, and Paul rejoiced when he heard about it.

CHALLENGE: Pray for someone today who is suffering. What are some ways can you love and serve them?

DAY 86 | 2 CORINTHIANS 8

HIGHLIGHT the verses that speak to you.

Write out the name of the book:

Which chapter and verse numbers stand out to you?

EXPLAIN what this passage means.

To whom was it originally written? Why?

How does it fit with the verses before and after it?

What is the Holy Spirit intending to communicate through this text?

APPLY what God is saying in these verses to your life.

What does this mean today?

What is God saying to you personally?

How can you apply this message to your life?

RESPOND to what you've read.

In what ways does this passage call you to action?

How will you be different because of what you've learned?

Write out a prayer to God in response to what you read today:

What Else Should I Know? The church began practicing sacrificial generosity from its very conception (see Acts 2:44-45); therefore, Paul reminded the church that generosity should be a fundamental part of their ministry to one another. He told the Corinthians about the generosity of the Macedonian churches, who, despite their own poverty, had raised money for the poor Christians in Jerusalem. Even though they were poor, they gave generously because the Christian community was in need.

Second Corinthians 8:9 reveals the motivation for all believers to willingly sacrifice of themselves for the sake of others in the community: Jesus' sacrifice for us. Jesus practiced and taught sacrificial giving. Gratitude for what Jesus has done for us motivates us to demonstrate responsible stewardship of our lives and our possessions. In verses 14-15, Paul reminded the Corinthians that because of their generosity to the Jerusalem Christians, other churches would be generous to them in their own time of need.

 QUESTION: What should the motivation be when you give?

DAY 87 | 2 CORINTHIANS 9

H

E

A

R

What Else Should I Know? Continuing the topic of giving from chapter 8, Paul wrote about his intent to return and collect the Corinthians' offering. He had spoken highly to the Macedonians about the Corinthians' generosity, but Paul's words in this letter suggest that their enthusiasm for giving may have waned since he first mentioned the offering. Therefore, he would bring a small contingent with him to motivate the Corinthians to collect the financial gift and have it ready to be delivered when he arrived.

Paul's words in this chapter focus on the attitude behind generosity rather than the act of giving itself. He challenged the Corinthians to give freely and cheerfully, not by compulsion, so that their gift would be a blessing, not only to the recipients but to the givers as well. As with all the other outworkings of a person's faith in God, generosity begins in the heart of the giver. When we have a generous heart, we reflect God's love and generosity to the world. Our generosity has the power to point people to Christ.

 QUESTION: What does your generosity say about your heart?

DAY 88 | 2 CORINTHIANS 10

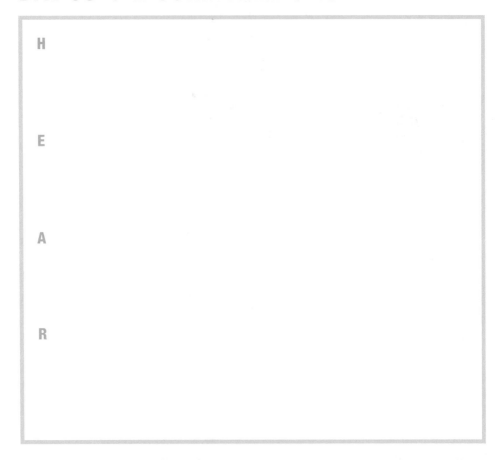

H

E

A

R

What Else Should I Know? In this chapter, Paul's critics questioned his authority as an apostle and accused him of lacking the boldness in person that he expressed in his letters (vv. 1-2). They tried to convince the Corinthians that Paul wasn't as powerful as he claimed to be in Christ, and they criticized his speaking abilities (vv. 7-10).

In response to these accusations, Paul argued that he belonged to God and that his motives for serving God were pure. In defending himself and his teaching, Paul reminded his readers then and now that we're in the midst of a very real spiritual battle, one that takes place largely in our minds (see vv. 3-5). In the battlefield of the mind, we must be on guard for and actively battle against wrong ways of thinking that can interfere with our personal growth in Christ and our witness to the world. By calling us to take our thoughts captive, Paul reminds us that we must actively align our thoughts with the mind of Christ.

 QUESTION: You are not a victim of your own mind. You get to choose to fight your thoughts. What thoughts do you need to take captive today?

DAY 89 | 2 CORINTHIANS 11

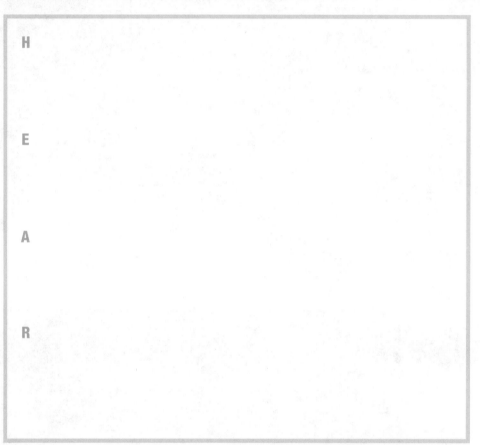

H

E

A

R

What Else Should I Know? Paul was the most famous missionary of their time, and his influence was well known throughout the region. To think he had to go to such great lengths to remind them of his authority and his calling from God undoubtedly felt foolish to him. But he offered a defense because he cared so much for the Corinthians, and he feared that false teachers were leading them astray by planting doubts about Paul in their minds and leading them into false teaching.

Paul reminded the Corinthians of his résumé, an impressive one by Jewish standards. He was a Hebrew, an Israelite, a descendant of Abraham, and a servant of Christ. But rather than focus on his knowledge, experience, and abilities, Paul cited his suffering as the clearest evidence of his integrity and devotion to Christ. Through all of these difficulties, Paul learned the life-changing truth that God's power is demonstrated in the midst of human weakness.

? **QUESTION:** How do the sufferings of Paul make you feel about your current sufferings?

DAY 90 | 2 CORINTHIANS 12

H

E

A

R

What Else Should I Know? Chapter 12 continues Paul's defense of his apostolic ministry that he began in chapter 11. In addition to his weaknesses, Paul highlighted a special vision and several "extraordinary revelations" (12:7) as evidence that his ministry efforts were rooted in God-given authority. These personal visions and revelations from God could have made it easy for Paul to become prideful in his ministry, but that was never the case, thanks in large part to the "thorn in the flesh" (v. 7) God gave him.

Much debate has been given to the identity of Paul's thorn, but the specifics don't matter for his argument. What matters is that this thorn constantly reminded Paul of his weakness and humility, compared with God's power and majesty. The thorn helped Paul remain dependent on God, whether or not his ministry thrived. Rather than removing Paul's suffering, however, God gave him something better: sufficient grace for Paul to rise above it by depending on God's power. Like Paul, we have weaknesses that can open the door for God's power to flow through us, changing not only our lives but also the lives of the people with whom we come into contact.

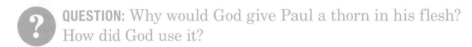

QUESTION: Why would God give Paul a thorn in his flesh? How did God use it?

MEMORY VERSE OPTIONS: Psalm 32:1; Proverbs 14:26-27; Matthew 5:38-39

DAY 91 | 2 CORINTHIANS 13

HIGHLIGHT the verses that speak to you.

Write out the name of the book:

Which chapter and verse numbers stand out to you?

EXPLAIN what this passage means.

To whom was it originally written? Why?

How does it fit with the verses before and after it?

What is the Holy Spirit intending to communicate through this text?

APPLY what God is saying in these verses to your life.

What does this mean today?

What is God saying to you personally?

How can you apply this message to your life?

RESPOND to what you've read.

In what ways does this passage call you to action?

How will you be different because of what you've learned?

Write out a prayer to God in response to what you read today:

What Else Should I Know? Paul closed his second letter to the Corinthians with a series of warnings. He would come to visit them for the third time, and he wanted to see true repentance of sin. Paul had invested much instruction, encouragement, and accountability in them, and he wanted to see spiritual growth in this area. He challenged the Corinthians to test themselves, meaning he wanted them to take a serious look at the validity and strength of their faith. Were they Christians? If the answer was yes, were they living like it, or were they living in unrepentant sin? Everything Paul had written was to build up their faith (see v. 10), in hopes that they would be convicted of their sin, repent of it, and grow in their faith.

Although we can't know for sure what the outcome of Paul's visit was, we know the church faithfully and generously gave the collection of money to the Jerusalem Christians. Paul's letter is a great reminder for believers today of the love we're to have for our brothers and sisters in Christ, the seriousness with which we're to take Scripture and its teaching, and the importance of personal spiritual growth.

QUESTION: Examine yourself today. Where are you putting your faith and trust?

DAY 92 | MARK 1

H

E

A

R

What Else Should I Know? Much of Mark's Gospel focuses on the actions of Jesus and the ways people responded to Him. Chapter 1 begins with the preparations made for Jesus' ministry. John the Baptist called for repentance from sin and proclaimed the One (Jesus) to follow him. Though Jesus had no sins for which He needed forgiveness, He presented Himself for baptism to identify with His people. Mark next introduced Jesus as a proclaimer of the message of good news with a call to repentance. Jesus formally invited four fishermen to follow Him.

Jesus further demonstrated His oneness with God by displaying authority over unclean spirits and healing many physical illnesses. Although many people sought Him because of His healing power, Jesus shied away from the crowds and devoted most of His time to training the twelve disciples. A final healing, however, showed Jesus' ministry to be marked by compassion for people in need. From the beginning of Mark's Gospel, we see that in Jesus' ministry, meeting people's spiritual and physical needs went hand in hand. This is the model He demonstrated for us.

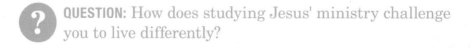

QUESTION: How does studying Jesus' ministry challenge you to live differently?

DAY 93 | MARK 2

Jesus CAME TO HEAL SICK PEOPLE.

H

E

A

R

What Else Should I Know? The healing of the paralyzed man is one of Jesus' most well-known miracles. When Jesus saw the faith of the man's friends, He was moved to extend spiritual healing to the man, the most important healing Jesus offers. Jesus' words "Your sins are forgiven" (v. 5) raised an issue with the teachers of the law who were present, because they knew God alone has the authority to forgive sins. Jesus, being God, knew their thoughts, so to validate His authority, He healed the man's paralysis as well.

Later, we see Jesus' encounter with the tax collector, Levi (Matthew), who would become one of Jesus' disciples and would write the Gospel of Matthew. Jesus' association with tax collectors and known sinners upset the religious leaders. Jesus took this opportunity to clearly articulate His mission: "It is not those who are well who need a doctor, but those who are sick. I didn't come to call the righteous, but sinners" (v. 17). All of us are born sick, born into sin. Jesus came to earth in order to heal humanity's brokenness and restore our relationship with God.

DAY 94 | MARK 3

H

E

A

R

What Else Should I Know? As Jesus traveled throughout Galilee teaching and performing miracles, large crowds began to follow Him. Mark pointed out that the evil spirits Jesus exorcised as part of His healings knew He was the Son of God, but Jesus wanted them to remain quiet until He was ready for His identity to be revealed.

While Jesus silenced the demons, the religious leaders accused Him of being one Himself. Jesus reminded them that His power was greater than Satan's, because He had the power to cast out spirits and forgive sin, both of which eliminate Satan's control over a person's life.

Jesus' statement about family that Mark included at the close of chapter 3 is an important word for readers then and now about the nature of a relationship with Jesus. Jesus considers anyone who follows Him a part of His family. Maybe you have a hard relationship with your family. Maybe your parents are divorced, or not everyone in your family goes to church. No matter what your earthly family is like, or what a relationship with Jesus may cost you, you're a part of God's family forever.

CHALLENGE: Read Ephesians 6. Put on the full armor of God today to protect yourself from the evil one.

DAY 95 | MARK 4

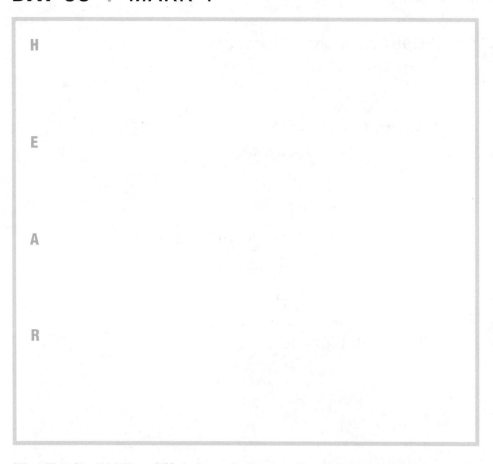

H

E

A

R

What Else Should I Know? Mark 4 records three parables and one miracle by Jesus. Each parable teaches key characteristics of the kingdom of God. The first one is the parable of the four soils. Jesus explained that the seed in the parable is the Word of God, taught by the sower. The different ways people hear and respond to the gospel are the different types of soil. People who respond positively to God's Word are those who accept it and put its truths into action.

In the second parable, the lamp represents the truths Jesus' disciples would be responsible for telling the world, a responsibility Jesus wanted them to take seriously. The parable of the growing seed continued the image He used in the first parable, this time teaching that God would make sure His kingdom grew and spread.

In verse 35, Mark shifted from a series of teachings to a series of miracles. When Jesus calmed the storm, He showed His power over creation, a power only God could possess. The same voice that spoke creation into being calmed it with just a word, leaving the disciples in a state of fear and awe as their understanding of Jesus continued to grow.

QUESTION: What parable stuck out to you the most in this chapter? Why?

W
E
E
K

20

DAY 96 | MARK 5

HIGHLIGHT the verses that speak to you.

Write out the name of the book:

Which chapter and verse numbers stand out to you?

EXPLAIN what this passage means.

To whom was it originally written? Why?

How does it fit with the verses before and after it?

What is the Holy Spirit intending to communicate through this text?

APPLY what God is saying in these verses to your life.

What does this mean today?

What is God saying to you personally?

How can you apply this message to your life?

RESPOND to what you've read.

In what ways does this passage call you to action?

How will you be different because of what you've learned?

Write out a prayer to God in response to what you read today:

What Else Should I Know? Mark 5 continues with three more miracles, each unique in demonstrating the type of work Jesus did and what the miracle revealed about Him. The first story recounts a time when Jesus exorcised a group of demons from a man powerless to resist them. When they saw Jesus, the demons immediately recognized Him as the Son of God and knew the power He had over them. Casting the demons out of the man, Jesus allowed them to enter a herd of pigs.

What follows is one of the most vivid New Testament descriptions of Jesus' saving work in a person's life. Verse 15 stands in direct contrast to verses 1-5. Rather than naked, the man was clothed. Rather than mentally insane from the demonic possession, he was now "in his right mind." Rather than being isolated from everyone, he was with Jesus. What an incredible picture of the saving grace Jesus offers us.

QUESTION: How do the stories of Jesus' healings impact your belief?

DAY 97 | MARK 6

H

E

A

R

What Else Should I Know? Mark 6 darted from event to event in Jesus' ministry, beginning with Jesus' reception in His hometown and ending with His miraculous walking on water. Evidently, Jesus' growing fame didn't impress the people in His hometown, and they refused to believe He was the Messiah. Their rejection didn't surprise Jesus, but it meant His ministry in Nazareth was limited. Instead, He and His disciples focused their efforts elsewhere, and He sent them out in pairs to call people to repentance. To validate their ministry, He gave them the authority to cast out demons and heal the sick. This marked the beginning of the disciples' ministry, which was modeled on that of Jesus.

The two miracles that close chapter 6 show readers that one reason Jesus performed miracles was to help His disciples understand who He was and realize the power He had. Only when His disciples truly understood Jesus to be the Son of God could they wholeheartedly commit to joining Him in His work of redemption.

 QUESTION: Just like Jesus and the disciples, who can you spend time investing in?

H

E

A

R

What Else Should I Know? As word about Jesus continued to spread, religious leaders came from Jerusalem to investigate Him. Among the things they didn't like about Him was His seeming disregard for their religious rules and rituals. Jesus didn't follow all their rules, and He didn't instruct His disciples to do so either. He used their questions and criticism as opportunities to correct their hypocritical nature.

The Pharisees had misplaced motives for obeying God and His law. Their appearance on the outside mattered more to them than the state of their hearts. In other words, they cared more about looking religious than loving God. Furthermore, they made up their own religious rules and placed them at a level of greater importance than God's law. This practice is seen most clearly in the ways they used obedience to their laws as an excuse to avoid helping people.

Verses 24-37 describe Jesus' ministry among people with whom the religious leaders would never have associated, including Gentiles (Greeks) and the demon-possessed. Mark repeatedly emphasized Jesus' compassionate heart, here showing how different it was from the hearts of the religious leaders. At this point in Jesus' ministry, His popularity had reached new heights, as had the religious leaders' hatred for Him.

RULES ≠ RELATIONSHIP

DAY 99 | MARK 8

H

E

A

R

What Else Should I Know? One important lesson in Mark's Gospel is Jesus' investment in His disciples. Occasionally, this meant they needed to hear the same lesson more than once, as in the case of the feeding of the multitudes. Like the miracle in Mark 6, this feeding showed Jesus' power to provide. It also showed that the disciples were slow to learn. Even though they had witnessed many of Jesus' miracles, they still doubted His power, and they still had difficulty understanding His teaching (see 8:14-21).

The healing of the blind man in the miracle that followed provided an instructive visual image for the disciples. The man was completely blind, but through a series of actions, Jesus restored his sight to the point that he could clearly see. Similarly, the disciples started out blind to Jesus' identity as the Messiah, the Son of God. But gradually, as they followed Him and learned from Him, they began to see Him for who He truly was. When Jesus asked them who they thought He was, Peter correctly answered, "You are the Messiah" (v. 29). Slowly but surely their eyes were being opened to who Jesus was and the hope He brought to the world.

 PRAY: Jesus, would You give me eyes to see more of who You are. I want to know You.

DAY 100 | MARK 9

H

E

A

R

What Else Should I Know? On a high mountain Jesus was transformed before Peter, James, and John. Elijah and Moses joined Him. Jesus used this event to further inform the disciples about His coming death and victorious resurrection.

As soon as they came down from the mountain, the disciples were reminded of the importance of faith in God as the foundation for ministry. A desperate father asked the disciples to cast a demon out of his deaf, mute son. They tried and failed. When Jesus discovered their inability to cast out the demon, He attributed it to a lack of faith on their part. In contrast, the father displayed faith by trusting Jesus to heal the boy.

 CHALLENGE: What is Jesus calling you to do? No matter what it is and what sacrifice it requires, it's vitally important to put your faith and trust in Him as you carry out that call.

Check In

WEEK 21

- ☐ Mark 10
- ☐ Mark 11
- ☐ Mark 12
- ☐ Mark 13
- ☐ Mark 14

MEMORY VERSES

OPTION 1: Psalm 34:8
OPTION 2: Proverbs 15:1-2
OPTION 3: Matthew 5:43-44

WEEK 22

- ☐ Mark 15
- ☐ Mark 16
- ☐ Romans 1
- ☐ Romans 2
- ☐ Romans 3

MEMORY VERSES

OPTION 1: Psalm 37:4-5
OPTION 2: Proverbs 15:16-17
OPTION 3: Matthew 5:45-46

WEEK 23

- ☐ Romans 4
- ☐ Romans 5
- ☐ Romans 6
- ☐ Romans 7
- ☐ Romans 8

MEMORY VERSES

OPTION 1: Psalm 37:23-24
OPTION 2: Proverbs 15:22-23
OPTION 3: Matthew 5:47-48

WEEK 24

- ☐ Romans 9
- ☐ Romans 10
- ☐ Romans 11
- ☐ Romans 12
- ☐ Romans 13

MEMORY VERSES

OPTION 1: Psalm 40:1-2
OPTION 2: Proverbs 16:9
OPTION 3: Matthew 6:1-2

SCAN THIS QR CODE TO ACCESS A FUN SURPRISE!

MEMORY VERSE OPTIONS: Psalm 34:8; Proverbs 15:1-2; Matthew 5:43-44

DAY 101 | MARK 10

HIGHLIGHT the verses that speak to you.

Write out the name of the book:

Which chapter and verse numbers stand out to you?

EXPLAIN what this passage means.

To whom was it originally written? Why?

How does it fit with the verses before and after it?

What is the Holy Spirit intending to communicate through this text?

APPLY what God is saying in these verses to your life.

What does this mean today?

What is God saying to you personally?

How can you apply this message to your life?

RESPOND to what you've read.

In what ways does this passage call you to action?

How will you be different because of what you've learned?

Write out a prayer to God in response to what you read today:

What Else Should I Know? Many times during His earthly ministry, Jesus predicted His death and the suffering His disciples would endure. He wanted those who followed Him to have a clear picture of the cost. Connecting with the mission of Jesus requires sacrifice. Contrary to the way the disciples viewed it, Jesus defined effective discipleship as humble service to other people, not attaining a position and power (see vv. 42-45). Real effectiveness in ministry comes through serving, not through being served.

This mindset was countercultural in Jesus' day, and it remains countercultural in ours. Serving others requires us to be actively attentive to people's needs and genuinely compassionate for their souls. How could we do anything less? This is how God loves us. When we recognize the love, compassion, and grace of God in our own lives, we can love others from an overflow of His love for us.

HIS LOVE FOR YOU
AS A DAUGHTER
SHOULD CHANGE
THE WAY YOU
love others.

DAY 102 | MARK 11

H

E

A

R

What Else Should I Know? Like all of the Gospel writers, Mark included the account of Jesus' entry into the city, which was the epicenter of Judaism in Jesus' day. This similarity with the other writers indicates how important and symbolic this event was for Jesus' time on earth. Most notably for Mark, the triumphal entry demonstrated Jesus' humble nature and divine mission. Riding on a donkey rather than a war horse highlighted that Jesus was a humble servant, while the acclamation of the people proclaimed His identity as the Messiah and King.

Once Jesus was in Jerusalem, his first act was cleansing the temple, which was bookended by the symbolic withering of the fig tree. Upon entering the temple, He found it overrun by greed and materialism. By quoting Isaiah, Jesus referred to the temple as "My house" (v. 17), again declaring His authority and unity with God.

Jesus used the symbolism of the withered fig tree to teach His disciples that the nation of Israel had become as spiritually fruitless as the tree Jesus cursed. This lesson is important for us to understand today. A person can look spiritually healthy on the outside, but the best indicators of spiritual health are a person's faith in God and love for others (see vv. 22-25).

CHALLENGE: Take some time and thank God for who He is and all He has done. Praise Him.

DAY 103 | MARK 12

H

E

A

R

What Else Should I Know? Mark 12 contrasts God's generous love with the self-gratifying nature of the religious leaders. The religious authorities knew they were the wicked tenants in the parable, and Jesus knew they would succeed in having Him killed. However, they didn't know they were acting in accordance with God's gracious plan to redeem His people and break down barriers that stood in the way of a relationship with Him.

Verses 13-34 document conversations Jesus had with the religious leaders as they searched to find the grounds to arrest or even kill Him. However, Jesus' responses displayed His superior understanding of God's law and His divine authority to speak on these matters.

The chapter ends with a warning against hypocrisy. The religious leaders did everything, even the most important aspects of religious life, for their own honor and glory. Jesus warned that their judgment was imminent. The poor widow, however, humbly and sacrificially gave to God above her means. When we truly understand the sacrifice Jesus made on our behalf, we can't help but give all of ourselves to Him in gratitude and service.

? QUESTION: What has God entrusted you to steward? How are you using that for His glory?

DAY 104 | MARK 13

H

E

A

R

What Else Should I Know? Jesus foretold the destruction of the temple in Jerusalem and the wrath of God's judgment on those who refuse to believe in Him. When pressed on the timing of these events, Jesus responded with signs of the end times and instructions on the way His followers should live in the meantime. Jesus encouraged them to stand firm in His teachings and not to be led astray by false teachers. He also prepared them to stand firm, through the power of the Holy Spirit, in the face of intense persecution that He knew would follow His death and resurrection.

The hope in the midst of all this hardship is the promise of verses 24-31: Jesus will return, and when He does, He will gather His children into His presence. We can't know when this day will come, but like the servants described in verses 34-37, we're to continually anticipate Jesus' return while we live for Him today.

? **QUESTION:** How can you live "ready" as you wait on Jesus' return?

DAY 105 | MARK 14

H

E

A

R

What Else Should I Know? Mark helps us understand that Jesus came as a humble servant whose singular focus was to pay the sacrifice for humanity's sin and restore their relationship with God. As the cross drew closer, Jesus had a few teachable moments left with His disciples, giving Him opportunities to prepare them for what was about to unfold. The first came when a woman interrupted dinner to anoint Jesus with expensive perfume. The disciples were shocked by the waste of expensive oil, but Jesus praised her action as a sacrifice for God and as preparation for His coming burial.

The second teaching opportunity came during the celebration of the Passover meal. Through His description of the bread and the cup as his body and blood, respectively, Jesus helped His disciples see that He was the ultimate Passover Lamb who would be sacrificed for their sins once and for all. Jesus' sacrifice wouldn't come without great personal agony, as His prayer in the garden of Gethsemane revealed. The humanity and vulnerability Jesus showed in the garden give even greater weight to the cross, further revealing the depths of Jesus' love for us.

 QUESTION: Jesus was betrayed, beaten, bore the burden of our sins. We have life because of His death. How does that change the way you live today?

DAY 106 | MARK 15

HIGHLIGHT the verses that speak to you.

Write out the name of the book:

Which chapter and verse numbers stand out to you?

EXPLAIN what this passage means.

To whom was it originally written? Why?

How does it fit with the verses before and after it?

What is the Holy Spirit intending to communicate through this text?

APPLY what God is saying in these verses to your life.

What does this mean today?

What is God saying to you personally?

How can you apply this message to your life?

RESPOND to what you've read.

In what ways does this passage call you to action?

How will you be different because of what you've learned?

Write out a prayer to God in response to what you read today:

What Else Should I Know? Jesus' trial began in Mark 14 in front of the Sanhedrin and the Jewish religious authorities, including Caiaphas, the high priest, and Pilate, the Roman governor. At the urging of the crowd, Pilate released a different prisoner, the murderer Barabbas, and sentenced Jesus to be crucified.

As Mark described the crucifixion, he payed special attention to individual people involved in or present for this event, including Simon, who carried Jesus' cross; the soldiers who cast lots for his clothes; people who walked by the cross and insulted Jesus; and Jesus' friends who were present for His death. Each face represented a person Jesus was sacrificing Himself for, whether or not they loved Him back.

Mark also highlighted some of the most significant events that accompanied Jesus' crucifixion, including two miracles: darkness overtook the land and the temple veil tore from top to bottom, symbolizing the union between God and humanity. The Son of God had accomplished His mission by giving up His life as the payment for our sin.

Fun Fact: The tearing of the veil symbolized that we now have access to the Holy of Holies—the presence of God. Now He lives in us.

DAY 107 | MARK 16

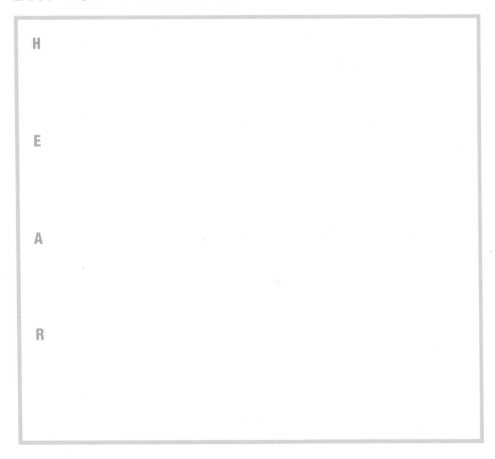

H

E

A

R

What Else Should I Know? All of Scripture points to the work and mission of Jesus, which seemed to end the day He hung on the cross at Calvary. At least that's how things appeared to His disciples, who watched the promised Messiah die. Little did they know the cross was only the first scene of Jesus' redemptive act. With His death on the cross, Jesus paid God's penalty for the sins of the world, sins that required a blood sacrifice to purify sinners. However, Jesus didn't remain in the grave. On the third day He rose from the dead and defeated death.

Mark's Gospel documents the moment when three of Jesus' faithful followers, all women, showed up at the tomb to anoint His body. There they encountered an angel, who told them the news of Jesus' resurrection. The angel also told them to take the news to the disciples and Peter. God wanted this great news to be conveyed as an offer of restoration and forgiveness. Through the death and resurrection of Jesus, God made a way for you—a sinful, broken daughter—to receive His forgiveness and grace and to be reunited with Him.

QUESTION: Who can you take the good news of Jesus to this week?

DAY 108 | ROMANS 1

H

E

A

R

We will never outgrow our need for the gospel.

What Else Should I Know? During his third missionary journey, Paul spent time in Greece, during which he wrote his letter to the Romans. Paul's plan was to visit Rome, so he wrote this letter to the Christians there in order to communicate his life calling and the message he longed to tell others. Paul was writing to proclaim the gospel, a message built on the foundation of the Old Testament and fulfilled in Jesus Christ. With this goal in mind, Paul's letter delays the customary greeting of his other letters and proceeds with a detailed description of Jesus (vv. 3-6) and a note about his desire to reach Rome and share the gospel there in person.

To establish how everyone needs the gospel, Paul pointed to the undeniable presence of sin in our world and our lives. At its core, sin is idolatry, the worship of the creation instead of the Creator. God made Himself known to people through creation, but people quickly turned to His creation to fulfill their needs. That exchange negatively affects everything in our lives, from relationships to worship. As a result, God allowed people to live in their sin, and Paul described the destruction that followed. In the closing verses of chapter 1, Paul painted a terrifying but realistic picture of who we are apart from Christ—people given over to sin and the destruction it creates.

DAY 109 | ROMANS 2

H

E

A

R

What Else Should I Know? Paul's description of sin continued in chapter 2, but he moved from what we might consider worldly sins to a word about God's judgment of people who judge the sins of others. Paul wanted to make one point clear: the depravity of sin affects every person who walks on the earth. Everyone is born a sinner; therefore, everyone deserves God's wrath and eternal judgment. Paul declared that God will judge those whose hearts are unrepentant. On the other hand, He will give eternal life to those who show by their actions that His law is written on their hearts.

Paul placed an emphasis on obedience, both of heart and of action. It isn't enough for us to simply listen to and know God's truths; we have to obey the law in order to receive God's favor, because obedience is the fruit of a heart changed by God. Obedience alone, however, won't save us. Paul's main point was that until we realize we're sinners by nature, we won't recognize our desperate need for salvation and appreciate God's grace. Once we come to that life-altering realization, He will change our hearts, and we'll desire to walk in obedience.

 QUESTION: In what areas have you gotten comfortable in your walk with Jesus?

DAY 110 | ROMANS 3

H

E

A

R

What Else Should I Know? Paul spent a significant portion of Romans helping the Jews understand that they needed God's grace as much as Gentiles (non-Jews) did. The truth that all people stand condemned for sin meant that Jews and Gentiles were equally guilty before God. Verses 9-18 culminate Paul's teaching that everyone is unrighteous and sinful. Because no one can be justified by the works of the law, everyone needs Jesus.

With the words "But now" in verse 21, Paul's letter turned from the negative reality of sinful humanity to the positive picture of God's saving work. God knew everyone deserved His wrath, yet He set into motion a plan to rescue His people from the consequences of sin. God wanted to restore His people to the relationship He had with them in the garden, before sin broke the fellowship He had with His creation. With that desire in mind, God made a way for unrighteous people to become righteous. Paul noted that all of Scripture, from the Law to the Prophets, points to God's gracious act of redemption through Jesus Christ. God made salvation available by grace through faith in His Son, Jesus. When people believe in Jesus for salvation, they're justified—declared righteous before God

 DEFINE: Look up the definition of righteousness. Write it out in your own words.

MEMORY VERSE OPTIONS: Psalm 37:23-24; Proverbs 15:22-23; Matthew 5:47-48

W
E
E
K

23

DAY 111 | ROMANS 4

HIGHLIGHT the verses that speak to you.

Write out the name of the book:

Which chapter and verse numbers stand out to you?

EXPLAIN what this passage means.

To whom was it originally written? Why?

How does it fit with the verses before and after it?

What is the Holy Spirit intending to communicate through this text?

APPLY what God is saying in these verses to your life.

What does this mean today?

What is God saying to you personally?

How can you apply this message to your life?

RESPOND to what you've read.

In what ways does this passage call you to action?

How will you be different because of what you've learned?

Write out a prayer to God in response to what you read today:

What Else Should I Know? One goal of Paul's letter was for his readers to clearly understand God's saving work, which includes justification from sin. Because a large number of Paul's audience was Jewish, he wanted them to understand that they were saved through Jesus' death and resurrection, not through their adherence to the law.

Paul reminded his Jewish readers that the covenant promises God made to Abraham and his descendants were assured by faith, not by the law. He pointed to Genesis 15:6 to prove his point: "Abram believed the Lord, and he credited it to him as righteousness." God's promises displayed grace to Abraham and to all who respond to God with faith like Abraham's—faith that trusts "the God who gives life to the dead and calls things into existence that do not exist" (Rom. 4:17). For Paul, Abraham's example proved that the gospel of Jesus Christ continued and fulfilled what had always been God's plan of salvation. People who come to God by placing their faith in Jesus are forgiven of sins and are made right with God.

 CHALLENGE: Look up in Scripture and find at least three promises God gives His children. What promises do you need to cling to in faith?

DAY 112 | ROMANS 5

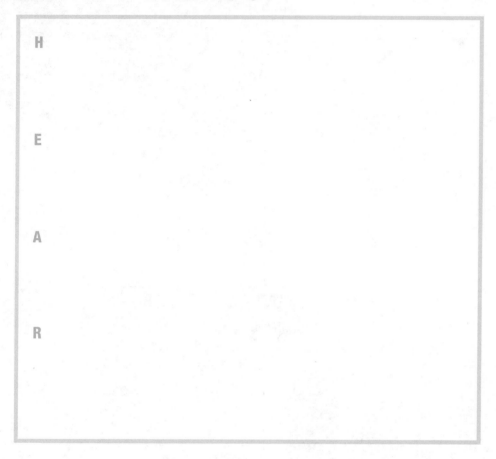

H

E

A

R

What Else Should I Know? Paul began Romans 5 by focusing on the benefits that come from justification, namely, peace, hope, and love from God. A believer can count on these benefits every day. The peace Paul had in mind is eternal peace with God that comes when He removes our condemnation for sin. In Christ we live in a state of peace that transcends our earthly circumstances, no matter how chaotic and disruptive they may feel.

Similarly, the hope Paul spoke of is hope in God's promises of eternity. Throughout Scripture, God promises to give an eternal home to His children so that they can live in His presence forever. He also promises that Jesus will return to call people to Himself. When Christians place their hope in these promises, they can face the sufferings and sorrows of life in a broken world.

God doesn't save us by grace only to make us try to live for Him in our own power. He gives us His grace to help us stand today, tomorrow, and on that future day when we'll appear before His throne. Paul also emphasized that God redeemed us when we were at our worst, demonstrating how great His grace is.

 QUESTION: How can you walk by the power of the Holy Spirit and not by your own power today?

DAY 113 | ROMANS 6

H

E

A

R

YOUR SIN DOES NOT HAVE TO DEFINE YOU. THERE IS FREEDOM IN JESUS FOR YOU TODAY.

What Else Should I Know? In Romans 6, Paul discussed reasons Christians can no longer think and live in the old ways of sin. Believers have died to the old life by being baptized into Jesus' death and raised into new life through His resurrection. We serve a new Master who liberated us from bondage to sin and empowers us to grow in faith, thus producing the spiritual fruit that shows we have eternal life. Through our obedience we display Christ and His character to the world.

Paul went on to contrast living as a slave to sin with living as a slave to Christ. He used the slavery analogy to help his readers understand what it meant to surrender their lives to following Christ. Paul argued that everyone is a slave to something, either to sin or to God. Christians aren't freed from sin to live as they please but rather to live in daily service to God and His will. This slavery to righteousness brings with it the benefits of holiness and eternal life, neither of which is possible apart from Jesus.

The good news Paul wanted to communicate is that because of Jesus' work, people no longer have to live as slaves to sin. Giving our lives to God is the most liberating choice we can make.

DAY 114 | ROMANS 7

H

E

A

R

You are not alone in your fight against sin.

What Else Should I Know? Paul opened chapter 7 by using marriage to illustrate the meaning of being dead to sin and free from the law's condemning power. Although we're set free from the power of the law and can freely serve God by His Spirit, the law still has good purposes in making us aware of our sinfulness and in guiding us to Christ.

Paul concluded chapter 7 by focusing on Jesus' power and presence in his life, in contrast with his struggle with sin. Verses 14-25 give readers an inside look at Paul's struggle with sin, one that should sound familiar to all of us. Paul hated sin, but no amount of hate was enough for him to completely avoid it. As long as we live in this broken world, we'll continue to struggle with sin. The good news for Christians is that Jesus gives us the power to withstand temptation and to choose not to sin, a power we lacked apart from Him. While this war wages within us, we can rest in the comfort that Jesus has won the battle for us and that someday our struggle with sin will be gone forever.

DAY 115 | ROMANS 8

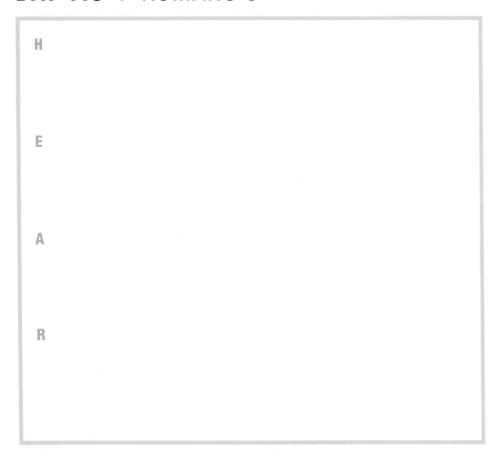

H

E

A

R

What Else Should I Know? Paul painted a detailed picture of a life given over to the sinful nature, in contrast with a life controlled by the Spirit. The former is identified by death, hostility to God, and enslavement to fear, while the latter is identified by life, peace, and sonship.

Specifically, Paul drew attention to the Spirit's help in resisting sin and making decisions. Furthermore, the Spirit confirms that we're God's children, adopted into His family, and we can address Him as Father. Therefore, nothing we face on earth can be compared to the glory that awaits us.

Paul closed Romans 8 by affirming that God is at work in all things. Whenever you feel crushed under the brokenness of this world, remember that even then God is working out His good plans and that nothing you face surprises Him or interferes with His work. God and His love will win in the end.

CHALLENGE: Set your mind on the Holy Spirit today. Keep refocusing your heart and mind on this truth every time you are tempted to doubt, worry or fear.

DAY 116 | ROMANS 9

HIGHLIGHT the verses that speak to you.

Write out the name of the book:

Which chapter and verse numbers stand out to you?

EXPLAIN what this passage means.

To whom was it originally written? Why?

How does it fit with the verses before and after it?

What is the Holy Spirit intending to communicate through this text?

APPLY what God is saying in these verses to your life.

What does this mean today?

What is God saying to you personally?

How can you apply this message to your life?

RESPOND to what you've read.

In what ways does this passage call you to action?

How will you be different because of what you've learned?

Write out a prayer to God in response to what you read today:

What Else Should I Know? In Romans 1–8, Paul had developed the doctrine of salvation by faith alone, concluding that God's purposes can never fail. However, it seemed that His purposes for the Israelites had indeed failed because most of them had rejected Jesus as their Messiah.

Paul addressed this issue in chapter 9, emphasizing that God is sovereign in all matters, including salvation. Next, to explain that God wasn't being unjust toward those He didn't choose, Paul focused on God's mercy, which is utterly undeserved and can never be earned. For the most part, the Israelites had tried to obtain salvation by obeying God's law, but no humans can ever save themselves. Faith—simply believing—and the grace that comes by it are the only ways to a right relationship with God.

Paul ended chapter 9 by noting where the nation of Israel stood in its relationship with God at the time of his writing. Paul referred to Jesus as the Jews' "stumbling stone" (v. 32) because they refused to believe in Jesus as their promised Messiah and instead had Him killed, causing them to remain in a state of unbelief and unrighteousness.

 DEFINE: Look up the definition of faith. write it out in your own words.

DAY 117 | ROMANS 10

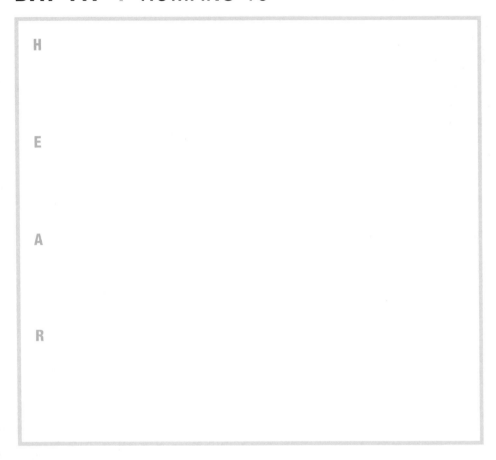

H

E

A

R

What Else Should I Know? Romans 10 begins with Paul's heartfelt plea for the Jews to come to know Jesus. Belief in the God of the Old Testament wasn't enough to save them if they rejected Jesus and His atoning work on the cross. According to Paul, the Jews had elevated the law to such a place of importance in their faith that it blinded them to the fulfillment of the law—Jesus—when He came to them.

Verses 8-13 provide one of the most succinct explanations of salvation in all of Scripture. Salvation comes not through obedience to the law but through believing and professing that Jesus is Lord and that He died and rose again. Paul described this as a heart transformation, stating that salvation is possible for anyone who calls on the name of the Lord.

To believe in this message of salvation, people must hear its message, so someone has to share it. This process of evangelism brought Paul great joy, and it was his life's mission. Unfortunately, not everyone who hears the gospel will believe it, but that doesn't diminish its impact, nor our need to share it.

PRAY: When was the last time you were burdened for the lost? Pray and ask God to soften your heart to those who need the gospel.

DAY 118 | ROMANS 11

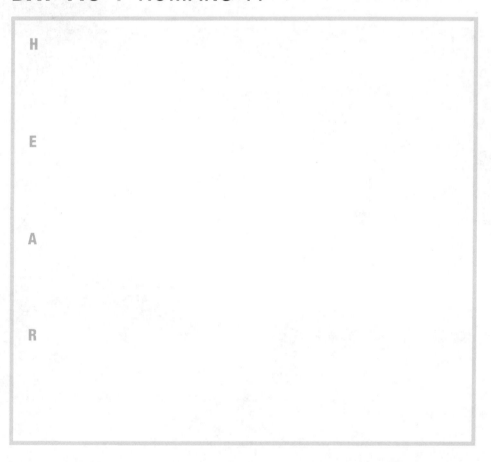

H

E

A

R

What Else Should I Know? At the time when Paul wrote, God's saving purposes centered on bringing many Gentiles to faith in God, but he wanted to make sure readers understood that God had never rejected Israel. God had broadened His offer of salvation, but it always remained available for the Israelites.

This fact is evident when we consider the remnant of Jews in the New Testament who believed in Jesus. Though the nation as a whole rejected Christ, heavily influenced by the religious leadership, many individual Jews who met Jesus or heard the gospel after His resurrection chose to believe in Him. Paul referred to them as "a remnant chosen by grace" (v. 5) and "the elect" (v. 7). Through the image of grafted branches, Paul reminded readers that God had made a covenant with the nation of Israel and that He's always faithful to His covenant promises. The Gentiles were grafted into God's covenant with Abraham through their belief in Jesus. The day will come when God's saving plan will be accomplished as both Jews and Gentiles acknowledge Him as Lord and Savior. Our response should be praise for the wonder of His saving plan.

 QUESTION: Jesus is in control over every detail of our lives. How does that free you to live today?

DAY 119 | ROMANS 12

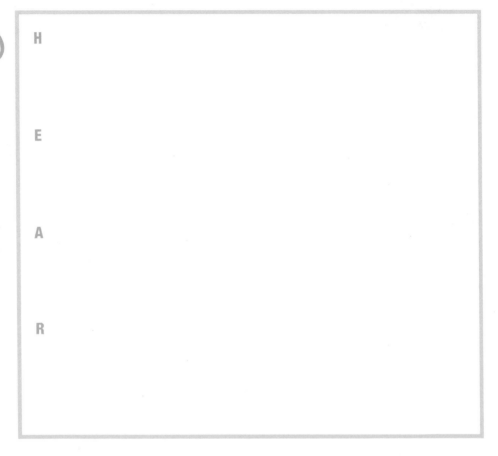

H

E

A

R

What Else Should I Know? "So what?" That's the important question Paul begins to answer in Romans 12. What difference should salvation make in a believer's life? In this chapter Paul focused on two specific impacts: the way we live and the way we love.

The first effect of salvation is that we offer our lives to God in sacrifice and worship by committing to live for Him. Paul used the phrase "a living sacrifice" (v. 1) to speak to the church body as a whole. To be the type of sacrifice God requires, we must let the Word of God transform our thinking, which will allow us to know and experience the will of God, as well as worship God.

Our salvation also affects the church body as we wisely use our spiritual gifts to serve others. Paul was aware that it's possible to exercise the gifts of the Spirit without displaying the fruit of the Spirit—specifically, love. For that reason he reminded his readers that Christian love is genuine, opposed to evil, and committed to what's good. Verses 9-21 include several practical examples of how Christ followers live set apart from "this age" (v. 2). Love modeled after the example of Jesus is at the heart of every example Paul provided.

 CHALLENGE: Have you surrendered every area of your life to Jesus? If not, what's holding you back?

DAY 120 | ROMANS 13

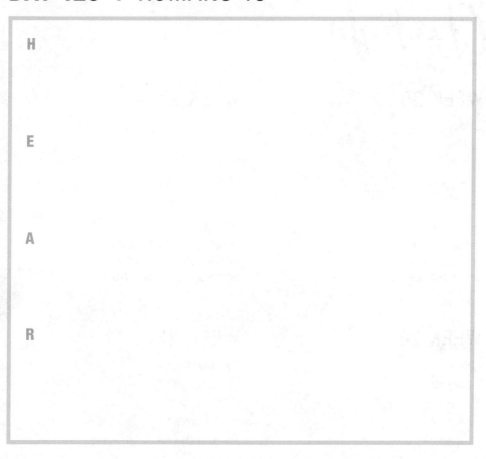

H

E

A

R

What Else Should I Know? In chapter 13 Paul provided instruction on the effects of salvation in a person's relationship with government and neighbors. We obey God by obeying the rules and rulers of our world. Christians are expected to show respect for leaders and to pay taxes. Paul reminded his readers that part of God's sovereign rule over the world means He rules over all earthly institutions as well. God appoints, or, at a minimum, allows all earthly rulers to rise to power, so to obey authority is to submit to the order of our world as God has orchestrated it. Paul's teaching on paying taxes is consistent with the teaching Jesus gave during His earthly ministry.

Paul again returned to the overarching theme of love when he reminded readers that the Ten Commandments teach us how to love our neighbors. Jesus' disciples are also expected to maintain high moral standards in daily relationships—specifically, in sexual behavior, sobriety, and integrity of speech. What's the motivation for following this Christian code of ethics? The answer, for Paul, is the imminent return of Jesus. Every day Jesus' return draws closer, so every day we must live ready to see Him face-to-face.

 CHALLENGE: Pray for those in authority over you today.

Check In

WEEK 25

- ☐ Romans 14
- ☐ Romans 15
- ☐ Romans 16
- ☐ Acts 20
- ☐ Acts 21

MEMORY VERSES

OPTION 1: Psalm 42:1-2
OPTION 2: Proverbs 17:27-28
OPTION 3: Matthew 6:3-4

WEEK 27

- ☐ Acts 27
- ☐ Acts 28
- ☐ Colossians 1
- ☐ Colossians 2
- ☐ Colossians 3

MEMORY VERSES

OPTION 1: Psalm 51:10-11
OPTION 2: Proverbs 18:21
OPTION 3: Matthew 6:7-8

WEEK 26

- ☐ Acts 22
- ☐ Acts 23
- ☐ Acts 24
- ☐ Acts 25
- ☐ Acts 26

MEMORY VERSES

OPTION 1: Psalm 46:10
OPTION 2: Proverbs 18:10
OPTION 3: Matthew 6:5-6

WEEK 28

- ☐ Colossians 4
- ☐ Ephesians 1
- ☐ Ephesians 2
- ☐ Ephesians 3
- ☐ Ephesians 4

MEMORY VERSES

OPTION 1: Psalm 51:12-13
OPTION 2: Proverbs 18:22
OPTION 3: Matthew 6:9-11

SCAN THIS QR CODE TO ACCESS A FUN SURPRISE!

DAY 121 | ROMANS 14

HIGHLIGHT the verses that speak to you.

Write out the name of the book:

Which chapter and verse numbers stand out to you?

EXPLAIN what this passage means.

To whom was it originally written? Why?

How does it fit with the verses before and after it?

What is the Holy Spirit intending to communicate through this text?

APPLY what God is saying in these verses to your life.

What does this mean today?

What is God saying to you personally?

How can you apply this message to your life?

RESPOND to what you've read.

In what ways does this passage call you to action?

How will you be different because of what you've learned?

Write out a prayer to God in response to what you read today:

What Else Should I Know? Paul's words in Romans 14 continue the focus on relationships with others by encouraging us to maintain unity by not judging others for their convictions and by not causing others to stumble into sin. The specific example Paul used is one addressed in many New Testament letters: eating meat previously sacrificed to idols. Paul took the stance that doing so wasn't a sin, but it might tempt and cause Christians who converted from paganism to sin.

Although the issue of sacrificed food isn't relevant today, we can think of many examples of not-necessarily-sinful choices that could cause a brother or a sister to sin. Whatever the specific issue, Paul encourages us to live in a way that brings love and encouragement to other people's lives. Everything we do, Paul says, is to be done for God's glory and purpose.

The heart of Paul's teaching in Romans 14 is found in verses 16-18: God's kingdom is more important than our rights, so we must always let love determine the way we act toward one another. When we do, the result is Spirit-filled peace and joy.

 PRAY: Jesus, would You help me to glorify You by my actions? Give me eyes to see those around me who need to know You.

DAY 122 | ROMANS 15

H

E

A

R

What Else Should I Know? In chapter 15, Paul offered two examples to help us understand how salvation changes our lives: the examples of Jesus and Paul himself. Verses 1-13 highlight the example of Christ. First and foremost, Jesus lived selflessly. Christ became a servant of the world in order to save the world. We glorify God by living in harmony with one another and by remembering the life of the Lord Jesus. Christians ought to treat others the same way Jesus treats His people—with compassion, sacrifice, and grace. Paul also encouraged the Romans to be filled with abundant hope through the Holy Spirit.

Verses 14-33 shift the focus to Paul's personal ministry and his relationship with the Christians in Rome. Like Jesus, Paul devoted his life to the glory of God. For Paul, this meant being wholeheartedly and selflessly committed to spreading the gospel wherever he could. This gospel message was the heart of his letter to the Romans, and he reminded them of its importance as he drew his letter to a close. Nothing was more important to Paul than introducing people to Jesus and His gospel of grace. Can you say the same?

CHALLENGE: Look for ways to selflessly serve today with no motive to get the credit.

DAY 123 | ROMANS 16

H

E

A

R

What Else Should I Know? Paul concluded his letter to the Romans with personal information about his plans to visit Rome and to spread the gospel even farther. He also sent personal greetings to many people he knew in the Roman church.

Paul's personal greetings are noteworthy in that they include men and women and in that they reveal the rapid, dedicated growth of the early church. Paul hadn't yet made it to Rome, but many people he knew had, and they were planting churches, meeting in homes, and going to prison for their faith. These people followed the example of Paul and, more importantly, the example of Jesus as they dedicated their lives to growing the church.

As he brought his letter to a close, Paul issued a brief warning against those who would disrupt the unity of the church, then complimented the Romans once more for their reputation. Fittingly, the final words of his letter are a doxology of praise to God for His greatness and glory.

DAY 124 | ACTS 20

H

E

A

R

What Else Should I Know? Acts 20 catalogs several stops on Paul's missionary journey, but two warrant special attention. While in Troas, Paul spent several hours one evening teaching in the upstairs room of a home. While listening, a man named Eutychus fell asleep and tumbled out of the window, dying instantly. However, Paul was able to raise him from the dead. Luke's account of this event is subtle; it mentions only that Paul put his arms around the man and proclaimed him to be alive. This event highlighted the power of God at work through Paul.

The second emphasis in this chapter was on Paul's words of encouragement to the leaders of the church in Ephesus and his anticipation of the dangers that awaited him in Jerusalem because of his faith. Several phrases in Paul's farewell speech highlight his overwhelming commitment to God's call and the great physical and emotional toll it took on him. Jesus said serving Him would come with a cost, and Paul's life exemplified that reality. But Paul's depth of love for these brothers in Christ and his laserlike focus on spreading the gospel show that living for Jesus makes it worth the cross He asks us to bear.

QUESTION: In what ways have you experienced the cost of following Jesus?

DAY 125 | ACTS 21

H

E

A

R

Fully convinced

What Else Should I Know? Despite several warnings and a good understanding of the suffering that awaited him, Paul continued to Jerusalem. Along the journey many people who dearly loved him (including Luke, the writer of Acts) begged him not to go, but he was determined. Even the prophet Agabus, who told Paul he would be arrested, couldn't dissuade him from his mission. In his own words, he was "ready not only to be bound but also to die in Jerusalem for the name of the Lord Jesus" (v. 13).

When Paul and his companions arrived in Jerusalem. Paul immediately went to meet with the leaders of the Jerusalem church, including James, the brother of Jesus. He shared with them the amazing work God was doing and He encouraged the believers in Jerusalem.

At the temple a mob of Jews attacked Paul, accusing him of teaching against Jewish laws, similar to the accusations leveled against Jesus prior to His crucifixion. He likely would have been killed if the Romans hadn't taken him into custody. We can be like Paul today: When we're fully convinced of who Jesus is and what He has done, we'll be obedient to His call and passionate about His priorities, no matter the cost.

W
E
E
K

26

DAY 126 | ACTS 22

HIGHLIGHT the verses that speak to you.

Write out the name of the book:

Which chapter and verse numbers stand out to you?

EXPLAIN what this passage means.

To whom was it originally written? Why?

How does it fit with the verses before and after it?

What is the Holy Spirit intending to communicate through this text?

APPLY what God is saying in these verses to your life.

What does this mean today?

What is God saying to you personally?

How can you apply this message to your life?

RESPOND to what you've read.

In what ways does this passage call you to action?

How will you be different because of what you've learned?

Write out a prayer to God in response to what you read today:

What Else Should I Know? Acts 22 describes Paul's imprisonment in Jerusalem. After he was arrested, Paul addressed the Jewish mob in the temple courtyard—the same mob that moments before had sought to kill him. Paul described Jesus' call on his life—a call he was being obedient to follow, even in chains. However, when Paul mentioned God's command to take the gospel to the Gentiles, he ignited the fury of the crowd. When the angry crowd abruptly ended Paul's speech, he was taken into the Roman barracks. A Roman centurion was ordered to flog and interrogate him to determine the true nature of the Jews' grievances against him.

Seeing Jewish men and women reject the mission of God deeply grieved Paul. In the midst of these circumstances, God reminded Paul that He's always at work and would empower him to preach the gospel in Rome.

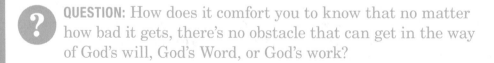

QUESTION: How does it comfort you to know that no matter how bad it gets, there's no obstacle that can get in the way of God's will, God's Word, or God's work?

DAY 127 | ACTS 23

H

E

A

R

What Else Should I Know? The Roman commander who had put Paul in prison wanted to learn more about why people so vehemently opposed him, so he took Paul to a meeting of the Sanhedrin, the Jewish ruling council. When the meeting grew violent, the commander, fearing for Paul's life, ordered his troops to remove Paul from the Sanhedrin. Verse 11 gives insight into Paul's relationship with God, who told him to "have courage" and promised that he would share the gospel in Rome. The rest of the chapter describes the plot to kill Paul, which has many similarities to the plot to kill Jesus, and the divine intervention of Paul's nephew and the Roman commander who had already spared Paul's life twice. God's sovereign control over Paul's life and protection of Paul's gospel ministry is a thread that runs throughout all of Acts, but it's seen even more clearly in these final chapters. Nothing was going to stop the gospel from reaching Rome.

 PRAY: Pray for your brothers and sisters in the faith that are persecuted all over the world.

DAY 128 | ACTS 24

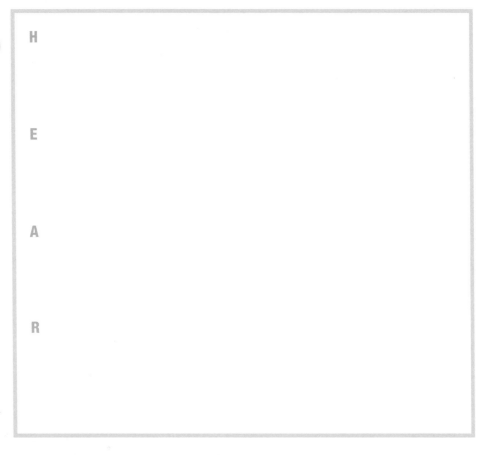

H

E

A

R

What Else Should I Know? Because of Paul's Roman citizenship, the commander sent Paul to Caesarea to appear before Felix, the Roman governor of Judea, who called for a formal hearing of Paul's case. Verses 5-6 record the official accusations against Paul: he was a troublemaker who upended the peace of the Jews wherever he traveled. The "sect of the Nazarenes" (v. 5), a term the Jewish leaders used to refer to the early Christians, pointed to Paul's leadership in the church as another of his offenses.

In his defense Paul argued that although he was a leader in the early church, he always acted peacefully and never stirred up trouble. Paul reminded his audience that when he entered the temple, he still adhered to the Jewish rituals and always acted with the best interests of others in mind. Although Paul's accusers brought serious charges against him, they were unable to prove his guilt, leading Felix to postpone the trial until a later date. Although Felix never reconvened Paul's trial, he kept Paul in confinement throughout the remaining two years of his term as governor.

QUESTION: Consider the boldness and suffering of Paul. How does that challenge you today?

DAY 129 | ACTS 25

H

E

A

R

What Else Should I Know? When Felix's replacement, Festus, came into office, the Jewish leaders requested that Paul be brought from Caesarea to Jerusalem for trial. They were persistent in their efforts against Paul, waiting for more than two years to try to have him condemned. They still lacked any real crime with which to charge Paul, and he defended himself against any violations of Jewish or Roman law. Festus also struggled to handle Paul's case since he could find no clear source of guilt, but he wanted to give the Jews a favor.

Realizing the danger to his life in traveling to Jerusalem, Paul exercised his right as a Roman citizen to appeal to Caesar. Festus hoped Agrippa would counsel him in what to do with this man who seemed to have broken no Roman laws. Throughout his ministry Paul seized every opportunity to share the gospel, and God continually opened doors for that purpose. He can do the same for you. When you truly grasp the love God demonstrated for us through Jesus' death and resurrection, you're compelled to live for Him and to share that good news with others.

 CHALLENGE: Walk slowly through your day. Don't hurry. Look around for ways to seize opportunities to love and serve others.

Jesus
CHANGES
EVERYTHING.

H

E

A

R

What Else Should I Know? Because King Agrippa expressed interest in hearing from Paul, the apostle had the opportunity to defend himself and his gospel ministry before the king. As he had done several times in Acts, Paul reminded Agrippa and the others listening that he had been raised a devout Jew and had lived as an obedient, faithful Pharisee. After Paul met Jesus, everything changed for him. Verses 16-18 clearly articulate the mission Jesus gave him, a mission to which Paul was being faithful even in this moment before Agrippa. Jesus sent Paul to turn people from darkness to light and to rescue them from sin and Satan.

As Paul demonstrated, our personal stories of God's work—our testimonies—are often the best way to share Jesus with others. Paul knew he was in prison because of his obedience to Jesus. Still, he pressed the king to acknowledge Christ as the Savior foretold by the prophets. The king rose to his feet and ended the hearing, clearly moved by Paul's words but unable to believe them yet. As he and Festus departed, the two agreed Paul was innocent. Paul was then sent to Rome to appear before Caesar.

MEMORY VERSE OPTIONS: Psalm 51:10-11; Proverbs 18:21; Matthew 6:7-8

DAY 131 | ACTS 27

HIGHLIGHT the verses that speak to you.

Write out the name of the book:

Which chapter and verse numbers stand out to you?

EXPLAIN what this passage means.

To whom was it originally written? Why?

How does it fit with the verses before and after it?

What is the Holy Spirit intending to communicate through this text?

APPLY what God is saying in these verses to your life.

What does this mean today?

What is God saying to you personally?

How can you apply this message to your life?

RESPOND to what you've read.

In what ways does this passage call you to action?

How will you be different because of what you've learned?

Write out a prayer to God in response to what you read today:

What Else Should I Know? On the way to Rome, Paul's party encountered a strong storm, causing their ship to sail off course. However, the delay to reach Rome didn't hinder Paul's evangelistic efforts. God gave Paul insight into the troubles that lie ahead, and Paul tried to warn the crew. When the crew failed to heed Paul's advice, disaster resulted in the form of a massive storm.

In the midst of the crew and passengers' despair, Paul predicted they would all be delivered, and the events unfolded just as he said. God was establishing Paul as a trustworthy leader in order to gain the listening ears of the crew. Because of Paul's leadership and the accuracy of his predictions, his life was spared once again. When the soldiers wanted to kill the prisoners, the centurion, their leader, came to Paul's defense, and neither he nor any other prisoners were killed.

Paul's life proves time and again that when we're faithful to God's direction, He protects and empowers us to carry out His will. You will face serious storms in your life—God's Word is filled with promises to help you endure them.

QUESTION: Based on the passage you just read, what does it teach you about learning to trust God in a storm?

DAY 132 | ACTS 28

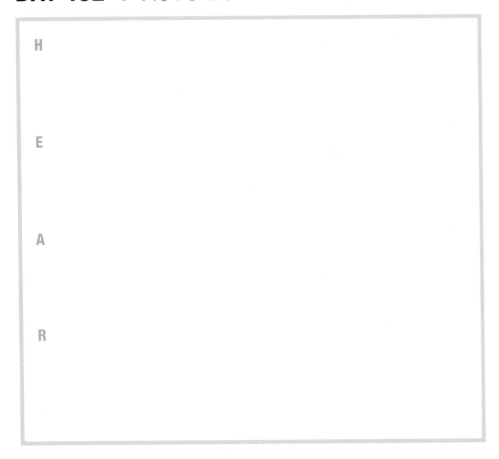

H

E

A

R

What Else Should I Know? The ship on which Paul was traveling wrecked on the island of Malta, south of Sicily. Paul immediately impressed the island's inhabitants when God delivered him unharmed from a viper's bite. As a result, Paul was able to carry out a ministry of healing among the islanders. After winter passed and the seas were again safe for travel, Paul's party secured passage to Italy. As they completed their journey to Rome on foot, two groups of Roman Christians came out to greet Paul.

Once in the city, Paul was allowed to live in an apartment rented at his own expense as long as he remained imprisoned under military guard. Luke's account ends with Paul's living under house arrest in Rome for two years as he awaited his hearing before Caesar. During that time he freely witnessed to all who came to hear him share the gospel. Paul could have easily allowed his circumstances to override his passion for sharing the gospel, but instead, he continued to proclaim God's love to all who would listen. We must do the same. There will never be circumstances in your life where you shouldn't share the gospel.

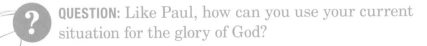

? **QUESTION:** Like Paul, how can you use your current situation for the glory of God?

DAY 133 | COLOSSIANS 1

Jesus IS NOT ONLY THE CREATOR BUT ALSO THE SUSTAINER OF ALL THINGS.

H

E

A

R

What Else Should I Know? Paul wrote his letter to the Colossians during his first imprisonment in Rome. The letter primarily served to correct misunderstandings in the church body that had been advanced by false teachers who were urging believers to blend other religious ideas with Christianity.

Though Paul didn't personally know many of these believers, he was concerned for their spiritual welfare. He began his letter to them by affirming and encouraging them in their faith and by sharing specific prayers for them. Paul prayed for their lives to bear the fruit of the gospel; an increased knowledge of God; and God-given endurance, patience, and joy.

Paul's teaching about Christ in verses 15-20 is one of the greatest affirmations of the person and work of Christ found in the New Testament. Paul affirmed Christ's deity as well as His lordship over all creation. He was able to bring about our reconciliation to God through His cross.

Making Jesus' name known was Paul's chief aim in life, and no amount of suffering would stop him from doing that. What are your main goals in life? The college you want to attend, the career you want, the life you want to build—everything should be secondary to sharing the message of Jesus Christ. Start today.

DAY 134 | COLOSSIANS 2

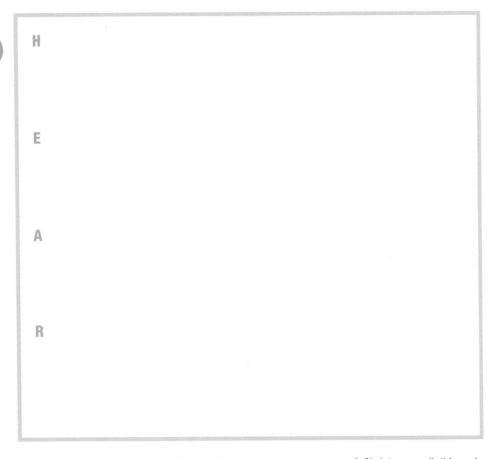

H

E

A

R

What Else Should I Know? After establishing the supremacy of Christ over all things in Colossians 1, Paul transitioned to the main point of his letter in chapter 2 by attacking a false doctrinal teaching that had become a problem for the Christians in Colossae. From Paul's letter we can get a sense of what this heretical teaching involved. Paul made several references to the mystery of God, now revealed in Jesus, which combated the heretical teaching that God reserved special or secret wisdom about His salvation for a limited number of people.

Paul challenged the believers to continue demonstrating commitment to Christ and gratitude for the privileges that belonged to them in Him. Our lives should be grounded in the supreme foundation of Jesus, and our faith should be fixed on Him as a result. That's who we truly are. That's what we were created for. That's how we're meant to see Jesus.

? **QUESTION:** How can you fix your eyes on Christ rather than your current circumstances?

DAY 135 | COLOSSIANS 3

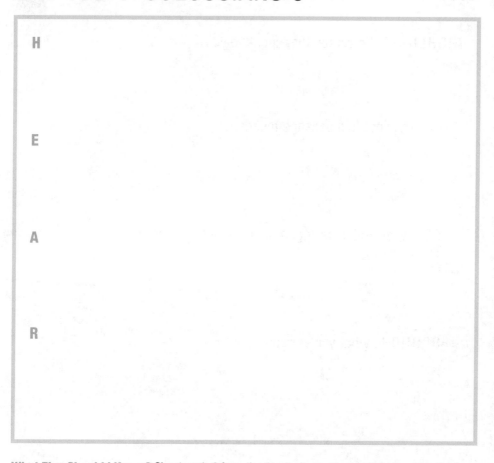

H

E

A

R

What Else Should I Know? Chapters 1–2 form the theological or doctrinal section of Colossians, while chapters 3–4 compose the practical part of Paul's letter. Paul reminded the Colossians that through their conversion experiences they had died to their old way of life and had risen with Christ to walk in newness of life, as symbolized by baptism.

Paul then addressed some of the most prevalent sins in the first-century Greco-Roman world, listing attitudes and behaviors the Colossians were to "put to death" (3:5) in their lives. In contrast, he also provided a list of virtues these believers were to "put on" (v. 12). If the Colossians were to genuinely serve Christ, they had to conduct their lives in a manner worthy of Him.

This message rings true for us today. We're responsible for reflecting Christ to the world. Being a Christian isn't about going to church or obeying rules. It's not even about following a Bible reading plan. It's about pursuing His holiness in all we say and do. That's why He died for us. It's a heavy call that demands a serious response.

 QUESTION: How are you pursuing holiness today?

W
E
E
K

28

DAY 136 | COLOSSIANS 4

HIGHLIGHT the verses that speak to you.

Write out the name of the book:

Which chapter and verse numbers stand out to you?

EXPLAIN what this passage means.

To whom was it originally written? Why?

How does it fit with the verses before and after it?

What is the Holy Spirit intending to communicate through this text?

APPLY what God is saying in these verses to your life.

What does this mean today?

What is God saying to you personally?

How can you apply this message to your life?

RESPOND to what you've read.

In what ways does this passage call you to action?

How will you be different because of what you've learned?

Write out a prayer to God in response to what you read today:

What Else Should I Know? Paul had opened his letter with an elaborate prayer for the Colossians, and in chapter 4 he asked them for prayer in return. Specifically, Paul asked for prayer for himself and his missionary team: that God would open doors for them to share the gospel and that they would clearly and boldly communicate it.

Paul then gave a final reminder to the Colossian believers to live in a way that points other people to Jesus. Like Paul, they were responsible for sharing the gospel with others, so Paul challenged them to do so in a way that was encouraging and hopeful. The words we say and the way we say them matter greatly when we tell others about Jesus.

Paul's letter to the Colossians reminds readers that Jesus is the foundation for all of spiritual life. No secret wisdom or set of rules can save a person; only belief in Jesus and His gospel message has the power to do that. The beauty of this message is that it's available to everyone.

CHALLENGE: Fill in the blanks:

Continue _____ in prayer.

Being _____ in it with _____.

DAY 137 | EPHESIANS 1

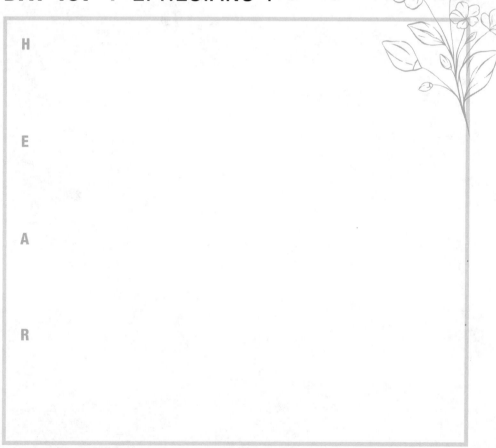

H

E

A

R

What Else Should I Know? Paul took advantage of his imprisonment in Rome to write letters to many different people and churches. His purpose in the letter to the Ephesians was to communicate God's redemptive plan and to challenge his readers to become everything God wanted them to be as His people.

At the start of his letter, Paul described at length the wonder of God's redemptive purpose in salvation. He revealed that God's plan is much more extensive than simply saving individual people in isolation—God gives believers His power to carry out His gospel mission in the world.

As he did in the letter to the Colossians, Paul also included a prayer for the Ephesian Christians, thanking God for their faith and praying for their increased knowledge of God. Then he reminded them of Jesus' supremacy and lordship over everything, including His church. The remainder of Paul's letter would instruct the Ephesians in how to live in unity with Christ and in unity with His body, the church.

 PRAY: Pray verses 15-23 over your life today.

DAY 138 | EPHESIANS 2

H

E

A

R

What Else Should I Know? In chapter 2, Paul reminded his readers of who they were before they came to know Jesus and who they were in Christ. He began by describing the desperation and depravity of their condition before they responded to the gospel (vv. 1-3). The "But God ..." statement in verse 4 is one of a handful of similar statements in Paul's letters, and it marks one of the most important contrasts in all of Scripture. Apart from Christ a person is dead. But in Christ—because of God's great love and mercy—a person is alive. The heart of the gospel is that God brings life to the dead and light to the darkness.

THE HEART OF THE GOSPEL IS THAT GOD BRINGS LIFE TO THE DEAD AND LIGHT TO THE DARKNESS.

Because we've received grace, our job is to reflect God's love and grace to others. The good works a believer does are to give glory to God so that others can know Him. What matters most about us isn't what the world tells us, the way people see us, or even the way we see ourselves. Our identity is determined by what God says about us. Apart from Christ we were dead and hopeless. But in Christ we're alive and will live forever with Him.

DAY 139 | EPHESIANS 3

H

E

A

R

What Else Should I Know? In Ephesians 3, Paul pointedly reminded the readers of his personal role in spreading the good news. Again the language of mystery surfaced as Paul described the revelation God gave him about the good news of Jesus and his personal call to open others' eyes to this mystery.

Paul's ministry was a gift of grace—an example of accepting opportunities to serve God. He viewed his time in chains, which gave him the opportunity to write these letters, as a divine appointment as well. God always puts us where He wants us. As we experience His strength, He will equip us with the things we need to fulfill all He calls us to. That's the theme Paul focused on in the second half of his epistle.

QUESTION: How does your perspective change knowing God is with you and He will strengthen you in your calling?

DAY 140 | EPHESIANS 4

H

E

A

R

What Else Should I Know? As Paul moved into the more practical portion of his letter, he reminded his readers to live lives worthy of their calling as disciples of Jesus. Though believers can do this in many ways, Paul gave a few specific examples: be humble, gentle, patient, and loving while living in oneness and peace. These are all Spirit-given traits that deeply affect our relationships with other believers.

With the role of the Holy Spirit in mind, Paul reviewed the matter of spiritual gifts. While Christians are united as one body in Christ, each individual believer possesses a unique set of gifts to strengthen the body as a whole. The Spirit gives these ministry gifts to the church for the specific purpose of "equipping the saints for the work of ministry, to build up the body of Christ" (v. 12).

Simply put, believers are to live differently from the world. Christians are meant to stand out: the way we act, the things we desire, the way we talk, the people we surround ourselves with, the things we prioritize—everything about us should point people to Christ.

 QUESTION: So what does the world see when it sees you? A person who is just like everyone else, or someone who is different and excited to share? Why?

Check In

WEEK 29

- ☐ Ephesians 5
- ☐ Ephesians 6
- ☐ Philippians 1
- ☐ Philippians 2
- ☐ Philippians 3

MEMORY VERSES

OPTION 1: Psalm 51:16-17
OPTION 2: Proverbs 18:24
OPTION 3: Matthew 6:12-13

WEEK 31

- ☐ Hebrews 4
- ☐ Hebrews 5
- ☐ Hebrews 6
- ☐ Hebrews 7
- ☐ Hebrews 8

MEMORY VERSES

OPTION 1: Psalm 63:1
OPTION 2: Proverbs 19:21
OPTION 3: Matthew 6:16-18

WEEK 30

- ☐ Philippians 4
- ☐ Philemon 1
- ☐ Hebrews 1
- ☐ Hebrews 2
- ☐ Hebrews 3

MEMORY VERSES

OPTION 1: Psalm 55:22
OPTION 2: Proverbs 19:17
OPTION 3: Matthew 6:14-15

WEEK 32

- ☐ Hebrews 9
- ☐ Hebrews 10
- ☐ Hebrews 11
- ☐ Hebrews 12
- ☐ Hebrews 13

MEMORY VERSES

OPTION 1: Psalm 67:1-2
OPTION 2: Proverbs 20:1
OPTION 3: Matthew 6:19-21

SCAN THIS QR CODE TO ACCESS A FUN SURPRISE!

W
E
E
K

29

DAY 141 | EPHESIANS 5

HIGHLIGHT the verses that speak to you.

Write out the name of the book:

Which chapter and verse numbers stand out to you?

EXPLAIN what this passage means.

To whom was it originally written? Why?

How does it fit with the verses before and after it?

What is the Holy Spirit intending to communicate through this text?

APPLY what God is saying in these verses to your life.

What does this mean today?

What is God saying to you personally?

How can you apply this message to your life?

RESPOND to what you've read.

In what ways does this passage call you to action?

How will you be different because of what you've learned?

Write out a prayer to God in response to what you read today:

What Else Should I Know? In Ephesians 5, Paul emphasized that, ultimately, we're called to imitate Christ. Because God is love, we're to extend His love to others. Because God is pure in speech and behavior, we're to behave with purity. Because God is light, we're to live as children of the light. Paul communicated a clear sense of urgency in living like Christ. We must make the most of every opportunity to reflect Jesus' love to others, because our days are numbered and eternity is at stake.

We're called to imitate Christ.

As Paul continued to address the way God expects His people to behave, he next considered family relationships. If our faith doesn't strengthen our relationships with the people we're related to, then how can we disciple others to get along with their families? We get along with people by yielding to their best interests out of love, a behavior rooted in our submission to Christ and our call to yield our entire lives to Him.

DAY 142 | EPHESIANS 6

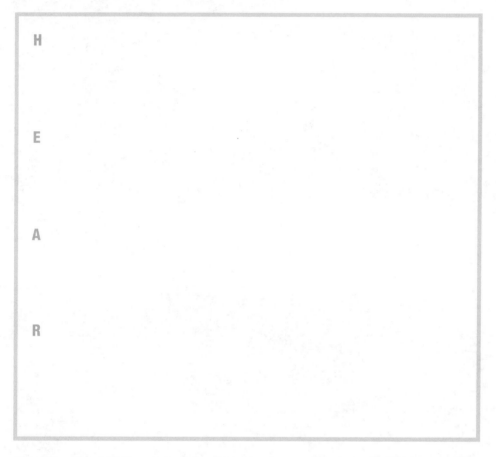

H

E

A

R

What Else Should I Know? Paul closed his letter with a call to be prepared for the spiritual battle the Christian life inevitably demands—to "put on the full armor of God" (v. 11). Paul's letters frequently encouraged his readers to be strong, withstand persecution, and endure in their faith. Here Paul explained why: The church is engaged in a very real spiritual battle with the enemy. This spiritual warfare is evident all around us every day, just as it confronted the believers in Ephesus. The only hope we have against this enemy is to stand strong and depend on God, fully dressed in the spiritual armor He has given us to engage in this battle.

A belt of truth, a shield of faith, a helmet of salvation, a sword of the spirit. This is the armor we have in Christ—not to fight against flesh and blood (v. 12), but to withstand sin. We must wear each piece of armor at all times. No matter what the world throws at you, no matter what sin you are facing, God's immovable strength and protection can help you withstand it.

 CHALLENGE: Before you do anything else today, put on the full armor of God. Prepare yourself for battle.

DAY 143 | PHILIPPIANS 1

H

E

A

R

What Else Should I Know? Paul wrote his letter to the Philippians while he was imprisoned in Rome. This letter was deeply personal because he considered the Christians in Philippi to be gospel partners. Paul began his letter by thanking the Philippians for their partnership with him. He prayed that their love would continue to grow as they discerned the most important things in life and prepared themselves to face God's judgment with confidence.

The apostle also wrote that he was convinced his imprisonment was causing the gospel to advance. He viewed his circumstances as a part of God's greater plan for the spread of the gospel; nevertheless, these verses reflect the tension he felt within himself. Paul wasn't afraid of death, but he felt torn between the desire to depart and be with Christ and the desire to remain in the flesh and help the Philippians and others grow in the faith. Paul also faced unimaginable suffering but expressed his ability to continue rejoicing. Whatever the outcome, Paul had assurance that Christ would be glorified and that the gospel wouldn't be defeated.

? **QUESTION:** How might God use your present circumstances to advance the gospel?

DAY 144 | PHILIPPIANS 2

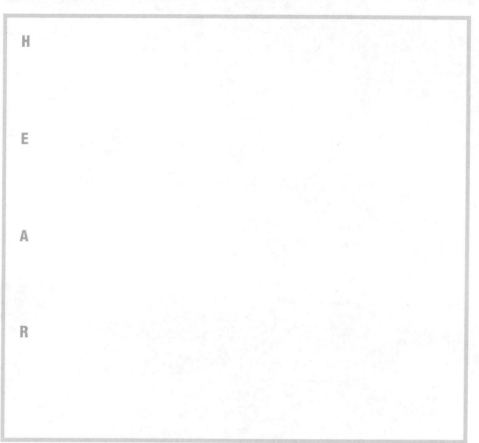

H

E

A

R

What Else Should I Know? A key theme of Paul's New Testament letters is unity. Paul challenged Christians to be united with Jesus in His will for their lives. If they were, then unity with one another would naturally follow. As Paul encouraged his friends to greater unity, he cited Christ's example to inspire them.

Specifically, Paul pointed to Jesus as the ultimate example of humility. To truly live in unity with God and others, we must tap into Spirit-given humility that empowers us to put the needs and interests of others ahead of our own. Jesus modeled humility when He gave up all the benefits of heaven to come to earth, live as a man in our broken world, and die on the cross to redeem our world from sin. Jesus knew the trajectory of His life on earth before He left heaven, yet He yielded to His Father's redemptive plan. This is humility and servanthood in its purest form, and Paul calls us to follow this example. When we imitate Christ, we shine as His light in the world, displaying to others the good news of the gospel.

 DEFINE: Look up the definition of humility. Write it out in your own words.

DAY 145 | PHILIPPIANS 3

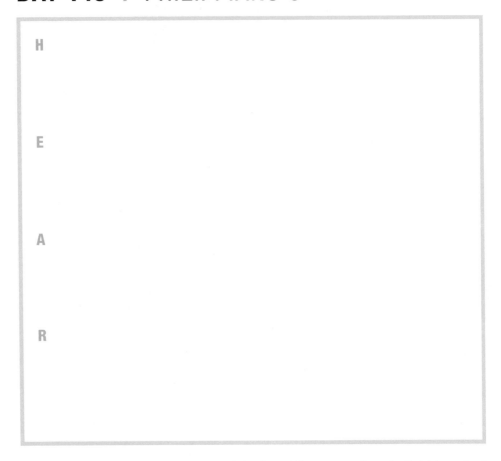

H

E

A

R

What Else Should I Know? In Philippians 3, Paul used his own experience in Christ to contrast his background in Judaism with his present life in Christ. Though Paul experienced every privilege Judaism offered, he didn't regret his decision to follow Christ. As a Christian, he continually strived to reach the goal of spiritual maturity. The prize he would earn when he reached this goal would be eternity in Jesus' presence. This single-minded focus on growing in Christlikeness motivated Paul in his missionary endeavors and in his writing.

In following Jesus' example, Paul made great sacrifices for the sake of discipleship. He gave up power and prestige as a Pharisee, relationships like marriage and family, and countless physical comforts. Like Paul, we'll also face sacrifices when we choose to follow Christ. But the goal of our lives shouldn't be the comforts of earth—it's unity with Jesus. Although we won't fully attain this goal until eternity, we can strive for it every day.

QUESTION: Just like Paul, what must we sacrifice when we choose to follow Jesus?

MEMORY VERSE OPTIONS: Psalm 55:22; Proverbs 19:17; Matthew 6:14-15

DAY 146 | PHILIPPIANS 4

HIGHLIGHT the verses that speak to you.

Write out the name of the book:

Which chapter and verse numbers stand out to you?

EXPLAIN what this passage means.

To whom was it originally written? Why?

How does it fit with the verses before and after it?

What is the Holy Spirit intending to communicate through this text?

APPLY what God is saying in these verses to your life.

What does this mean today?

What is God saying to you personally?

How can you apply this message to your life?

RESPOND to what you've read.

In what ways does this passage call you to action?

How will you be different because of what you've learned?

Write out a prayer to God in response to what you read today:

What Else Should I Know? Paul concluded his message to his friends in Philippians 4 by challenging, instructing, and thanking them. Throughout this letter Paul had challenged the Philippians to seek unity in Christ. In this chapter he mentioned a specific relationship that needed unity and healing. Euodia and Syntyche were two women who had partnered with Paul in gospel ministry but found themselves in a contentious relationship. Paul encouraged them to work toward unity and encouraged the other believers to assist them. The work of Christ is too important to be sidetracked by relational discord.

Verses 4-9 issued final challenges for the Philippian believers to live in Christ. They were to rejoice in the Lord, be steadfast in prayer, and meditate on attitudes consistent with the faith they professed to believe. Though the Philippians had struggles, Paul still loved them and encouraged them to grow in their relationship with Christ and to focus on eternity at all times. In Christ, he said, they could be content in any and every circumstance, trusting in God's provision.

 QUESTION: In what area is God asking you to be content?

DAY 147 | PHILEMON

H

E

A

R

What Else Should I Know? The letter of Philemon was written to a single person believed to have been a wealthy member of the church in Colossae. Paul's letter had a very narrow focus: to restore the relationship between Philemon and Onesimus, one of Philemon's slaves who had run away. When Onesimus escaped to Rome, he met Paul, heard his teaching, and became a Christian. Paul felt that the two needed to restore their relationship now that they were brothers in Christ (see v. 16). Specifically, Paul challenged Philemon to welcome Onesimus home in the same manner he would welcome Paul. Onesimus and Paul had grown close during their time together, and Paul would have even preferred for Onesimus to stay with him in Rome.

Paul's call to forgiveness and restoration is relevant to all our relationships today. Jesus modeled forgiveness for us when He died on the cross to forgive us of our sins. Throughout His teachings He also urged His followers to forgive (see Matt. 5:23-24; 6:14-15; 18:21-22; Luke 17:3-4). Forgiveness isn't optional for followers of Christ. We must do everything we can to make sure our relationships with others are healthy, reflecting the love, grace, and mercy God has shown us.

 CHALLENGE: Examine yourself and your relationships. Is there any area that needs restoration?

DAY 148 | HEBREWS 1

H

E

A

R

What Else Should I Know? Although the writer of the Book of Hebrews is unknown, the purpose was clear: To give encouragement to the Hebrew (Jewish) Christians to grow into mature followers of Christ. One theme throughout Hebrews is Jesus' superiority to everything the Jews' religious system offered. This emphasis was intended to encourage readers to persevere in the faith.

The writer began by declaring that in the past God had spoken through the prophets, but now God spoke through His Son, Jesus. He went on to list five ways to describe Jesus that highlighted His deity: the heir of all things, the radiance of God's glory, the sustainer of all creation, the purifier of sins, and the superior to the angels. A series of quotations from the Old Testament follow that support Jesus' deity and superiority to every created being. From the beginning of the book, readers learn that Jesus is the Son of God, the Creator and Sustainer of the universe, and the eternal Ruler of God's kingdom. He's worth persevering for, and always worthy of our worship.

PRAY: Jesus, I want to know You more as my Father, my Maker, and my Creator. Would You show me more of who You are today?

DAY 149 | HEBREWS 2

H

E

A

R

What Else Should I Know? In light of Jesus' superiority, which was established in chapter 1, the writer of Hebrews warned believers against neglecting the salvation God provided through His Son.

First-century Hebrew Christians converted from Judaism, a religion steeped in tradition, rituals, and family heritage. It would have been easy for them to drift back into Judaism in the face of persecution or hardship. The writer urged readers to listen to the truths of salvation and the movement of the Holy Spirit in their lives. We stay rooted in our faith when we actively listen to God and remind ourselves of the gospel.

The writer then explained why God's Son had come to earth in the form of a man. Genesis 3 makes clear that sin had prevented people from fulfilling God's purpose for them. Hebrews 2 shows that Jesus became human to provide a solution for humankind's sin problem, doing for people what they couldn't do for themselves. Through His death He made salvation available. In this way Jesus is the High Priest who sacrificed Himself for human sin so that people could be forgiven. Only through faith in Christ can people fulfill all God created them to be.

 DEFINE: Look up the definition of propitiation. Write it out in your own words.

DAY 150 | HEBREWS 3

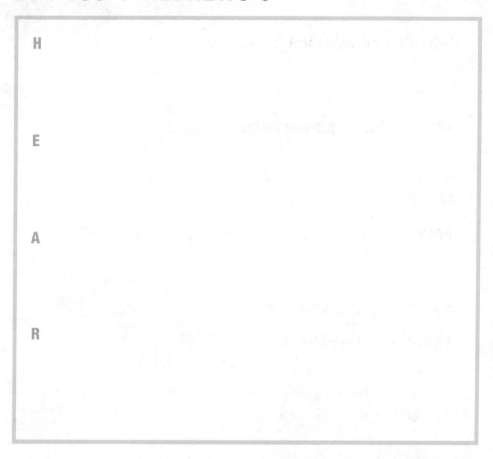

H

E

A

R

What Else Should I Know? In chapter 3, Jesus and Moses become our models of faithfulness. These Jewish converts would have looked to Moses as the model of faith. In the same way the writer established Jesus' superiority to the angels, he pointed to Jesus' superiority to Moses as well. The image of the builder and the house portrayed Jesus as "the one who built everything" (v. 4). While Moses was a faithful servant *among* God's people, Jesus was the faithful Son *over* God's people.

Verses 7-19 present readers with the second of the writer's warnings, this time against slipping into unbelief, or turning away from God. He pointed to the Israelites who wandered in the desert as an example of the danger of unbelief. Although they had witnessed some of God's greatest miracles and faithfulness—from the parting of the Red Sea to the provision of quail and manna—they repeatedly turned from God toward idolatry, discontentment, and faithlessness. The readers of Hebrews were warned not to harden their hearts against God's will or to allow unbelief to turn them away from Him. Rather, they were to encourage one another daily and to be true to their professions of faith in Christ.

 QUESTION: In what areas do you struggle to believe God?

WEEK 31

DAY 151 | HEBREWS 4

HIGHLIGHT the verses that speak to you.

Write out the name of the book:

Which chapter and verse numbers stand out to you?

EXPLAIN what this passage means.

To whom was it originally written? Why?

How does it fit with the verses before and after it?

What is the Holy Spirit intending to communicate through this text?

APPLY what God is saying in these verses to your life.

What does this mean today?

What is God saying to you personally?

How can you apply this message to your life?

RESPOND to what you've read.

In what ways does this passage call you to action?

How will you be different because of what you've learned?

Write out a prayer to God in response to what you read today:

What Else Should I Know? In chapter 4 the writer of Hebrews expressed his desire for his readers to obey God and enter His rest, a spiritual reality symbolized by the promised land. For the Israelites who wandered in the desert, the promised land was a place that offered physical rest from the exhaustion of wandering and homelessness. At the same time, it offered spiritual rest by fulfilling God's promise to His people.

The Sabbath rest encouraged in Hebrews 4 signifies the rest that comes from a relationship with Jesus. While this rest is partly physical—a day set aside for rest and worship—it's also spiritual, a rest for weary souls that can be found only in a relationship with Jesus. Jesus alone brings peace to the turmoil and restlessness caused by sin, and a relationship with Him brings the promise of eternal rest in God's presence. The writer stressed that genuine believers have entered God's rest through faith and obedience. Because God sees us as we are, we must confess and repent of our sins so that we can be forgiven. Then we'll find true, unshakable rest that transcends the circumstances of life.

 CHALLENGE: Pick an entire day this week and spend it with the Lord. Stop your work. Put away your phone. Practice silence and listening to God's voice.

DAY 152 | HEBREWS 5

JESUS IS QUALIFIED, AS GOD'S SON WHO DIED FOR OUR SINS, TO BE THE SAVIOR AND HIGH PRIEST FOR EVERYONE WHO TRUSTS HIM.

H

E

A

R

What Else Should I Know? In previous chapters, the writer of Hebrews made a case for Jesus' greatness compared to the angels and Moses. In chapter 5, he also established Jesus' greatness compared to the high priests of Judaism.

The Old Testament described the high priest as the person God chose to represent the people before Him. The high priest served in the temple, and once a year on the Day of Atonement, he entered the inner sanctuary of the temple and offered a sacrifice on behalf of everyone's sins. This practice foreshadowed Jesus' role as our great High Priest who became the once-for-all atoning sacrifice for the sins of the world. Just as God called the Israelites' high priests to their roles, He also called Jesus to be the ultimate High Priest. Unlike human high priests, however, Jesus was sinless; He didn't need to offer sacrifices for Himself.

Inasmuch as Jesus was God incarnate, He was also fully human, and His sacrifice on our behalf cost Him greatly. His example of obedience is a model for every Christian to follow.

DAY 153 | HEBREWS 6

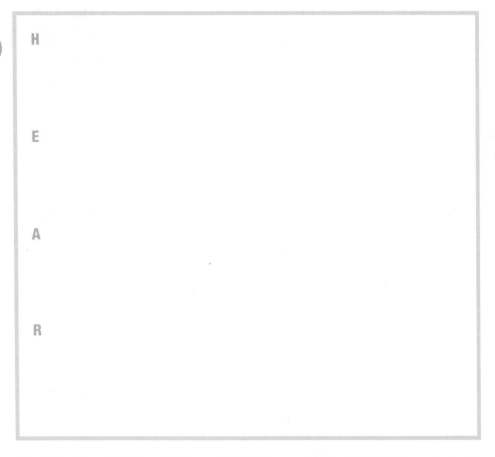

H

E

A

R

What Else Should I Know? Hebrews 5:11–6:12 presents the writer's third warning to his readers. Lamenting the fact that his readers should have been more spiritually mature, he warned them not to fall into a permanent state of spiritual immaturity and lack of growth. Though no true follower of Christ can lose his or her salvation, faith must be fed to grow.

Using the image of an infant who survives on the nourishment of milk alone, unlike an adult who needs solid food to survive, the writer told his readers they needed someone to teach them basic Christian doctrines. Because they were still spiritual infants, he advised them to take deliberate action to grow in their faith, love, and hope. Rather than becoming lazy, they should imitate worthy examples of faith and perseverance.

The writer's warning against falling away was direct and harsh. Anyone who turned away from Jesus could expect judgment from God. His gift of salvation was too costly to be taken lightly.

Verses 13-20 remind us that God's faithfulness should encourage believers to maintain our hope in Him and in eternity. Our hope is in Jesus, anchored in the sacrifice He made on our behalf.

 QUESTION: In what ways do you need to be deliberate about growing in your faith?

DAY 154 | HEBREWS 7

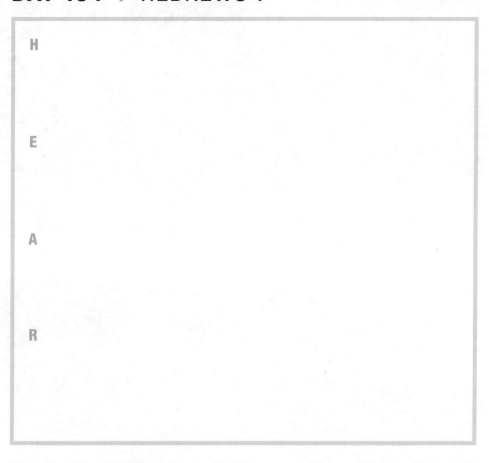

H

E

A

R

What Else Should I Know? Chapter 7 of Hebrews used the example of a priest named Melchizedek to foreshadow Jesus as High Priest. Melchizedek is mentioned in only three places in Scripture: Genesis 14; Psalm 110; and Hebrews 5–7. In Genesis 14:17-20, we learn that Melchizedek was a priest and a king who blessed Abraham and to whom Abraham paid a tithe. In both the Psalms and Hebrews passages, he's mentioned as a foreshadowing of Jesus, the great High Priest and King of kings. The writer of Hebrews argued that if the sacrificial system under Aaron's priestly line could have redeemed people, a high priest in Melchizedek's order wouldn't have needed to come. Because the sacrificial system couldn't save, however, Jesus came as a High Priest in that order.

The writer of Hebrews pointed to five attributes of Christ that qualified Him to serve in this priestly role: He is holy, innocent, undefiled, separated from sinners, and exalted above the heavens. Jesus is the Son of God. Because His priesthood is forever, Jesus' work on the cross to save sinners is permanent, and believers' hope is secure.

PRAY: Jesus, thank you that my hope is secure in You. You are holy. You are more than enough for me.

DAY 155 | HEBREWS 8

H

E

A

R

What Else Should I Know? In Hebrews 8, the writer continued his emphasis on Jesus as the High Priest believers need by bringing attention to God's Old Testament covenant and the tabernacle under Moses. Previously, the writer had presented the need for a high priest who was greater than Aaron; here, he explained the need for a new covenant that was greater than the old.

The old covenant refers to the law God gave to Moses, beginning with the Ten Commandments (see Ex. 20:1-17), and expanded on throughout Deuteronomy and Leviticus. God established this law not only to guide His people, but also to highlight their sin and their need for Him. No one can live up to the standards of the old covenant on their own. We need a Savior.

The prophet Jeremiah foretold this new covenant—not one that centered on rules and standards, but on heart change. Jesus ushered in this new covenant with His atoning work on the cross. The tearing of the temple curtain at the time of Jesus' death shows that through Him all people have access to God and that their hearts are permanently changed by the Holy Spirit's presence. Thankfully, because of Jesus, obedience to the new covenant is possible. God's love and grace can change our hearts forever.

 PRAY: Jesus, I need You. Thank You for Your covenant that makes a way for me to know You. You are so good!

DAY 156 | HEBREWS 9

HIGHLIGHT the verses that speak to you.

Write out the name of the book:

Which chapter and verse numbers stand out to you?

EXPLAIN what this passage means.

To whom was it originally written? Why?

How does it fit with the verses before and after it?

What is the Holy Spirit intending to communicate through this text?

APPLY what God is saying in these verses to your life.

What does this mean today?

What is God saying to you personally?

How can you apply this message to your life?

RESPOND to what you've read.

In what ways does this passage call you to action?

How will you be different because of what you've learned?

Write out a prayer to God in response to what you read today:

What Else Should I Know? In chapter 9 the writer of Hebrews continued his contrast between the old covenant and the new covenant. The writer described Jesus as the Priest of the true tabernacle and the Mediator of a better covenant. The tabernacle and its rituals were symbols that pointed forward to Jesus and the redemption from sins His sacrifice would bring. He offered the perfect, once-and-for-all sacrifice: Himself. This superior sacrifice can cleanse us and make us fit to serve God.

To ratify the old covenant, Moses sprinkled the blood of sacrifices on "the tabernacle and all the articles of worship" (v. 21). To ratify the new covenant, Jesus offered His own blood. The permanence and power of Jesus' sacrifice to atone from sin reach far beyond what a ritual sacrifice could accomplish. With His death Jesus offered us permanent forgiveness for sins and eternal life in the presence of God.

Jesus suffered on the cross to ensure that we don't have to suffer for eternity. Now Jesus continues to do the work of a priest by interceding for us in God's presence. Because our relationship with God is rooted in Jesus and sustained by Him, we're secure in Him forever.

We're secure in Jesus forever.

DAY 157 | HEBREWS 10

H

E

A

R

What Else Should I Know? The writer emphasized the Jewish sacrificial system's inability to make anyone right with God and to bring them to spiritual maturity. The writer used the Old Testament to demonstrate that Jesus accomplished what the old covenant's sacrificial system couldn't. Through Jesus' perfect sacrifice, people of faith are made right with God and are set on a path to spiritual maturity.

In verse 19 the author moved from theological to practical teaching by giving direction on the way people live out their faith in Jesus and His sacrifice. Our behavior should reflect our belief that Jesus is the sinless, eternal High Priest who offered Himself as the perfect, once-for-all-time sacrifice for our sins. The writer urged his audience to draw near to God in faith and purity, holding firmly to their confession of hope with the assurance of God's faithfulness. He challenged them to encourage one another to love and do good works while consistently meeting together. He warned them against the danger of sin and the threat of persecution. The instructions in Hebrews 10 remind us that we can't pursue God and accept sin at the same time in the Christian life.

? **QUESTION:** How does reading this passage change the way you approach God?

DAY 158 | HEBREWS 11

H

E

A

R

What Else Should I Know? Often referred to as the hall of faith, Hebrews 11 catalogs men and women who displayed exceptional faith in God. First the writer defined *faith* as trusting God to the extent of having assurance in His promised blessings. Noting that a person can't please God without faith, the writer pointed to Noah and Abraham as examples of men who demonstrated faith by their actions.

A major component of faith is trusting God when we don't experience the fulfillment of all His promises, as Abraham and Sarah modeled. Sometimes we experience tests of our faith, like Abraham and Moses. Numerous other Old Testament saints demonstrated faith in God; Rahab, the judges, David, and Samuel are just a few. They didn't see God's ultimate promise fulfilled in Jesus, but through their faith God bore witness to its fulfillment.

We demonstrate genuine faith when we obey God's promises. Each hero of the faith reminds us that sustaining faith is possible throughout any and all circumstances. Genuine faith means trusting God with our lives and our futures. That's the kind of faith God is looking for in His people.

 QUESTION: How can you actively trust God while waiting in His provision?

DAY 159 | HEBREWS 12

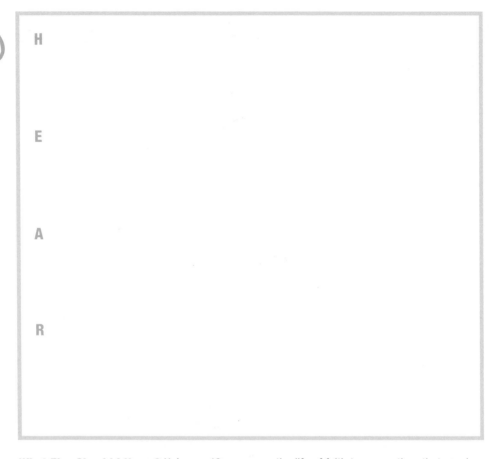

H

E

A

R

What Else Should I Know? Hebrews 12 compares the life of faith to a marathon that requires great endurance. Along the way we'll face difficulties, some of which come as discipline from God. We can endure these seasons by growing spiritually through them. This chapter also challenges us to strive for spiritual health and holiness while encouraging us to greater service. When we truly understand the sacrifices God has made to draw us to Himself, we'll desire to show gratitude to Him, primarily through serving and worshiping Him. Through Christ we're also united with one another in deeper community.

The writer cautions us not to reject God's grace when He pursues us. God's offer of grace is available only until Jesus returns, a day we can't predict, so postponing this decision makes no sense. We aren't guaranteed another opportunity, and the consequence of missing God's grace is eternal. This warning should motivate us to a greater sense of urgency to share the message of God's grace with others.

CHALLENGE: Take a minute and write down the name of someone who needs to hear the gospel. Begin to pray over them today. Ask God to open a door for you to share.

DAY 160 | HEBREWS 13

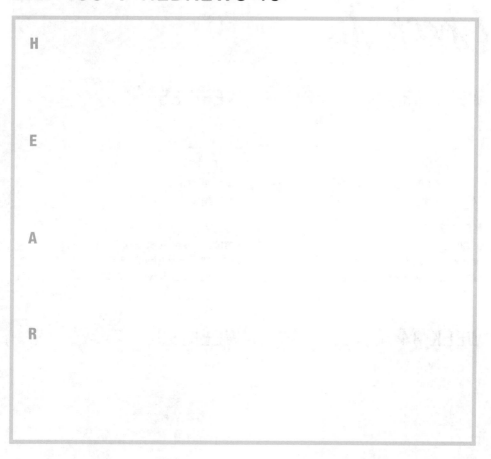

H

E

A

R

What Else Should I Know? The writer's specific challenges in this chapter are themes that repeatedly appear throughout Hebrews and the New Testament as a whole: love, hospitality, compassion, sexual morality, contentment, generosity, trust and confidence in God, gratitude for spiritual leaders, a call to worship, and obedience to authority. Each theme is rooted in love for God and the desire to make His love evident to those around us.

The closing verses of Hebrews remind us that who we are and how we live ultimately reflects Jesus' work in our lives. He's the One who deserves glory and who equips us to live the life of faith to which we're called. It's not easy to be the type of person these teachings challenge us to be. But God's new covenant makes it possible. The Spirit of God is working in us, molding us into the image of Jesus day by day.

 CHALLENGE: Circle which one you need Jesus' help with the most

| Love | Hospitality | Compassion | Sexual Purity | Contentment |

| Generosity | Obedience to Authority | Confidence in God | Call to Worship | Trust |

Check In

HOW'RE YOU DOING?! TEXT A FRIEND + HOLD EACH OTHER ACCOUNTABLE TO STAYING IN THE WORD TOGETHER!

WEEK 33

- ☐ 1 Timothy 1
- ☐ 1 Timothy 2
- ☐ 1 Timothy 3
- ☐ 1 Timothy 4
- ☐ 1 Timothy 5

MEMORY VERSES
OPTION 1: Psalm 68:5
OPTION 2: Proverbs 20:19
OPTION 3: Matthew 6:22-24

WEEK 35

- ☐ Titus 1
- ☐ Titus 2
- ☐ Titus 3
- ☐ 1 Peter 1
- ☐ 1 Peter 2

MEMORY VERSES
OPTION 1: Psalm 82:3-4
OPTION 2: Proverbs 21:1
OPTION 3: Matthew 6:27-28

WEEK 34

- ☐ 1 Timothy 6
- ☐ 2 Timothy 1
- ☐ 2 Timothy 2
- ☐ 2 Timothy 3
- ☐ 2 Timothy 4

MEMORY VERSES
OPTION 1: Psalm 81:10
OPTION 2: Proverbs 20:27
OPTION 3: Matthew 6:25-26

WEEK 36

- ☐ 1 Peter 3
- ☐ 1 Peter 4
- ☐ 1 Peter 5
- ☐ 2 Peter 1
- ☐ 2 Peter 2

MEMORY VERSES
OPTION 1: Psalm 84:10
OPTION 2: Proverbs 21:15
OPTION 3: Matthew 6:29-30

SCAN THIS QR CODE TO ACCESS A FUN SURPRISE!

MEMORY VERSE OPTIONS: Psalm 68:5; Proverbs 20:19; Matthew 6:22-24

DAY 161 | 1 TIMOTHY 1

HIGHLIGHT the verses that speak to you.

Write out the name of the book:

Which chapter and verse numbers stand out to you?

EXPLAIN what this passage means.

To whom was it originally written? Why?

How does it fit with the verses before and after it?

What is the Holy Spirit intending to communicate through this text?

APPLY what God is saying in these verses to your life.

What does this mean today?

What is God saying to you personally?

How can you apply this message to your life?

RESPOND to what you've read.

In what ways does this passage call you to action?

How will you be different because of what you've learned?

Write out a prayer to God in response to what you read today:

What Else Should I Know? In addition to the letters Paul wrote to churches, he also wrote letters to individuals he discipled to be leaders and pastors. Timothy was one of them. Acts 16 records the beginning of their ministry partnership and gives insight into Timothy's spiritual heritage. Paul began investing in Timothy's life when Timothy was probably still a teenager, and Timothy accompanied Paul on his missionary journeys. The letters of 1–2 Timothy reveal the close bond the two shared in life and ministry. From the beginning Paul referred to Timothy as "my true son in the faith" (1 Tim. 1:2).

Paul began his first letter to Timothy by warning him about false teachers and instructing him on the importance of sound Christian doctrine to combat heresies. Next Paul humbly reminded Timothy of his own sinfulness and need for Christ's forgiveness. Paul's letters to Timothy include several sayings that Paul deemed "trustworthy" (v. 15), including a reminder of Jesus' grace for sinners. Paul knew in order to be an effective minister of the gospel, Timothy needed to continually remind himself of the power and extent of God's grace in his own life and in the lives of those to whom he would minister.

 PRAY: Just like Paul invested in Timothy, spend time thinking and praying about a girl you could pour into.

DAY 162 | 1 TIMOTHY 2

H

E

A

R

What Else Should I Know? After Paul gave Timothy instructions for combating false teaching and claiming the truths of the gospel, he gave him specific instructions about church and worship practices. Chapter 2 focuses on general worship practices. Paul began with the importance of congregational prayer. Corporate prayers of intercession and thanksgiving should be made on behalf of all people, including kings and people in authority.

The way people conduct themselves in worship matters because it reflects their relationships with God and the state of their hearts. Paul's instruction for men to "pray, lifting up holy hands" has less to do with posture and more to do with purity of heart. Paul called them to be prayer warriors, free from anger and arguments that could divide the church. Paul's instructions to women had a similar purpose. God wants people pure of heart, dedicated to loving Him and serving others.

QUESTION: How would you describe the way you worship? Worship isn't about what you wear, how high you lift your hands, or what else is going on in your life. It's about what's inside your heart.

DAY 163 | 1 TIMOTHY 3

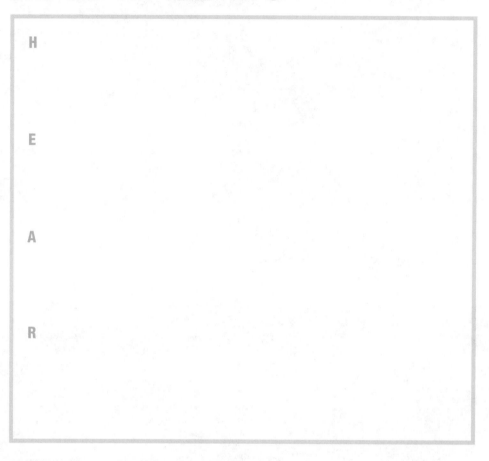

H

E

A

R

What Else Should I Know? Paul continued his instructions on church practice in chapter 3, which shifts the focus to leaders. Paul focused his instructions on two groups of church leadership: elders (or overseers) and deacons. Speaking specifically to elders, Paul noted that they shouldn't be new to the faith. Elders are the leaders of the church, so it's important that they have strong, tested, and steadfast relationships with God, as well as a deep, personal knowledge of Scripture.

While elders are the leaders and overseers of the church, deacons are the servant leaders. The same godly character is expected of them, although they don't have the added burden of church oversight. Their leadership is more narrow in its focus.

Verse 15 reminds readers of the reason these instructions about church practice matter: the church is "God's household," and its mission is to share the gospel of Jesus Christ with the world. This task should never be taken lightly, and nothing is to get in its way.

CHALLENGE: Pray for your church and your church leaders today. Send them a letter, email, or text to encourage the leaders today.

DAY 164 | 1 TIMOTHY 4

H

E

A

R

What Else Should I Know? In 1 Timothy 4, Paul focused his pastoral instructions on Timothy's personal ministry. At the time Paul wrote this letter, Timothy was leading the young church in Ephesus, a church Paul had started. When the church came under the influence of false teachers who were leading people away from the basic tenets of the gospel, Paul sent Timothy to lead the church back to its roots.

Paul called Timothy to be a leader who stood in contrast to these false teachers. He reminded Timothy that he had been placed in a position of responsibility to be a good example to other believers. Paul told Timothy not to be discouraged by his youth—spiritual maturity is what matters for church leadership. The most important thing for a Christian leader is for his life to be firmly rooted in godliness. Another of Paul's trustworthy sayings appears here: our hope is in the living God. Leaders must believe this truth and teach it to others.

We can take hope and instruction from this chapter. God expects the same thing from a 16-year-old that he does a 60-year-old: a life of godliness. You can be a leader today wherever He has placed you.

 CHALLENGE: Think about how you can use the area of influence God has given you. Don't delay your obedience.

DAY 165 | 1 TIMOTHY 5

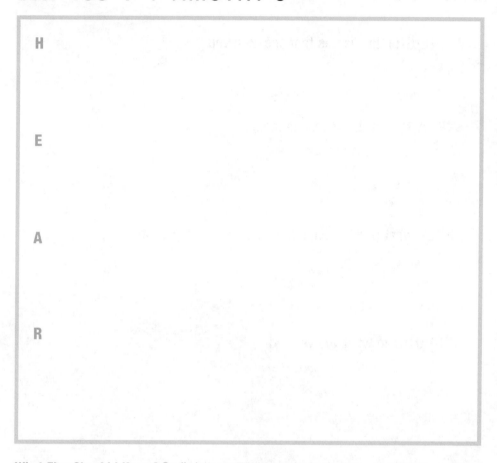

H

E

A

R

What Else Should I Know? Paul's letter to Timothy continues with more detailed instructions about how Timothy should interact with the widows and elders in his church. Paul wanted Timothy to understand that an exemplary Christian leader should respect people in different life stages, including compassion and admonition to those who need it.

Paul prioritized service to widows with the greatest needs, prioritizing widows who didn't have children or grandchildren to take care of them. He also gave Timothy the responsibility to protect and advocate for the elders, as well as to hold them accountable to their calling. Paul knew the elders would be in a position to receive the criticism and complaints of the church, so he encouraged Timothy to defend them as needed.

This chapter is clear that the call to church leadership is a serious one. God holds church leaders to a higher standard than anyone else because they have the responsibility to shepherd His children. Pray for your church leaders today.

QUESTION: How can you lead and serve in your church?

W E E K 34

DAY 166 | 1 TIMOTHY 6

HIGHLIGHT the verses that speak to you.

Write out the name of the book:

Which chapter and verse numbers stand out to you?

EXPLAIN what this passage means.

To whom was it originally written? Why?

How does it fit with the verses before and after it?

What is the Holy Spirit intending to communicate through this text?

APPLY what God is saying in these verses to your life.

What does this mean today?

What is God saying to you personally?

How can you apply this message to your life?

RESPOND to what you've read.

In what ways does this passage call you to action?

How will you be different because of what you've learned?

Write out a prayer to God in response to what you read today:

What Else Should I Know? Paul drew his letter to a close with a final pastoral charge for Timothy. The issue of money was important for Timothy to handle from a godly perspective. It's evident from verses 3-5 that false teachers were preaching for financial gain. They exploited people by accepting a profit in exchange for their teaching.

Paul wanted Timothy to understand the foolishness of greed and the wise pursuit of godliness. The love of money is a terrible trap, but people whom God has blessed with riches are expected to use them for the good of God's kingdom. Rather than focus time and energy on getting rich, Paul told Timothy to flee from greed and other sins and to spend his days pursuing "righteousness, godliness, faith, love, endurance, and gentleness" (v. 11).

This teaching was the culmination of Paul's letter to Timothy. The pursuit of godliness is essential to the Christian life; it's the way we ensure that we're following God and growing in our faith.

? **QUESTION:** What things do you need to flee today in order to pursue holiness?

DAY 167 | 2 TIMOTHY 1

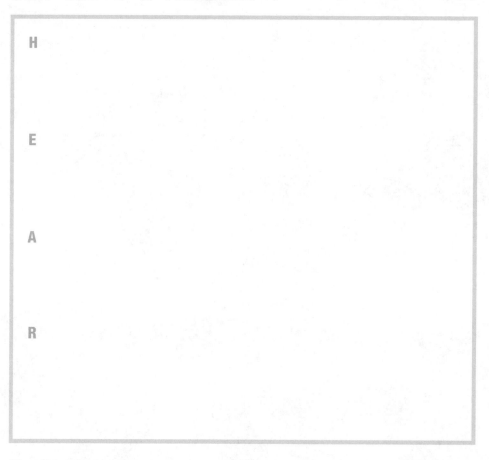

H

E

A

R

What Else Should I Know? The exact amount of time between Paul's first and second letters to Timothy is unknown, but it's clear Paul's circumstances had drastically changed. The Book of 2 Timothy is thought to be Paul's last letter, written from a prison cell in Rome just prior to his execution. A sense of urgency is evident throughout this letter.

Because Paul and Timothy were very close as ministers of the gospel, we shouldn't be surprised that Timothy was one of the last people Paul wrote to before his death. Paul reminded Timothy of the content of the gospel message, which is built on Jesus. Just as Jesus immensely suffered to bring the gospel to us, sharing the gospel with others may bring us suffering, as it had for Paul. That reality should only strengthen our ministry efforts, however, because it means the power of the gospel is evident in and through our lives.

Using himself as the model, Paul reminded Timothy that discipleship should be paramount in his ministry. At its core, discipleship is about sharing the "sound teaching" (v. 13) of Scripture with others in order to help them grow in their faith. This was the ministry to which God had called Timothy in Ephesus, and He fully equipped Timothy to live out that calling.

QUESTION: Who is God calling you to disciple? What are some steps you can take to make that happen?

DAY 168 | 2 TIMOTHY 2

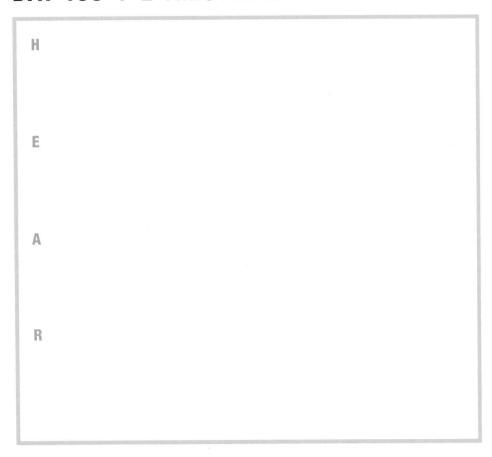

H

E

A

R

What Else Should I Know? Paul began 2 Timothy 2 with a series of commands that challenged Timothy in his ministry and faith: be strong, commit, share in suffering, and remember (vv. 1-8). Paul warned Timothy that the days of ministry ahead of him would be difficult and that he could expect to suffer in ways similar to Paul. To help Timothy understand what to expect as a gospel servant, Paul used several illustrations of people who endure hardship to achieve a worthwhile goal: soldiers, athletes, and farmers. Each group must make sacrifices to do its work well.

Unlike those groups, however, the ultimate sacrifice had already been made for believers. Nothing Christians suffer can compare to the suffering of Jesus. Because of Jesus' victory over death, we know our future is secure. No amount of suffering on earth can change the fact that we're God's children and that we'll spend eternity with Him.

QUESTION: How does knowing your future is secure in Jesus change the way you live today?

DAY 169 | 2 TIMOTHY 3

H

E

A

R

What Else Should I Know? Paul identified nineteen sinful behaviors that will characterize unbelievers living in the last days, from ingratitude and unholiness to abusiveness and greed. The issue at the root of all these behaviors is placing love of self over love of God. Verse 5 indicates that even seemingly religious people will be among those Paul described.

Timothy was to avoid these behaviors and the people practicing them. Instead, Timothy's responsibility was to emphasize God's truth. Because of the degradation of the world around him, persecution for his faithfulness was all but guaranteed. Paul encouraged Timothy not to give up the fight, though, because he had the power of God and His Word on his side. The truth of Scripture would stand up against anything Timothy faced because it's the Word of God, breathed out by God Himself. God's Word convicts of sin and teaches us how to pursue righteousness. Scripture reveals who God is and how to live for Him. Timothy was a student of the Word, as all Christians should be, because the Bible is the tool we need to live out the mission God has given us. Through Scripture we learn how to be disciples who make disciples—the goal of the Christian life.

 QUESTION: What should it look like for you to be a student of God's Word?

DAY 170 | 2 TIMOTHY 4

H

E

A

R

What Else Should I Know? In chapter 4, Paul continued to warn Timothy about the last days, emphasizing the need to be prepared for persecution and equipped for right living. Timothy's guide through all these difficulties must be the inspired Word of God, which would profit him in all areas of belief and behavior.

Because of the power of God's Word and the prevalence of sin in society, Paul reminded Timothy to preach the Word at all times and in all seasons. Preaching means more than standing behind a pulpit to deliver a sermon. We all have opportunities to make known the truth of God's Word. You can be a preacher wherever you are—in fact, God calls you to be.

Paul's image of pouring himself out as a drink offering (see v. 6) was his way of telling Timothy that he was about to make the ultimate sacrifice for God: he was going to die for his faith. To do so was to live life to the fullest, in Paul's mind. He had faithfully committed his life to the mission Jesus had given him on the road to Damascus, and he couldn't wait to spend eternity in God's presence.

There will be seasons when our faith will be stretched further than we can imagine, but we must stand firm in the Lord. Eternity is at stake.

W
E
E
K

35

DAY 171 | TITUS 1

HIGHLIGHT the verses that speak to you.

Write out the name of the book:

Which chapter and verse numbers stand out to you?

EXPLAIN what this passage means.

To whom was it originally written? Why?

How does it fit with the verses before and after it?

What is the Holy Spirit intending to communicate through this text?

APPLY what God is saying in these verses to your life.

What does this mean today?

What is God saying to you personally?

How can you apply this message to your life?

RESPOND to what you've read.

In what ways does this passage call you to action?

How will you be different because of what you've learned?

Write out a prayer to God in response to what you read today:

What Else Should I Know? Like 1–2 Timothy, the letter to Titus is another Paul wrote to an individual. Also like Timothy, Titus was most likely introduced to Christianity by Paul, and he accompanied Paul on part of his missionary journey, traveling to Crete, the largest Greek island, located in the Mediterranean Sea.

Titus was Greek, so when Paul decided someone needed to stay and oversee the new churches in Crete, it made perfect sense for it to be him. Paul never forgot his partners in ministry, and Titus was no exception. This letter was one way Paul continued to equip and encourage him after they parted ways.

Titus' job was to bring leadership and structure to the new churches on the island. Verses 6-9 reminded him of the essential characteristics for the role: blameless, monogamous, humble, self-controlled, hospitable, and holy. The reason? Young Christians in Crete were in danger of believing the lies of false teachers. Strong leadership in the church would help protect their growing faith.

? **QUESTION:** How can you be intentional with new believers as they learn to walk with Jesus?

DAY 172 | TITUS 2

H

E

A

R

What Else Should I Know? Titus 2 identifies the clearest way to offset the dangers of false teaching: teach the Bible. A faith rooted in God's Word alone is the surest way to avoid being led astray from the gospel. This is why it was so important for Titus and the other leaders of the church to "proclaim things consistent with sound teaching" (v. 1).

Paul gave specific instructions to show Titus how to lead various groups in the church. Although each group was different, the same themes applied to everyone: godliness, self-control, reverence, and commitment to the gospel.

Verses 11-14 summarize Paul's instructions with a word for all believers. Christians are to behave in the manner Paul described because God's grace has been made known to them. When we understand and accept God's gift of grace, it transforms us from people who are worldly and self-consumed to people who pursue lives of godliness as we wait for Jesus' return. These traits make our lives look markedly different from the world around us. We begin to look more and more like Jesus, and this resemblance draws other people to Him.

QUESTION: What traits mentioned in this passage do you need help to work on?

DAY 173 | TITUS 3

H

E

A

R

What Else Should I Know? While Titus 2 focused on relating to one another in the church, chapter 3 broadens that instruction to include the way believers conduct themselves in the world. This teaching includes being obedient, kind, peaceful, humble, and submissive to governmental leaders.

Why does a Christian's attitude matter? Paul explained in verses 3-8 that knowing Christ dramatically changes a person's life, and that change should be evident in behaviors and attitudes as well. The traits Paul encouraged the Christians in Crete to express are characteristics Jesus modeled while on earth. They're also fruit of the Spirit that should mark the life of every believer. Paul presented a stark contrast between who these believers were before they knew Jesus and who they were in Him; the same comparison defines the life of every Christian today.

Paul wanted Titus to remind those to whom he ministered that Christ had changed them and that their lives should give evidence of that transformation. This letter reminds us of the importance of sound doctrine and godly living as the foundations of healthy church life and of our witness to the world.

 QUESTION: Does your attitude reflect the fruit of the Spirit? Why or why not?

DAY 174 | 1 PETER 1

H

E

A

R

What Else Should I Know? In this first letter, Peter addressed both Jewish and Gentile Christians who were experiencing violent persecution. He encouraged his readers to persevere in their faith and to brace for future attacks.

Peter addressed the sufferings his readers were experiencing. Interestingly, though, he did more than acknowledge their suffering; he described suffering as something that builds our faith—a theme we've seen throughout the New Testament. Verse 8 is a testimony to the faith of the early Christians. Through faith they loved Jesus and were wholeheartedly and joyfully committed to living for Him, no matter what they faced.

Verses 13-25 called readers to an active faith that has the pursuit of holiness as its goal. These teachings have implications for our lives as Christ followers today. The basis for Christian hope is Jesus' resurrection and the promise of eternal life. Our trials are temporary. They refine our faith and make us stronger. They show our obedience to God and give us a chance to reflect His holiness in our behavior. All this is possible because Jesus has redeemed us from our old, sinful way of life.

CHALLENGE: On a separate piece of paper, write out a testimony of how God has used a past trial for your good.

DAY 175 | 1 PETER 2

H

E

A

R

What Else Should I Know? In chapter 2 Peter used several images to help us understand how Christ has changed us.

We've received a new diet, which Peter described as spiritual milk, that helps us grow in Christlikeness (vv. 1-3). When we pursue Christ by studying His Word and discipling with other believers, God empowers us to live godly lives that are set apart from the characteristics of the world—malice, deceit, hypocrisy, envy, and slander.

- The second image Peter used was a new spiritual house (vv. 4-8). This image refers to the church, which Peter described as a group of people growing into Christlikeness together.
- The third image Peter included was a new family (vv. 9-10), described by such phrases as "a chosen race, a royal priesthood, a holy nation, a people for his [God's] possession" (v. 9).

Each phrase reminds us that we're children of God, brothers and sisters united in His mercy and grace. God made us His children so that we'll tell the world about who He is and what He has done to redeem us.

QUESTION: Based on this passage, what does God give us when we experience salvation?

DAY 176 | 1 PETER 3

HIGHLIGHT the verses that speak to you.

Write out the name of the book:

Which chapter and verse numbers stand out to you?

EXPLAIN what this passage means.

To whom was it originally written? Why?

How does it fit with the verses before and after it?

What is the Holy Spirit intending to communicate through this text?

APPLY what God is saying in these verses to your life.

What does this mean today?

What is God saying to you personally?

How can you apply this message to your life?

RESPOND to what you've read.

In what ways does this passage call you to action?

How will you be different because of what you've learned?

Write out a prayer to God in response to what you read today:

What Else Should I Know? Peter continued his instruction by turning his attention to Christian marriages. He began with counsel for wives, whom he challenged to focus on inner purity and extending goodwill toward others. One motivating factor was to win over spouses who weren't yet Christians, a common situation among the first converts to Christianity. Peter's hope was that the women would point their husbands to Christ with their words and actions—an example he finds in the Old Testament story of Sarah.

Peter challenged husbands to honor their wives and provide spiritual leadership. More broadly, He encouraged believers to get along with one another, blessing one another through sympathy, compassion, love, and humility.

Repeatedly throughout his letter Peter returned to the topic of suffering. When Christians respond to suffering with hope, they put God's power and love on display. This is why it was so important for Peter's audience to be fully prepared to share the gospel, the "reason for the hope that is in you" (v. 15). Our lives should always glorify God, even in our trials.

 PRAY: Jesus, I want to honor You. Would You give me a deeper passion for Your gospel and for lost people?

DAY 177 | 1 PETER 4

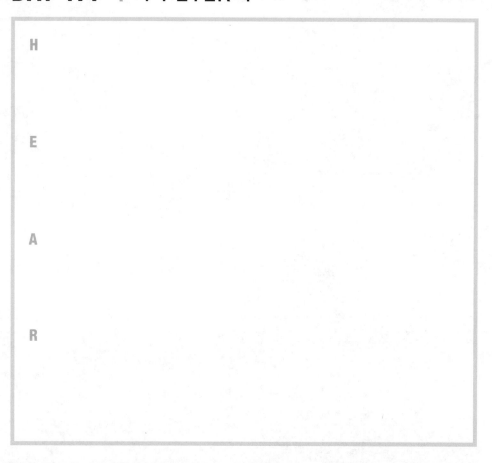

H

E

A

R

What Else Should I Know? Chapter 4 emphasizes sharing in Christ's suffering and resting in the promises that come through His victory over sin and death on the cross. With Christ as our example, we're to demonstrate the same resolve with which Jesus obeyed God's will and served others, with our focus always on the promise of eternity. Peter reminded his readers of their lifestyle before they met Christ, and he warned that many people would tempt them to fall back into their previous sins. Because this temptation would be great, it was important for them to keep the gospel at the forefront of their minds. Peter reminded them that the wicked would have to give an account to the Lord, who judges "the living and the dead" (v. 5).

Peter returned to the issue of suffering in verse 12. Suffering for our faith shouldn't come as a surprise; Jesus endured it, and He repeatedly warned His followers they would, too. But the Holy Spirit empowers us to endure suffering and to live for Christ. So take heart. God sees your suffering and hears your prayers. There's good news in suffering for the faith. It shows that you're faithfully living for God—and that other people notice it.

 QUESTION: How can suffering be good in your life?

DAY 178 | 1 PETER 5

H

E

A

R

What Else Should I Know? Peter closed his first letter by encouraging church leaders to take their spiritual calling seriously. They were to be active shepherds who protected and cared for the people entrusted to them. They were also to serve with humility and compassion. Shepherding people through such tumultuous times wouldn't be easy, but church leaders could find strength and motivation in the future glory of Christ.

The theme of humility runs through the rest of Peter's instructions in this chapter. In verse 5 he turned his attention to those who were younger, urging them to respect and submit to their leaders. Peter warned against the rise of pride in a person's life and expected all believers to relate to one another and to God in humility. Peter's exhortation is especially important in light of the presence of the devil, who still actively targets Christians today. The image of Satan as "a roaring lion, looking for anyone he can devour" (v. 8) paints a vivid picture of his predatory, deadly behavior. The only appropriate response to him is to resist him through faith in Jesus.

Peter concluded his letter by encouraging Christians to stand firm in the gospel: a promise that the sovereign God would help them endure any trial that came their way.

QUESTION: In what ways do you struggle with pride? How can you combat a prideful heart?

DAY 179 | 2 PETER 1

H

E

A

R

What Else Should I Know? Believing his life would soon end (see 1:14), Peter wrote this letter to provide urgent instructions and warnings he wanted to give to the early church. Peter described the power of God, which transforms the Christian heart. Through His power we're able to flee sinfulness and pursue godliness. Peter went on to list characteristics of godliness the Holy Spirit produces in our lives: goodness, knowledge, self-control, endurance, godliness, brotherly affection, and love. These qualities motivate us to pursue God more deeply and to share His love with others.

Peter wanted his readers to firmly plant their faith in Scripture and believe it could be trusted as the primary source and guide for their spiritual lives. Believers' lives are to be rooted in their faith in God, which will grow as they practice it and seek God as He has revealed Himself in Jesus Christ. The gospel the apostles preached is a trustworthy source for this knowledge, and it remains as true for us today as it was when they spoke it.

? **QUESTION:** Read back over the attributes mentioned in this chapter. Which one do you have the hardest time with? Why?

DAY 180 | 2 PETER 2

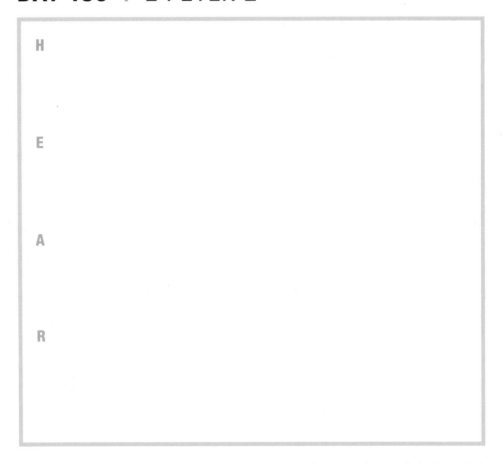

H

E

A

R

What Else Should I Know? In chapter 2 Peter explained why his readers needed to base their faith in God on the truth of the gospel: because there were counterfeiters among them. Peter painted a scathing picture of these false teachers. They were primarily motivated by greed, which led them to teach any lie they thought would bring them the most money. At its extreme, this false teaching denied Jesus and His work on the cross altogether. However, the judgment of God was waiting for these false teachers.

Peter called to mind Noah and Lot as examples of people who pursued righteousness in the midst of unrighteousness and, as a result, received God's grace rather than judgment. Peter encouraged his readers to be like Noah and Lot, remaining committed to God and His truths, no matter how people tried to influence them. Peter implored his readers to avoid these teachers at all costs and to hold firm to the truth of the gospel that came from those who actually lived with Jesus and witnessed His teachings.

 PRAY: Jesus, help me to be wise as You are wise. Would You help me to discern lies from truth?

Check In

WEEK 37

- ☐ 2 Peter 3
- ☐ John 1
- ☐ John 2
- ☐ John 3
- ☐ John 4

MEMORY VERSES

OPTION 1: Psalm 85:6-7
OPTION 2: Proverbs 21:23
OPTION 3: Matthew 6:31-32

WEEK 39

- ☐ John 10
- ☐ John 11
- ☐ John 12
- ☐ John 13
- ☐ John 14

MEMORY VERSES

OPTION 1: Psalm 90:12
OPTION 2: Proverbs 22:6
OPTION 3: Matthew 7:1-2

WEEK 38

- ☐ John 5
- ☐ John 6
- ☐ John 7
- ☐ John 8
- ☐ John 9

MEMORY VERSES

OPTION 1: Psalm 86:5
OPTION 2: Proverbs 22:1
OPTION 3: Matthew 6:33-34

WEEK 40

- ☐ John 15
- ☐ John 16
- ☐ John 17
- ☐ John 18
- ☐ John 19

MEMORY VERSES

OPTION 1: Psalm 96:2-3
OPTION 2: Proverbs 23:13-14
OPTION 3: Matthew 7:3-4

SCAN THIS QR CODE TO ACCESS A FUN SURPRISE!

W
E
E
K

37

DAY 181 | 2 PETER 3

HIGHLIGHT the verses that speak to you.

Write out the name of the book:

Which chapter and verse numbers stand out to you?

EXPLAIN what this passage means.

To whom was it originally written? Why?

How does it fit with the verses before and after it?

What is the Holy Spirit intending to communicate through this text?

APPLY what God is saying in these verses to your life.

What does this mean today?

What is God saying to you personally?

How can you apply this message to your life?

RESPOND to what you've read.

In what ways does this passage call you to action?

How will you be different because of what you've learned?

Write out a prayer to God in response to what you read today:

What Else Should I Know? Peter's examination of the false teachers reached a climax in chapter 3, in which he reminded his readers to remember what the prophets and apostles had spoken. It's clear that a chief argument of the false teachers was that Jesus wasn't coming back, and they used the delay since His ascension as proof for their case.

Peter, however, reminded readers of the power of God to act swiftly whenever He chooses, as He did with creation and again with the flood. Jesus' return will be the precursor to God's final judgment of the world, so any delay of that return is an act of mercy and patience on God's part, not evidence that He has failed to keep His promises. God is patient. He wants everyone to come to know Him through repentance and faith (see v. 9).

Jesus will come back "like a thief" (v. 10)—unexpectedly—which means a day will come when His offer of grace and salvation will no longer be available. Rather than watching the clock for Jesus to return, we should share the gospel and help Him draw people everywhere into a relationship with Him while time remains.

 QUESTION: How can you make Jesus known to those around you at school or in your neighborhood?

DAY 182 | JOHN 1

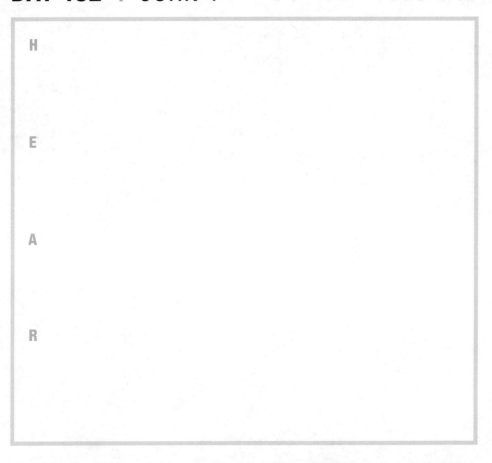

H

E

A

R

What Else Should I Know? John, one of Jesus' apostles, wrote his Gospel to prove that Jesus is God incarnate, the divine Son of God who came to earth as a man. John 1 focuses on Jesus' divinity and role in creation, as well as the start of His earthly ministry. The Word, Jesus, is divine, distinct from God the Father but one with Him. God created everything through the Word. Nothing came into being without His direct involvement. Life came through Jesus, who provided the light of God's love and guidance. Just as physical light dispelled the darkness on the first day of creation (see Gen. 1:3), Jesus' light pierced the darkness of sin to provide eternal salvation for those who believe in Him. Although the Word created the world, people didn't recognize or respond to Him. Despite that rejection, some people accepted Jesus, believing in Him as Savior.

John's Gospel also emphasizes the humanity of Jesus. By coming in human form, Jesus allowed us to see the glory of God. John the Baptist's witness proved true as Jesus' life, ministry, death, and resurrection revealed God's grace and truth. In Jesus we find grace, truth, and salvation. Once Christ changes our lives, we, like the first disciples, are compelled to live in a way that demonstrates the power of the gospel, pointing other people to Jesus.

DEFINE: Look up the definition of incarnate. Write it out in your own words.

DAY 183 | JOHN 2

H

E

A

R

What Else Should I Know? John marked the beginning of Jesus' earthly ministry with the account of the first miracle Jesus performed. Jesus and His mother, Mary, were attending a wedding celebration, and the hosts ran out of wine. Jesus used the opportunity to give the people closest to Him a glimpse of who He was and of His power. John noted that this miracle solidified His disciples' faith in Him and first revealed His glory to the world.

Following this miracle, Jesus traveled to Jerusalem for the Passover. When He went into the temple and found it overrun by vendors and money changers, He cast them out. His reference to the temple as "my Father's house" (v. 16) was a clear statement of His divinity and of His relationship with God the Father. The temple, which should have been devoted to worshiping God, had been turned into a marketplace where people attempted to turn worship into profit. Jesus' action made the point that one reason He came was to draw people and their worship back to God. This event also established His religious authority and initiated the tensions that would escalate between Himself and the Jewish religious leaders—a tension that would eventually lead to the cross.

QUESTION: What does this passage teach you about Jesus? How can you be more like Him?

DAY 184 | JOHN 3

H

E

A

R

What Else Should I Know? In John 3, Jesus encounters Nicodemus, a Pharisee and religious leader. Having witnessed some of Jesus' miracles and seeing the authority with which He spoke, Nicodemus was curious to seek Jesus out and discover what else He could learn about Him.

Nicodemus believed God had sent Jesus, but he didn't know Jesus was the promised Messiah, the Savior the Jews were waiting for. Their conversation leaves no doubt about what's required for a person to enter the kingdom of God: a relationship with Jesus. At the heart of Jesus' teaching is the concept of being born again—the life-changing effect of the Holy Spirit in a person's life. This change takes place as people confess their belief that Jesus is the Son of God, who died to pay the price for their sins. John 3:16-18 gives Jesus' first concise explanation of why He came to earth: to save people from their sins.

 QUESTION: In this passage, what does Jesus share about His purpose on earth?

DAY 185 | JOHN 4

H

E

A

R

What Else Should I Know? In John 4 we read about another important conversation Jesus had early in His ministry. During His travels Jesus passed through Samaria. While in the town of Sychar, Jesus stopped to rest at a well when a woman came to draw water. The woman Jesus met that day couldn't have been more different from Nicodemus. Although she had no idea who Jesus was when she met Him, she knew He was a Jew, and as a Samaritan woman, she wasn't supposed to associate with Him.

Jesus used this opportunity to describe the new life available in Him as "living water" (v. 10). The image of living water that forever satisfies a person's thirst represents eternal life with God. The woman's belief in Jesus is evident in verses 28-29,39-42, in which we read that she told everyone she met about her conversation with Jesus and that those people sought out Jesus too.

Both of the spiritual conversations in John 3–4 make it clear that Jesus is the only way to salvation. A relationship with Him is the only way to find spiritual satisfaction and fulfillment.

QUESTION: What does it mean to be satisfied with Jesus alone? How does that change the way you live?

MEMORY VERSE OPTIONS: Psalm 86:5; Proverbs 22:1; Matthew 6:33-34

DAY 186 | JOHN 5

HIGHLIGHT the verses that speak to you.

Write out the name of the book:

Which chapter and verse numbers stand out to you?

EXPLAIN what this passage means.

To whom was it originally written? Why?

How does it fit with the verses before and after it?

What is the Holy Spirit intending to communicate through this text?

APPLY what God is saying in these verses to your life.

What does this mean today?

What is God saying to you personally?

How can you apply this message to your life?

RESPOND to what you've read.

In what ways does this passage call you to action?

How will you be different because of what you've learned?

Write out a prayer to God in response to what you read today:

What Else Should I Know? John 5 presents another miracle that highlights Jesus' role as the divine Son of the Trinity. In order to heal the lame man beside the pool of Bethesda, Jesus did nothing more than speak, telling him to get up and walk. Jesus didn't even touch him. But because the Creator of the universe spoke these words, they had the power to heal and restore this man.

The trouble was that Jesus healed on the Sabbath, violating the pharisaical law. However, Jesus was the Lord of the Sabbath, and His response to the critics, "My Father is still working, and I am working also" (v. 17), was both a statement of His authority as the Son of God and a point of great contention with the Pharisees. Instead of running when the Jews grew angry with Him, Jesus took the opportunity to describe in great detail who He was.

His testimony teaches us that as the Son, Jesus followed the Father's instructions and obeyed the Father's commands. In obedience to His Father, Jesus said He would fulfill His roles as both Savior and Judge. There was no doubt: the prophecies of John the Baptist and the Old Testament prophets were spoken about Him.

 PRAY: Jesus, help me to believe and trust in You. Protect me against a critical spirit toward Your works.

DAY 187 | JOHN 6

H

E

A

R

What Else Should I Know? While the four Gospels have many points of similarity, they also have considerable differences because each Gospel writer wanted to communicate a unique message to a particular audience. Among the teachings unique to John's Gospel are the "I am" statements of Jesus, the first of which appears in John 6. John had just recorded Jesus' testimony that He was the Son of God, and with each of these "I am" statements, Jesus revealed some of His attributes and functions as the Son, using images that would be easy for listeners to understand.

John 6 begins with the miracle of Jesus feeding the 5,000. By meeting the people's physical need for food and then declaring Himself to be the Bread of life, Jesus helped the people see that He alone could satisfy their spiritual hunger.

Everyone is born with spiritual hunger—a hole in our hearts that we attempt to fill with religion, materialism, and relationships. But the only thing that can satisfy our spirit is to know Jesus as our loving, all-sufficient Savior.

? **QUESTION:** Are you hungry for the things of this world or for Jesus? Why is Jesus the only One who can satisfy?

DAY 188 | JOHN 7

H

E

A

R

What Else Should I Know? As Jesus had explained to Mary at the wedding reception (see John 2:4), Jesus knew the time for the culmination of His ministry hadn't yet arrived.

In contrast, when Jesus went and taught in the temple, He pointed listeners to the glory and honor of God. Not surprisingly, the words Jesus spoke created more controversy, with some people affirming that He was the Christ and others refusing to believe because He didn't fit the image of the Messiah they expected (see 7:40-43).

Jesus continues to be as controversial and divisive today as He was for the Jews. Thankfully, our faith isn't founded on what we imagine Jesus should be like or what He should do for us. It's founded on what He already did—dying for our sins on the cross.

QUESTION: How do you respond in the face of controversy surrounding the conversation about Jesus?

DAY 189 | JOHN 8

H

E

A

R

What Else Should I Know? John 8 focuses on the second of Jesus' "I am" statements. In addition to calling Himself the Bread of life, Jesus proclaimed, "I am the light of the world" (v. 12). Darkness versus light is a frequent symbol throughout the Bible, with darkness symbolizing evil and light symbolizing good. By calling Himself "the light of the world" and "the light of life" (v. 12), Jesus claimed that all goodness originates with Him and that He alone is a person's hope to escape the darkness of the world. This was a symbolic way of describing the gospel, the salvation from sin and death available to all people through belief in Him.

In the dialogue that continued throughout this chapter, Jesus condemned the Jews for their lack of belief in Him, saying they would die in their sins and be eternally separated from God because of their unbelief. In contrast, Jesus affirmed the faith and eternal security of people who believed. To those people He spoke these beautiful words. Let them encourage you as you live for Him—and let them spur you to share His message of hope: "You will know the truth, and the truth will set you free" (v. 32).

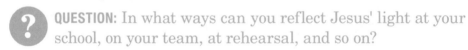

QUESTION: In what ways can you reflect Jesus' light at your school, on your team, at rehearsal, and so on?

DAY 190 | JOHN 9

H

E

A

R

What Else Should I Know? The chapter begins by describing an encounter Jesus and His disciples had with a blind man. The disciples asked a common question in Jesus' day: "Who sinned, this man or his parents, that he was born blind?" (v. 2). In that day people often blamed sin as the reason for a person's physical ailments. Jesus challenged this belief by stating the opposite: this man was blind so that God's glory and works would be displayed. Jesus, the Light of the world, would bring this blind man out of both blindness by restoring his sight. The symbolism is striking.

With each chapter of John's Gospel, the gap between belief and unbelief widened. While the blind man was able to proclaim, "One thing I do know: I was blind, and now I can see!" (v. 25), the Pharisees became increasingly more blind in their disbelief (see v. 41). Jesus didn't come to save people who are sinless; Scripture makes it clear such a person doesn't exist. Jesus came to save sinners who recognize their sinfulness—their spiritual blindness. To them—to all of us—Jesus, our Savior, offers sight.

PRAY: How is it hard for you to see, believe, or understand about Jesus? Ask Him to help you in these areas.

MEMORY VERSE OPTIONS: Psalm 90:12; Proverbs 22:6; Matthew 7:1-2

WEEK

E

E

K

39

DAY 191 | JOHN 10

HIGHLIGHT the verses that speak to you.

Write out the name of the book:

Which chapter and verse numbers stand out to you?

EXPLAIN what this passage means.

To whom was it originally written? Why?

How does it fit with the verses before and after it?

What is the Holy Spirit intending to communicate through this text?

APPLY what God is saying in these verses to your life.

What does this mean today?

What is God saying to you personally?

How can you apply this message to your life?

RESPOND to what you've read.

In what ways does this passage call you to action?

How will you be different because of what you've learned?

Write out a prayer to God in response to what you read today:

What Else Should I Know? Two "I am" statements by Jesus appear in John 10, and both use the illustration of a shepherd and his sheep to help readers better understand Jesus' identity. The first appears in verses 7-9, in which Jesus stated, "I am the gate for the sheep" (v. 7). Like the image of the Light of the world, this statement also describes Jesus as the only way to God.

Secondly, Jesus described Himself as the Good Shepherd (see v. 11). As the Shepherd, Jesus provides food and comfort for the sheep, protects them from predators, knows them personally, and even dies for them. The sheep recognize their Shepherd's voice and can even distinguish it from the voices of other shepherds. They obey their Shepherd's commands because they know He's working for their good and is always looking out for them. This knowledge allows them to fully trust His love and give Him control of their lives. This is how Jesus wants us to live in a relationship with Him. He wants us to know that He loves us and will always take care of us, and He wants us to trust Him with our lives.

 QUESTION: How are you actively seeking to hear the Shepherd's voice?

DAY 192 | JOHN 11

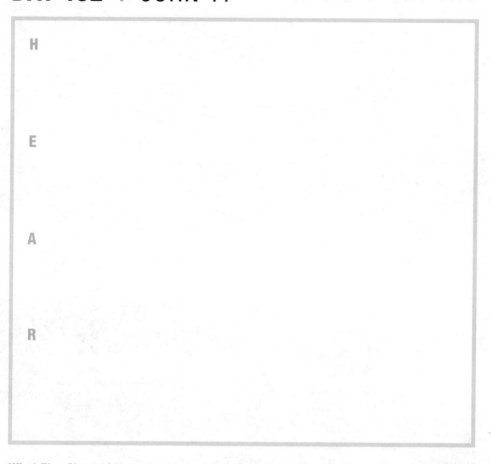

H

E

A

R

What Else Should I Know? John 11 records one of Jesus' greatest miracles: the resurrection of Lazarus. Lazarus was the brother of Mary and Martha, two women who figured prominently in Jesus' life and ministry. When Lazarus grew sick, his sisters turned to Jesus. Having seen Him heal many people before, they knew He could save their brother's life. Although Jesus affirmed that like the affliction of the blind man, Lazarus's sickness was for God's glory, He didn't rush to heal him. Instead, Lazarus died and was buried. When Jesus arrived four days later, the sisters questioned His lack of action, but their belief and faith in Him didn't waver.

Lazarus's death presented Jesus with the opportunity to further establish His authority by showing that He had authority even over death, something only God Himself could claim. His proclamation, "I am the resurrection and the life" (v. 25), shows that only through a relationship with Jesus is eternal life in God's presence possible. But it would come at a cost. After this miracle the threat against Jesus' life intensified, and the cross drew nearer.

QUESTION: What do you learn about Jesus' humanity in this passage? Why do you think Jesus waited four days to come and see Lazarus?

DAY 193 | JOHN 12

H

E

A

R

What Else Should I Know? John 12 serves as the transitional chapter between Jesus' earthly ministry and the events surrounding His death. Opposition to Him rapidly increased after He raised Lazarus from the dead. Soon, His own death was approaching. Jesus' knowledge of His impending death made the scene in which Mary publicly anointed Him with burial oils even more symbolic. In John's account of this scene, readers learn more about Jesus' understanding of the upcoming events and gain insight into the greed that would lead to Judas's betrayal.

If the Gospel of John is a case for Jesus' divinity, John 12 is a final public call to believe in Jesus as the Light of the world. Jesus referred to the events that would come, His death and resurrection, as His time to be glorified and the reason for His coming to earth. Jesus left the crowds with the call to believe in Him while they had the chance. The benefits then are the same for those who believe in Jesus today: we become "children of light" (v. 36) and gain eternal life with the Father.

CHALLENGE: In this chapter, you read about Mary anointing Jesus with expensive perfume worth about a years' wages. Her action was worship. Respond with worship today for all God has done for you.

DAY 194 | JOHN 13

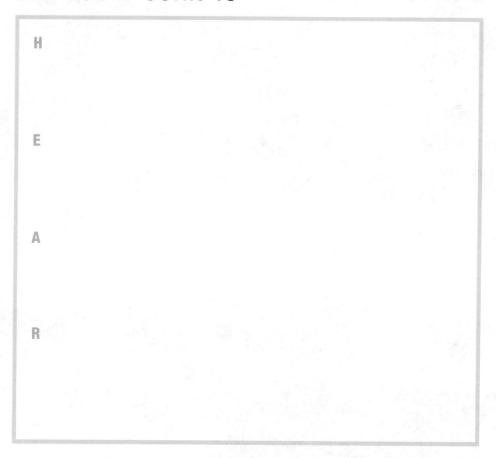

H

E

A

R

What Else Should I Know? Jesus' sacrificial death occupies a central focus in John's Gospel as the events moved toward a climax at the cross and Jesus' triumph through the resurrection. In chapter 13 the focus shifts to Jesus' final meal with His disciples before His arrest, death, and resurrection. With little time remaining, Jesus turned His attention to His disciples, both to prepare them for the coming events and to teach them the kingdom qualities of humility, service, and love. They would be called to embody these traits when they took on Jesus' ministry after His ascension to heaven.

Jesus knew He would be betrayed by Judas and denied by Peter. Yet despite the disciples' unfaithfulness, Jesus demonstrated a servant attitude toward them. He washed their feet. What a picture of humility and love for us today. God calls us to serve everyone—even those who betray us. Facing death, abandoned by those He loved most, Jesus remained the ultimate servant.

 QUESTION: How do you respond when people hurt you?

DAY 195 | JOHN 14

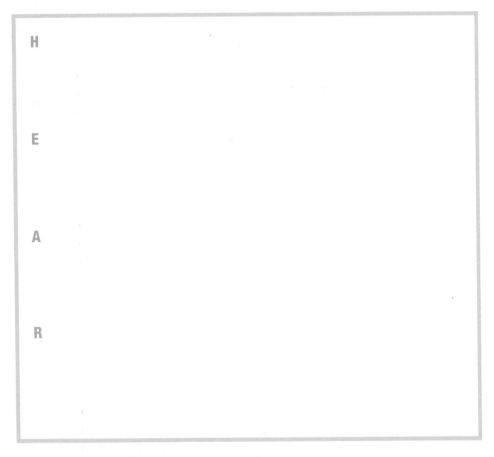

H

E

A

R

What Else Should I Know? After Jesus washed the feet of the disciples, He outlined His expectations for them after His death. Anticipating the sorrow His disciples would experience at His departure, Jesus offered a message of comfort to enable them to live confidently. In another of His "I am" statements, Jesus referred to Himself as "the way, the truth, and the life" (v. 6). Jesus is the single, reliable source of redemptive revelation. There is no other way to know God.

Another means of comfort for Jesus' disciples would be the presence of the Holy Spirit, whom Jesus promised to send in His place. The Holy Spirit serves as a Counselor and Teacher. He brings peace and comfort to a believer's soul, and He increases our understanding of God and His will for our lives. In this teaching Jesus also included a call to obedience. Believers listen to Jesus and do what He says. Obedience to God doesn't guarantee a person's salvation—only believing in Jesus alone can do that—but if Jesus has truly changed a person's heart, obedience to Him will follow.

? **QUESTION:** In what ways is the Holy Spirit at work in the life of a believer?

DAY 196 | JOHN 15

HIGHLIGHT the verses that speak to you.

Write out the name of the book:

Which chapter and verse numbers stand out to you?

EXPLAIN what this passage means.

To whom was it originally written? Why?

How does it fit with the verses before and after it?

What is the Holy Spirit intending to communicate through this text?

APPLY what God is saying in these verses to your life.

What does this mean today?

What is God saying to you personally?

How can you apply this message to your life?

RESPOND to what you've read.

In what ways does this passage call you to action?

How will you be different because of what you've learned?

Write out a prayer to God in response to what you read today:

What Else Should I Know? The images in John 15 describe Jesus' relationship with believers in two ways: a vine and branches, and a master and friends. This chapter also includes Jesus' final "I am" statement: "I am the true vine" (v. 1).

As branches, we abide in Him faithfully and obediently in order to produce fruit for the kingdom of God. God is the Master Gardener, cutting off branches that show no signs of life and pruning fruitful branches to help them yield even more. The point of this image is clear: our growth in our relationship with God depends on our abiding connection to Jesus, the Vine.

Jesus wanted His disciples to understand that His mission will put us at odds with the world. But persecution shouldn't discourage us. It should give us hope: It shows we're bearing fruit. It proves we're abiding in Him.

 QUESTION: How can you stay connected to the vine?

DAY 197 | JOHN 16

H

E

A

R

What Else Should I Know? In the final instructions Jesus gave to His disciples, Jesus promised He would ask the Father to send the Holy Spirit to them (see 14:16). The Holy Spirit would be their Counselor (see 14:26), testify about Jesus Christ (see 15:26), and enable believers to testify also (see 15:27).

In this chapter, Jesus gave His disciples more insight into the role of the Holy Spirit. The Spirit would convict people of sin, righteousness, and judgment, guiding believers into all truth. Only through the Spirit's strength are we able to find the hope and confidence Jesus gave at the close of this chapter: "Be courageous! I have conquered the world" (v. 33).

Yet at the same time, Jesus never abandons His followers. He is always there for us as our intermediary. While the Holy Spirit is at work in our lives, Jesus sits with His Father in heaven, interceding on our behalf as the One through whom we're made right with God.

 QUESTION: How are you living dependent on the Holy Spirit?

DAY 198 | JOHN 17

H

E

A

R

What Else Should I Know? John 17 is often referred to as Jesus' High Priestly prayer. Jesus' prayer on the eve of His arrest and trials included a prayer for Himself, a prayer for His disciples, and a prayer for future believers of every age. Jesus prayed that He would glorify His Father through His death—the culmination of His mission on earth.

Jesus then prayed that His disciples would glorify the Father by preserving the unity they had with Jesus. Jesus petitioned the Father to protect His disciples from the evil one. He also asked God to grow them in Christlikeness as they continued His mission of drawing people to the Father.

Finally, Jesus prayed for all who would come to believe in Him in the future. He wanted believers to experience unity with the Father and the Son, growing in their knowledge and love. That unity would show unbelievers the gospel. Jesus' selfless prayer while facing imminent danger is a model for all believers today—nothing, not even death, can get in the way of the gospel.

 PRAY: Pray for unity among you and your Christian friends. Ask Jesus to use your unity to demonstrate the gospel to those who don't know Him.

DAY 199 | JOHN 18

H

E

A

R

What Else Should I Know? John began with Judas' betrayal and Jesus' surrender to the soldiers and religious leaders. From the beginning of this narrative, John highlighted the fact that Jesus knew what was happening and allowed it to happen. As the divine Son of God, Jesus was always in control, even when He was betrayed and put to death. He willingly gave His life to save ours.

John next recorded a portion of Jesus' trial, a scene that also includes the first two of Peter's denials of Jesus. While Jesus was defending His identity as the Messiah before Israel's leaders, Peter cowered, denying any relation to Him. The contrast is striking and intentional on John's part.

After Jesus appeared before the religious leaders, He was sent to Pilate, the Roman governor. John highlighted in detail the conversation between these two men, in which Jesus defended His kingship. Although Pilate seemed to believe Jesus, He didn't defend Him. Pilate chose not to be on the side of truth, a choice with devastating, eternal consequences.

QUESTION: How did Jesus respond in the face of betrayal and questioning?

DAY 200 | JOHN 19

H

E

A

R

What Else Should I Know? Pilate had found no basis for the charges brought against Jesus, but he wasn't willing to sacrifice his political interests to set Him free. Therefore, he yielded to the religious leaders' demands for Jesus' death.

Though Pilate handed Jesus over to the Jews to be crucified, it's important to note that Jesus willingly gave Himself to die a sacrificial death for the sins of the world. John emphasized Jesus' control of these events. He also recorded many unique elements of the crucifixion that gave further evidence of Jesus' divinity, including fulfillments of Old Testament prophecy and Jesus' declaration "It is finished" (19:30).

Jesus' crucifixion occurred during the season of Passover, showing that He died as the Lamb of God (see 1:29,36). Just as the blood of lambs had spared the Israelites in Egypt (see Ex. 12:13), Jesus' blood "cleanses us from all sin" (1 John 1:7). Jesus died for us.

PRAY: Jesus, thank You for dying for my sins. Your grace for me doesn't make sense. I love You.

Check In

WEEK 41

- [ ] John 20
- [ ] John 21
- [ ] 1 John 1
- [ ] 1 John 2
- [ ] 1 John 3

MEMORY VERSES

OPTION 1: Psalm 100:4-5
OPTION 2: Proverbs 24:16
OPTION 3: Matthew 7:5-6

WEEK 42

- [ ] 1 John 4
- [ ] 1 John 5
- [ ] 2 John 1
- [ ] 3 John 1
- [ ] Jude 1

MEMORY VERSES

OPTION 1: Psalm 103:1-2
OPTION 2: Proverbs 25:11-12
OPTION 3: Matthew 7:7-8

WEEK 43

- [ ] Revelation 1
- [ ] Revelation 2
- [ ] Revelation 3
- [ ] Revelation 4
- [ ] Revelation 5

MEMORY VERSES

OPTION 1: Psalm 103:3-4
OPTION 2: Proverbs 26:20
OPTION 3: Matthew 7:9-10

WEEK 44

- [ ] Revelation 6
- [ ] Revelation 7
- [ ] Revelation 8
- [ ] Revelation 9
- [ ] Revelation 10

MEMORY VERSES

OPTION 1: Psalm 103:11-12
OPTION 2: Proverbs 27:17
OPTION 3: Matthew 7:11-12

SCAN THIS QR CODE TO ACCESS A FUN SURPRISE!

DAY 201 | JOHN 20

WEEK 41

HIGHLIGHT the verses that speak to you.

Write out the name of the book:

Which chapter and verse numbers stand out to you?

EXPLAIN what this passage means.

To whom was it originally written? Why?

How does it fit with the verses before and after it?

What is the Holy Spirit intending to communicate through this text?

APPLY what God is saying in these verses to your life.

What does this mean today?

What is God saying to you personally?

How can you apply this message to your life?

RESPOND to what you've read.

In what ways does this passage call you to action?

How will you be different because of what you've learned?

Write out a prayer to God in response to what you read today:

What Else Should I Know? In John 17, Jesus referred to a time when He would be glorified. That glorification came to fruition in chapter 20 with John's description of Jesus' resurrection from the dead. For John, this was the ultimate proof that Jesus was the Son of God. Though all the Gospel writers included the resurrection, John's account highlights specific conversations Jesus had with His disciples afterward. We see ways His resurrection affected their faith and should affect ours as well.

The evening after Mary found the tomb empty, Jesus appeared to the disciples, who were huddled behind locked doors. To these disciples Jesus brought words of peace, comfort, and commission. Jesus appeared again a week later to the disciples, including Thomas, who had difficulty believing the news. Jesus invited Thomas to see and touch His scars, but Thomas responded in faith without touching His wounds.

John's purpose in writing his Gospel was to call people to believe in Jesus as the Son of God who offers eternal life. As believers, that's our purpose too.

Fun Fact: Jesus appeared first after His resurrection to a woman, Mary Magdalene. Mary carried the message to the disciples that He was risen.

DAY 202 | JOHN 21

H

E

A

R

What Else Should I Know? Jesus' final appearance was to Peter and six other disciples on the seashore as they were fishing. To make His presence known, Jesus performed a miracle similar to the one He had done when He first called His disciples, bringing their experience with Him full circle. Before Jesus died, Peter had denied knowing Him three times, just as Jesus had predicted. Here, Jesus asked Peter three times to declare his love for Him. Every time, Peter emphatically affirmed His love for Jesus. Jesus followed each affirmation with a call to minister to His people, His sheep.

This scene gives us great insight into what Jesus expects of His disciples. Being a disciple means loving people. If we really love Jesus and want to follow Him, we'll serve Him by caring for other believers. Peter was listening—he became one of the most influential apostles in the early church, and his life exemplified wholehearted, selfless faithfulness to Jesus' mission.

 QUESTION: How is God calling you to minister to His sheep?

DAY 203 | 1 JOHN 1

H

E

A

R

What Else Should I Know? In addition to the Gospel of John, the apostle wrote four other books: 1 John; 2 John; 3 John; and Revelation. John wrote his Gospel to call people to believe in Jesus as the Son of God, but he wrote 1 John to people who were already Christians.

Like Peter's first letter, John's first letter is one of assurance and comfort to Christians. He began with a description of Jesus that emphasized both His humanity and His divinity. Continuing the metaphor of light versus darkness from his Gospel, John used the image of walking in the light to help believers understand what the Christian life looks like. John described people who walk in the light of Christ as those who have fellowship with God and one another.

At the heart of fellowship with God is confession of sin. John reminded his readers that a repentant heart, not sinlessness, is the aim of a Christian's life. Sinning is inevitable on our side of eternity, but a heart that Jesus has truly changed confesses sin and accepts God's forgiveness.

? **QUESTION:** How does God's Word help us walk in the light of Christ?

DAY 204 | 1 JOHN 2

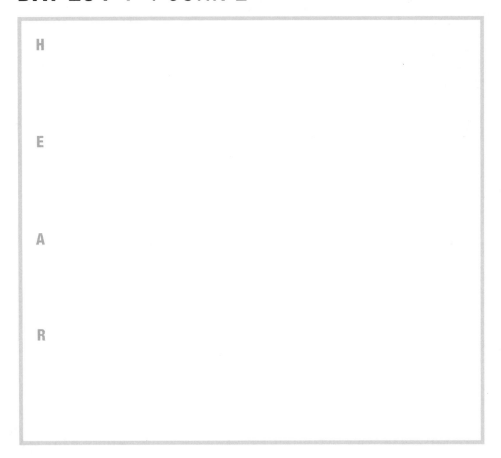

H

E

A

R

What Else Should I Know? In chapter 1, John noted how important it is for Christians to confess their sin. In chapter 2, he encouraged his readers to avoid sin altogether. Jesus' grace isn't a license to sin more; rather, it should motivate us to pursue sinless lives modeled on the life of Jesus. That pursuit can feel defeating because of the inevitability of sin, but Jesus' atoning work on our behalf should encourage us. Because of Jesus, God doesn't count our sin against us.

We display evidence of a genuine relationship with God by obeying His commands, walking as He walked, and loving others as He did. These themes appear again and again in John's letter. For John, the clearest indicator of a person's relationship with Jesus is love for others. Our love for others is modeled on Jesus' love for us—sacrificial, costly, selfless.

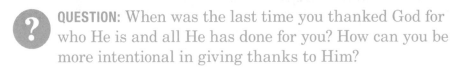

QUESTION: When was the last time you thanked God for who He is and all He has done for you? How can you be more intentional in giving thanks to Him?

DAY 205 | 1 JOHN 3

H

E

A

R

What Else Should I Know? John returned to the themes of love and obedience in chapter 3. He began by emphasizing God's love for us, which motivates us to obey His commands. God's love shapes our identity and encourages us to pursue sinlessness.

John communicated to his readers the weight and danger of sin by reminding them that Jesus died to take away sin's power over us. False teachers in John's day were likely trying to convince believers their sin wasn't a grave matter. John was emphatic to say that couldn't be further from the truth. Unrepentant sin cannot coexist with godliness.

At the close of chapter 3, John challenged Christians to model Jesus' love in their relationships with others. We do that when we meet people's needs and share God's truth with them. In this way our lives are consistent with Jesus' life on earth. Jesus expressed His love for others by meeting all their needs, both physical and spiritual.

 QUESTION: How can you share God's love today?

WEEK 42

DAY 206 | 1 JOHN 4

HIGHLIGHT the verses that speak to you.

Write out the name of the book:

Which chapter and verse numbers stand out to you?

EXPLAIN what this passage means.

To whom was it originally written? Why?

How does it fit with the verses before and after it?

What is the Holy Spirit intending to communicate through this text?

APPLY what God is saying in these verses to your life.

What does this mean today?

What is God saying to you personally?

How can you apply this message to your life?

RESPOND to what you've read.

In what ways does this passage call you to action?

How will you be different because of what you've learned?

Write out a prayer to God in response to what you read today:

What Else Should I Know? Like Peter and Paul, John addressed the issue of false teachers who were interfering with the spread of the gospel. This was a serious problem for the early church. Because of the dangerous threat false teachings posed to the believers' faith, John urged his readers to use the Word of God to test all human teachers who claimed to speak with spiritual authority. The mark of genuine faith is the confession that Jesus Christ came in the flesh, an all-important belief the false teachers denied. The truth about the nature of Christ is so basic to Christianity that it can never be compromised. Jesus was both fully God and fully man.

IT IS IMPORTANT TO ALWAYS GO TO THE WORD OF GOD IN THE FACE OF QUESTIONS OR CONFUSING TEACHING. ALWAYS SEEK WISE COUNSEL.

John abruptly turned from a discussion of true and false spirits to an appeal for believers to love one another. Christians should love one another because God loved them first. Again John reminded readers that God's love was supremely demonstrated when He sent His Son to be a sacrifice for our sins. This is foundational to the gospel—but it was in danger of being undermined by false teachers.

DAY 207 | 1 JOHN 5

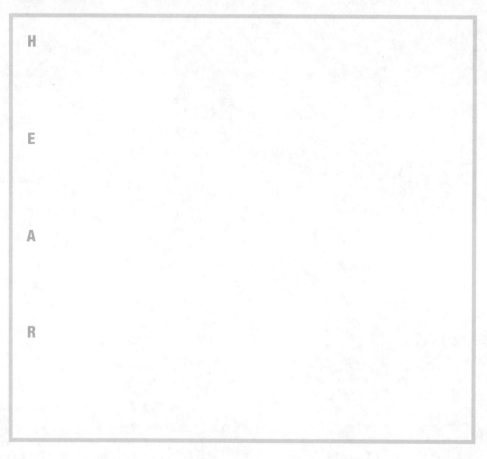

H

E

A

R

What Else Should I Know? In chapter 5 John called readers to lives of faith, love, and obedience. Verse 1 states the gospel as plainly as possible: belief is rooted in Jesus, who is the Christ, the Son of God. When we believe in Jesus, the natural result is that we love one another and obey God's commands. In the event that his readers felt overwhelmed by the call to obedience, John reminded them that God's law brings freedom rather than burden. Christ frees us from the bondage of sin and empowers us to live for God alone.

John did everything he could to help people know Jesus as the Son of God and receive the gift of eternal life. One thing he emphasized is prayer—a major way we articulate our love for God and show we love one another. Believers can have confidence in prayer, in victory over sin, and in eternal security. These are key truths of the faith John wanted every believer to claim.

CHALLENGE: Take a second and evaluate your prayer life. Be deliberate and intentional about making time to talk to your Father.

DAY 208 | 2 JOHN

H

E

A

R

What Else Should I Know? Though 2 John shares its main themes with the Letter of 1 John, it's very different. Like Paul's letters to Titus and Philemon, 2 John is a personal letter. John addressed his letter to "the elect lady and her children" (v. 1). There's much debate about whether this address refers to a specific person or to a specific church that John referred to in female terms, like the bride of Christ. Whichever interpretation is true, John's main points remain the same.

To combat the dangers of false teachers, John emphasized the importance of walking in the truth of God's Word and loving one another. When these two pillars of the Christian faith are upheld in the local church, false teachers and their lies hold no power over the people. The best way to guard against them, John says, is to love God and obey His commands. The Book of 2 John is a short and succinct, but it's an important personal note about the foundations of our Christian faith.

CHALLENGE: Fill in the blanks:

_____ *God.*

_____ *His commandments.*

DAY 209 | 3 JOHN

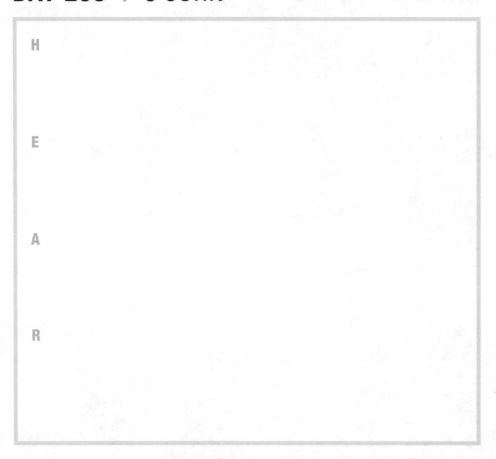

H

E

A

R

What Else Should I Know? In this letter, John wrote to a man named Gaius and he commended Gaius for showing hospitality and love to traveling preachers and missionaries who came through his town. As people traveled throughout the region spreading the gospel in its early days, they relied on the housing, food, and financial support of the people in the towns they visited. Gaius's hospitality was so important and meant so much to John because it showed other Christians a clear way they could put Jesus' command to "love one another" (John 13:34) into practice. By loving people this way, Gaius partnered with them in their gospel work.

Gaius's example stands in direct contrast to that of Diotrephes, whose actions showed that he didn't walk in the truth or love others. Actions always speak louder than words. You can talk about your faith all day, but until you put that faith into action, it's dead (James 2:26). God values a heart that loves Him and puts that love to work by loving others.

QUESTION: How can you be hospitable and loving toward others this week?

DAY 210 | JUDE

H

E

A

R

What Else Should I Know? The final personal letter in the New Testament is the Letter of Jude. This is the only book in the biblical canon written by Jude, the brother of Jesus and James. Jude's primary audience was Jewish Christians, but his letter is relevant to all believers.

Like John, Jude warned against the dangers of false teachers, specifically teachers who tried to downplay sin. Some teachers argued that because of grace, people could behave in whatever way they wanted. However, this teaching stood in direct contrast to Jesus' call to pursue holiness. Jesus' grace is a wonderful gift that should push us toward Him rather than toward sin.

Although Jesus changed the way God deals with our sin, He didn't lessen its severity. That's why sanctification, the process of growing in Christlikeness, is an essential part of the Christian faith. Once we're united with God through salvation, it's essential that we continue to grow in our knowledge of Him and strive toward even greater obedience, ensuring that our faith is solid so we can't be swayed by anyone who seeks to undermine it.

QUESTION: How can you grow in your knowledge of Jesus?

MEMORY VERSE OPTIONS: Psalm 103:3-4; Proverbs 26:20; Matthew 7:9-10

DAY 211 | REVELATION 1

HIGHLIGHT the verses that speak to you.

Write out the name of the book:

Which chapter and verse numbers stand out to you?

EXPLAIN what this passage means.

To whom was it originally written? Why?

How does it fit with the verses before and after it?

What is the Holy Spirit intending to communicate through this text?

APPLY what God is saying in these verses to your life.

What does this mean today?

What is God saying to you personally?

How can you apply this message to your life?

RESPOND to what you've read.

In what ways does this passage call you to action?

How will you be different because of what you've learned?

Write out a prayer to God in response to what you read today:

What Else Should I Know? The Bible begins in Genesis 1 with a picture of creation, when God gave shape and life to the world and established His relationship with humanity. After sin entered the world, that relationship was broken. The rest of Scripture describes the great lengths God went to in order to draw people back to Himself.

In the Book of Revelation, the final book of the Bible, we get a glimpse of the time when Jesus will return, God will complete His redemptive work, and people who believe in Him will receive final victory over sin. Revelation is John's record of a vision God gave him of the events that will happen when Jesus returns and God completes His redemptive work in the world.

Revelation 1 includes a vision of Jesus that proves He's alive, portraying a glory far beyond what we could ever imagine. John's response to this vision shows us that Jesus deserves our worship. The better we understand who He is, the better we'll understand how to worship Him.

Jesus deserves our worship.

DAY 212 | REVELATION 2

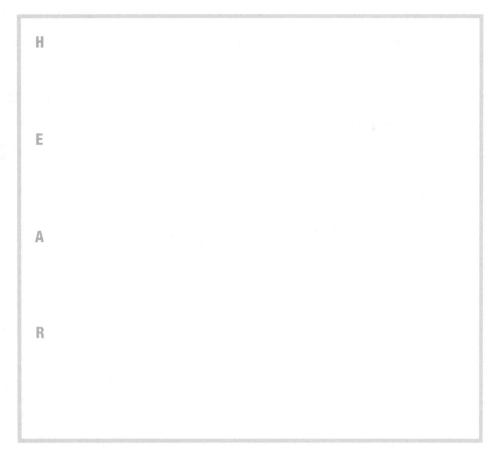

H

E

A

R

What Else Should I Know? Before Jesus showed John a vision of the last days, He gave him messages for seven churches located in present-day Turkey. The first letter was to the church in Ephesus. In it Jesus affirmed several qualities about the church, including their faithfulness to God, perseverance through persecution, and testing of false prophets. His criticism of this church was "You have abandoned the love you had at first" (v. 4), meaning love for God and others was no longer their primary focus. To love God and others is the greatest commandment, in Jesus' own words (see Matt. 22:37-40). No other Christian work matters if we aren't expressing that love.

The church in Smyrna received a letter of hope and encouragement, while the churches in Pergamum and Thyatira received words of praise and warning. Both churches were faithful in persevering through persecution, but both embraced false teaching. As we've seen, false teaching is a common theme in the New Testament. But God won't tolerate it—then, or now. He alone is worthy of our worship. Nothing else.

 QUESTION: Is your primary focus on Jesus? If not, how can you refocus back on Him?

DAY 213 | REVELATION 3

H

E

A

R

What Else Should I Know? Revelation 3 contains the last three church letters from Jesus, including the two most critical ones. The church in Sardis didn't receive any encouragement or praise from Jesus, only criticism. Jesus declared them dead inside, meaning their faith was lifeless, and He called them to repent of their sins or face eternal judgment. In contrast, the church in Philadelphia received only praise from Jesus because of their endurance through suffering.

The final letter to the church in Laodicea, however, may be the most uncomfortable to read because it hits close to home today. Jesus accused this church of being lukewarm in their faith. Wealthy and self-sufficient, the church in Laodicea failed to realize their need for Jesus. Jesus urged them to repent of their sins and renew their trust in Him alone.

At the center of each of the seven letters is a call that's still important to the body of Christ today: remain true to the risen Christ regardless of your present circumstances. Jesus knew these churches well, just as He knows us well. He spoke to them in truth because He loved them. He does the same to us today.

 QUESTION: Take time to examine your spiritual life. Are you hot, cold, or lukewarm? Why?

DAY 214 | REVELATION 4

H

E

A

R

What Else Should I Know? In Revelation 4, John shifts to a detailed picture of heaven and the end times. The goal of the vision was to establish hope and confidence in God's victory over sin and in the completion of His redemptive work that began with the incarnation of His Son.

According to chapter 4, the setting of this vision is the throne room of heaven, which John described in intricate detail. Each character represented in the vision is vividly portrayed and is shown to be worshiping the One who sits on the throne forever. Rich in allusions to the Old Testament, particularly Ezekiel 1:5-10 and Isaiah 6:1-4, the picture of the throne room validated the events John would describe next.

The description of the creatures and the elders who never stop praising God is humbling and convicting. That's the worship God deserves. Like the twenty-four elders John describes, we should continually lay our crowns at God's feet in an act of worship and surrender to the only One who deserves our praise.

 CHALLENGE: Your future in heaven will be filled with worship. Find time to get alone today and worship your Heavenly Father.

DAY 215 | REVELATION 5

H

E

A

R

What Else Should I Know? John described how the One on the throne, God the Father, was holding a scroll in His right hand, but John wept because nobody was worthy even to look at what it said. His tears didn't last long, however, for the Lion of the tribe of Judah, who had the appearance of a slaughtered Passover Lamb, proved His worthiness to take the scroll and open it.

That Lion and Lamb was Jesus. The description of Jesus is rich in symbolism that represents both His humility and His power. The entire company of the throne room fell down and worshiped Him just before He was to open the seals one by one. The scroll described here represents the events of the end times, as the following chapters of Revelation reveal.

Scholars debate the whether the elements of John's vision were literal or figurative, but the main point is broader: God knows how His story will end, and He remains in control of His world until the end. Jesus is the main character of this vision, as He is for the whole of Scripture, so we know God's story will end triumphantly for everyone Jesus calls His own.

QUESTION: Why is it comforting to know that God is in control of this world and your life?

MEMORY VERSE OPTIONS: Psalm 103:11-12; Proverbs 27:17; Matthew 7:11-12

W
E
E
K

44

DAY 216 | REVELATION 6

HIGHLIGHT the verses that speak to you.

Write out the name of the book:

Which chapter and verse numbers stand out to you?

EXPLAIN what this passage means.

To whom was it originally written? Why?

How does it fit with the verses before and after it?

What is the Holy Spirit intending to communicate through this text?

APPLY what God is saying in these verses to your life.

What does this mean today?

What is God saying to you personally?

How can you apply this message to your life?

RESPOND to what you've read.

In what ways does this passage call you to action?

How will you be different because of what you've learned?

Write out a prayer to God in response to what you read today:

What Else Should I Know? Revelation 6 begins a new section of John's vision as Jesus opened God's scroll and began to reveal its contents. This section of the vision emphasizes the stages of God's judgment that are coming on the world. The acts described in this chapter aren't exclusive to John's vision; similar end-time prophecies are included in the Book of Daniel and in Jesus' teachings in Matthew 24 and Mark 13.

The seals speak to an increasing degree of judgment by God. The first four seals opened to reveal riders on horses that enacted judgments against the earth. The fifth seal revealed a scene from heaven in which Christian martyrs awaited their glorification for their suffering. The sixth seal opened to reveal an earthquake that showed God's glory and wrath.

The words at the close of chapter 6 serve as a warning to everyone who rejects Jesus today, but they also serve as a motivation for believers to work tirelessly to bring people to Jesus. Only those who know Jesus as their savior can stand in the face of God's wrath.

 QUESTION: How does reading about the end times change the way you will live today?

DAY 217 | REVELATION 7

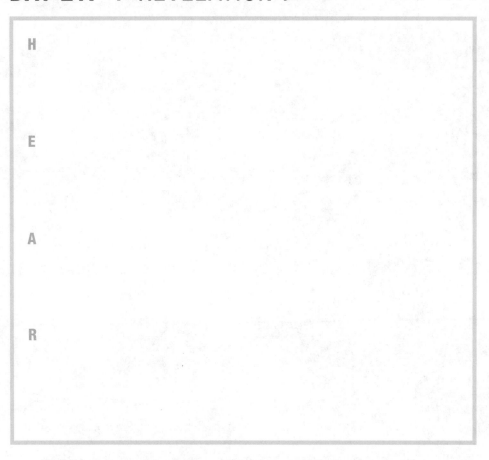

H

E

A

R

What Else Should I Know? Chapter 7's description of angels holding back the winds of the earth provides a beautiful picture of God restraining His judgment to protect those who belong to Him. God marked 144,000 people as His own and protected them from the end-time events. Even in the midst of great judgment, we're reminded that God cares for and protects His own.

The scene of the multitude of people in heaven gives a similar picture of protection and hope. This group was faithful to God through their suffering. Two important things stand out: the recognition that salvation occurs only through God (v. 10), and the promise of redemption in verses 15-17. God must judge sin, and He must hold Satan and his followers accountable for their wrongs, but even then God will continue to draw people to Himself until the end. Our hope today as believers is that God promises enduring care for those who follow Him. We can always count on His protection and love.

QUESTION: In what ways has God shown His protection and love in your life?

DAY 218 | REVELATION 8

H

E

A

R

What Else Should I Know? Now that God's people had been sealed for Him, judgment was no longer withheld. Verses 3-5 suggest that this judgment came in response to requests for justice from God's people. Many of John's readers had questioned God's justice as they had watched suffering take place for a long time. This scene reassured them that God heard their prayers and would act justly against evil in the world.

The trumpets in this chapter describe scenes of more global, permanent destruction as aspects of creation were destroyed. All of creation is gone: the ground, the sea, the rivers and streams, the sun, moon, and stars. With the fourth trumpet one-third of day and night was gone as well.

God promised to fully redeem His broken creation, but that redemption wouldn't come without great cost—an image we've already seen through the death of Jesus. Sin is catastrophic. When we see the pains God must go to in order to right His world, it should humble us, turn us from sin, and leave us thankful that He sent his Son to take our place.

 QUESTION: How should it comfort you to know that God will bring justice against every evil?

DAY 219 | REVELATION 9

H

E

A

R

What Else Should I Know? God's judgments grew more severe with each stage. With the fifth trumpet, God demanded the release of demonic forces from hell that resembled locusts, while the sixth trumpet released four horsemen, who killed one-third of the earth's population.

Amid such a grave picture of future events, readers can't miss John's note in verses 20-21. Even with God's judgment raining down around them, some people still refused to repent of their sins and turn to God. This is a tragic reflection on the depravity of the human condition. We interact with many people today who feel the same way. They're so immersed in their own lives that they fail to see the ways God is at work around them. They're too caught in their own sin that they can't see their desperate need for Him. The stories of Revelation aren't meant to scare us—they're meant to motivate us to do everything we can to help people see the reasons they need Christ and the hope He can bring to their lives.

 PRAY: Take time and pray for your lost friends today.

DAY 220 | REVELATION 10

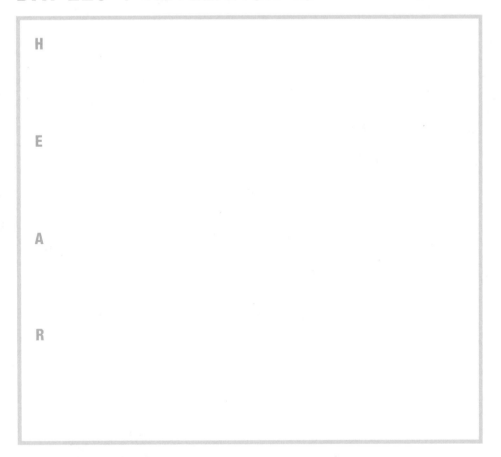

H

E

A

R

What Else Should I Know? While the visions of Revelation 8–9 gave readers a sobering picture of God's future judgment, Revelation 10 dramatically sets the stage for God's final, most severe judgments. The angel in this part of John's vision announced that the end was at hand and that the blowing of the seventh trumpet would set its events in motion. This angel also carried with him a scroll, which he told John to eat. The scroll turned his stomach sour, revealing the difficulty John would have in warning people about the final judgments.

We also learn from this chapter that John heard about particular end-time events that he was instructed not to write down. God has prepared us in large part for what the future holds, but He has withheld some details we don't need to know. Our job is to trust Him. We don't need to know all the hows, whens, and whys of God's plan to know that He loves us and will protect us. We can have faith in Him today while eagerly anticipating the victory and rewards He promises.

 **QUESTION:** While it's important to trust God in the end times, how can you trust Him today?

Check In

TAKE A MINUTE AND THANK THE LORD FOR ALL HE HAS TAUGHT YOU OVER THE LAST SEVERAL MONTHS!

WEEK 45

- ☐ Revelation 11
- ☐ Revelation 12
- ☐ Revelation 13
- ☐ Revelation 14
- ☐ Revelation 15

MEMORY VERSES

OPTION 1: Psalm 106:1
OPTION 2: Proverbs 27:19
OPTION 3: Matthew 7:13-14

WEEK 47

- ☐ Revelation 21
- ☐ Revelation 22
- ☐ Matthew 1
- ☐ Matthew 2
- ☐ Matthew 3

MEMORY VERSES

OPTION 1: Psalm 119:11
OPTION 2: Proverbs 28:18
OPTION 3: Matthew 7:17-18

WEEK 46

- ☐ Revelation 16
- ☐ Revelation 17
- ☐ Revelation 18
- ☐ Revelation 19
- ☐ Revelation 20

MEMORY VERSES

OPTION 1: Psalm 119:9-10
OPTION 2: Proverbs 28:13-14
OPTION 3: Matthew 7:15-16

WEEK 48

- ☐ Matthew 4
- ☐ Matthew 5
- ☐ Matthew 6
- ☐ Matthew 7
- ☐ Matthew 8

MEMORY VERSES

OPTION 1: Psalm 119:105
OPTION 2: Proverbs 29:18
OPTION 3: Matthew 7:19-20

SCAN THIS QR CODE TO ACCESS A FUN SURPRISE!

Circle the verse you want to memorize this week.

MEMORY VERSE OPTIONS: Psalm 106:1; Proverbs 27:19; Matthew 7:13-14

DAY 221 | REVELATION 11

HIGHLIGHT the verses that speak to you.

Write out the name of the book:

Which chapter and verse numbers stand out to you?

EXPLAIN what this passage means.

To whom was it originally written? Why?

How does it fit with the verses before and after it?

What is the Holy Spirit intending to communicate through this text?

APPLY what God is saying in these verses to your life.

What does this mean today?

What is God saying to you personally?

How can you apply this message to your life?

RESPOND to what you've read.

In what ways does this passage call you to action?

How will you be different because of what you've learned?

Write out a prayer to God in response to what you read today:

What Else Should I Know? Revelation 11 leaves no doubt about God's power and glory through the description of two prophets sent by God. It's clear from the description of these men that God would protect them so that their message could be communicated—however, God allowed His prophets to be killed by "the beast that comes up out of the abyss" (v. 7). The gloating and celebrating that followed the death of God's servants showed just how far the world had fallen from Him. However, God resurrected His prophets, and their ascension to heaven marked the beginning of the end.

After a massive earthquake shook earth, God's awesome power was enough to convince some of those left to finally respond to Him. With that the seventh trumpet of judgment was blown, and John heard the declaration that the time for God's final judgment was at hand.

 QUESTION: How can you find comfort in God's power today?

DAY 222 | REVELATION 12

H

E

A

R

What Else Should I Know? As John's vision continued to unfold, he witnessed the culmination of the conflict between God and Satan. John described two signs he saw in heaven: The first was that of a woman in labor, likely symbolizing Israel, and the second was a red dragon. John's vision gives readers a behind-the-scenes look into the conflict between God and Satan at the time of Jesus' birth (see v. 5). Although God continues to permit Satan to have some power today, Jesus defeated Satan when He conquered death by rising from the dead.

The quotation in verses 10-12 reveals the eternal impact that Jesus' resurrection had on Satan. He was defeated once by the empty tomb, and he was permanently cast out of God's presence by the conflict John described in this chapter. As with much of Revelation, the timing and literal nature of the events described in this chapter are much debated, but the message is clear: Jesus established His power over Satan when He died on the cross for our sins. While we wait for Jesus to return, we cling to the promise of definitive victory in the future to help us endure our trials today.

 PRAY: Reflect on Jesus' power over Satan and the victory that is ours. Take time to thank Jesus.

DAY 223 | REVELATION 13

H

E

A

R

What Else Should I Know? The vision John received shows Satan and his two beasts as an evil trinity bent on deceiving the people of earth by leading them away from the one true God. The beast of the sea had become known as the antichrist because his authority stood in direct contrast to Jesus. Having been given power over all peoples and nations, and having become the object of many unbelievers' worship, he turned many people away from following God.

The second beast was the beast of the earth. Later referred to as the false prophet, this beast opposed the Holy Spirit. As the Holy Spirit points to Jesus, the false prophet pointed people to the antichrist as their object for worship.

Amid the conflict and terror of this scene, a couple verses bring readers great hope. In verses 9-10, John reminded readers that those who oppose God will get what they deserve. It may not happen as soon as we would like, but John reminded us that God is faithful to His Word, and in the meantime we must endure in the faith, trusting God to bring His justice and to redeem His world.

 QUESTION: How can you keep your mind and heart from being led astray?

DAY 224 | REVELATION 14

```
H


E



A



R
```

What Else Should I Know? The chapter begins with a vision of the Lamb and the 144,000 who had been sealed by God. Unlike those marked by the beast, these individuals bore the names of the Father and the Son, eternally linking them with God. These faithful followers of Christ joined in the eternal worship John had described in Revelation 4–5. What better motivation could there be to faithfully endure the persecution and trials we must face during this life?

In the next part of his vision, John saw three angels who each declared different events about to unfold. First, the gospel was proclaimed with the final call to obedience before God's great judgment. Second, Babylon had fallen. Third, people marked by the beast would fall into eternal torment, but those who died as Christians would receive a special blessing.

Again John took the opportunity to call his readers to faithful, patient endurance while they waited for Jesus' return. The image of the harvest that closes the chapter provided a symbolic look at God's final judgment, the details of which were about to be revealed. The time had come for God to rid the world of evil and to complete the victory Jesus had guaranteed on the cross.

 QUESTION: Based on this passage, describe how you imagine what the eternal worship of Jesus will look and feel like.

DAY 225 | REVELATION 15

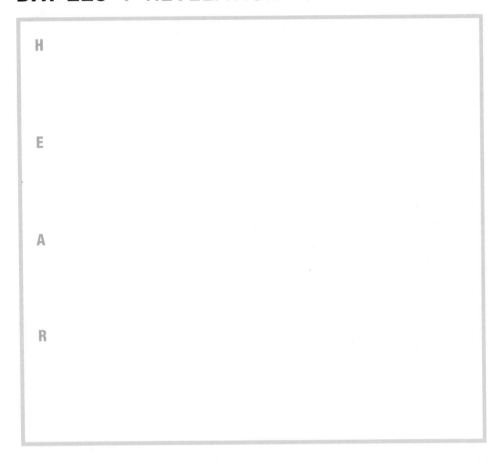

H

E

A

R

What Else Should I Know? Since Revelation 6, the drama depicting God's judgment of the world had been building. In chapter 15, John gave readers another glimpse into heaven when he saw seven angels who held the seven bowl judgments. Before the first bowl was poured out, however, John described the victorious saints he witnessed before the throne of God. These saints sang a worship song that proclaimed God's glory, sovereignty, justice, holiness, and righteousness. It's important to remember each of these attributes of God as we read about the wrath and judgment that follow.

God was right to judge the evil in the world. He had created the world to reflect Him and His glory. Ever since the world had been broken by sin, God had been on a mission to redeem it and restore it to its original glory, but that couldn't happen without destroying the evil that had originally broken it. After this reminder of God's righteousness and glory, John's vision reached the climactic unveiling of the seven bowls of God's wrath.

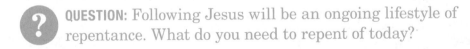

QUESTION: Following Jesus will be an ongoing lifestyle of repentance. What do you need to repent of today?

DAY 226 | REVELATION 16

HIGHLIGHT the verses that speak to you.

Write out the name of the book:

Which chapter and verse numbers stand out to you?

EXPLAIN what this passage means.

To whom was it originally written? Why?

How does it fit with the verses before and after it?

What is the Holy Spirit intending to communicate through this text?

APPLY what God is saying in these verses to your life.

What does this mean today?

What is God saying to you personally?

How can you apply this message to your life?

RESPOND to what you've read.

In what ways does this passage call you to action?

How will you be different because of what you've learned?

Write out a prayer to God in response to what you read today:

What Else Should I Know? Revelation 16 focuses entirely on the seven bowl judgments. These judgments were painful, akin to the plagues upon Egypt found in Exodus. People broke out in sores, oceans and rivers turned to blood. Yet even though people were living in agony, they still refused to acknowledge God's holiness and turn to Him. The sixth bowl described Satan's preparation for Armageddon, the great battle between good and evil. He gathered his army as God prepared the earth for battle. The seventh and final bowl judgment produced an earthquake and a hailstorm greater than any the world had ever seen.

The people left on earth cursed God because it was clear who was to blame for what was happening. That might seem crazy, but people do something similar today when they say they believe God exists but refuse to trust Him with their lives. Revelation is a sobering reminder of why it's so important to believe in Jesus and why we should devote ourselves to the mission of the gospel while people still have time to repent and believe in Him.

QUESTION: In reading this book, how has your view on sharing your faith changed?

DAY 227 | REVELATION 17

H

E

A

R

What Else Should I Know? Revelation 17–18 provides readers with greater detail and symbolism related to the fall of Babylon. The primary images in this chapter are a woman and a beast. The woman most likely represents worldly temptation and the corrupt world powers that stand in opposition to God. Throughout Revelation, Babylon symbolizes rebellion against God.

The lures of power, wealth, and self-gratification have always pulled people away from God. Here, the connection between this woman and the beast, Satan, makes it clear that the angel was describing a time when immorality will reign and people will align themselves with the beast, setting themselves up in opposition to Jesus, the Lamb.

Verses 14-17 hold the key to this chapter: the powers of the world and of Satan are no match for the Lamb. God is the One in charge, the only One who will orchestrate the world's events up to the very end.

 QUESTION: What temptations drive you away from God?

DAY 228 | REVELATION 18

H

E

A

R

What Else Should I Know? Babylon remains the subject of chapter 18. This great city built for itself immense wealth and conducted itself with blasphemous arrogance in the face of God.

In this chapter, John recorded the song of victory over the beast who rose up against God, sung by an angel whose splendor illuminated the earth. This angel announced the fall of Babylon, an event prophesied throughout Scripture. John also recorded another voice, likely Jesus or God the Father, calling for God's people to turn their backs on Babylon, which represents the world's idolatrous pursuits and sinful living.

The lusts of the world have a strong, tempting pull on our lives, but God wants His people to completely separate from them in order to avoid being caught up in the world's sins and therefore its judgments. None of the things that appeal to us in our world—money, power, fame, lust—will go with us into eternity. To pursue them is to place our hope in something that has no lasting value. Only a relationship with God has eternal worth.

 QUESTION: What are some things you are trying to pull into your relationship with Jesus that don't belong?

DAY 229 | REVELATION 19

H

E

A

R

What Else Should I Know? Chapter 19 continues the celebration begun by the magnificent angel in chapter 18, and a vast multitude in heaven rejoiced at God's victory. Our God avenges injustice. In this chapter we again see the great multitude, elders, and creatures from chapters 4–5 who worship at the foot of God's throne. Their praise now included celebration of God's victory over sin.

John then witnessed the announcement of a wedding ceremony between the Lamb and His bride. This was the second coming of Jesus, the event for which all Christians live in great anticipation. John's description of Jesus includes many titles that capture His character: Faithful and True, just Judge, Word of God, King of kings, and Lord of lords.

With Jesus' entry to claim victory over Babylon and the beast, John witnessed the final defeat of the beast and his armies. As Christians, we find strength and hope for life by realizing that when Jesus comes again, He will defeat the forces of evil. This truth should amaze us, but it should also compel us to share our hope in Christ with everyone we know so they can share in the same promise.

 QUESTION: Who do you need to share this hope of the future with today?

DAY 230 | REVELATION 20

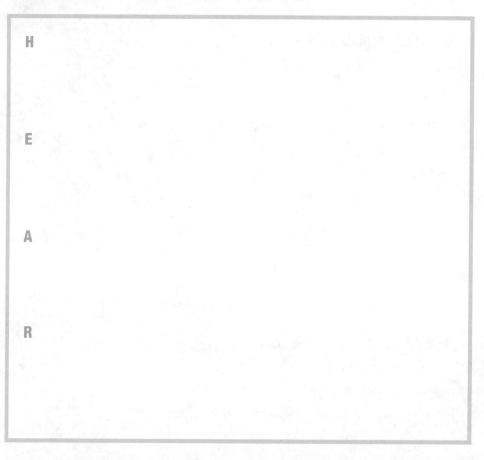

H

E

A

R

What Else Should I Know? The final three chapters of Revelation focus on Satan's ultimate defeat and a look ahead at our eternal future with God. John's vision describes a thousand-year period after Jesus returns when He will reign on the earth. During this time Satan will be bound and held captive.

After Jesus' thousand-year reign, John recorded, Satan will make one last push against God. He'll again build an army in an attempt to overthrow Jesus, but they won't even reach the point of battle before God will defeat them and throw them into hell forever. With that God's judgment of evil will be complete.

The final scene in this chapter is often called the great-white-throne judgment, which refers to God's judgment of all humankind. People who have faith in Jesus will dwell with God for eternity; those who don't will join Satan in eternal torment. The Book of Revelation constantly draws us back to God's sovereignty and to the promise of His ultimate victory over sin, death, and hell.

 CHALLENGE: Take time today and write out a letter thanking Jesus for your salvation.

MEMORY VERSE OPTIONS: Psalm 119:11; Proverbs 28:18; Matthew 7:17-18

WEEK 47

DAY 231 | REVELATION 21

HIGHLIGHT the verses that speak to you.

Write out the name of the book:

Which chapter and verse numbers stand out to you?

EXPLAIN what this passage means.

To whom was it originally written? Why?

How does it fit with the verses before and after it?

What is the Holy Spirit intending to communicate through this text?

APPLY what God is saying in these verses to your life.

What does this mean today?

What is God saying to you personally?

How can you apply this message to your life?

RESPOND to what you've read.

In what ways does this passage call you to action?

How will you be different because of what you've learned?

Write out a prayer to God in response to what you read today:

What Else Should I Know? Revelation 21 describes the new heaven, new earth, and new Jerusalem, a holy city. Verses 3-4 affirm the great hope of every Christian: eternally dwelling with God in a place devoid of sin, pain, and death. The redemptive plan God had initiated in Genesis 3 will be complete. Time and again in Scripture we've seen that both creation and humanity were broken by sin; here we see that God will once and for all make all things new, just as He promised.

The description of the city in verses 9-21 is strikingly detailed, although we can only imagine how far human words fall short in capturing this glorified state. In verses 22-27 John commented on the absence of a temple in the holy city. This is the most important detail about our future home: We'll live in the presence of God forever. His glory will shine so brightly that we won't need a sun or a moon. Everything in the city will reflect His glory, His holiness, and His purity, and we'll spend all our days worshiping and serving Him.

? **QUESTION:** How does your perspective of today change knowing there is no hurt or pain in Heaven?

DAY 232 | REVELATION 22

H

E

A

R

What Else Should I Know? John closed his book by describing the river of life, which symbolizes the eternal life Jesus makes available to us. Just as the Bible began with a description of Eden, it ends with this description of a new Eden, which will endure forever because of Jesus' redemptive work. The curse from Genesis 3 will be gone.

As Jesus concluded His vision to John, He issued an urgent call to faith. He promised to return, and He's always faithful to keep His promises. The names Jesus included in His final statement to John reinforce His faithfulness: the Alpha and the Omega, the First and the Last, the Beginning and the End. His faithfulness is clear, from the account of creation in Genesis to the promise of the new creation in Revelation.

Jesus wants all people to know Him, but as the vision in Revelation makes clear, a time is coming when unbelievers will no longer have the hope of redemption from their sin and the offer of eternal life with God. It's on us today to guide those around us to know Him personally.

? **QUESTION:** How have you seen God's faithfulness displayed in Scripture? What about in your own life?

DAY 233 | MATTHEW 1

H

E

A

R

HE IS THE IMMANUEL FOR YOUR TODAY AND TOMORROW. HE IS WITH *you*.

What Else Should I Know? The Gospel of Matthew was written to a Jewish audience to demonstrate that Jesus was the fulfillment of the Old Testament Scriptures. This explains why Matthew began with Jesus' genealogy. The genealogy affirms that Jesus descended from Abraham, Judah, and David, fulfilling various Old Testament prophecies about the Messiah.

Following the genealogy, Matthew focused on events surrounding Jesus' birth, beginning with the angel's appearance to Joseph. Matthew was the only Gospel writer to include this interaction. The angel told Joseph that Jesus had been conceived of the Holy Spirit, a detail that underscores His divine nature—Immanuel, "God is with us" (v. 23). This scene also gives insight into Joseph's faithfulness to God and to Mary. From the beginning of Matthew's Gospel, the faithfulness of God's chosen people was on display.

DAY 234 | MATTHEW 2

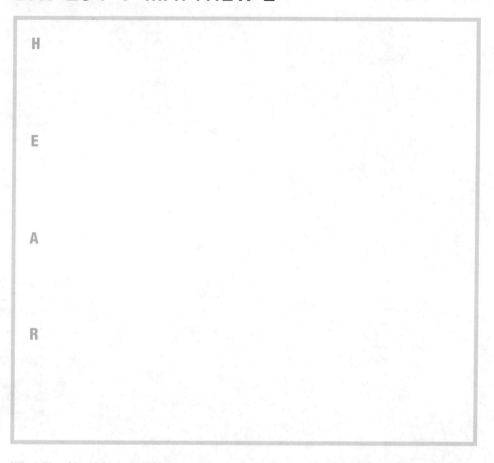

H

E

A

R

What Else Should I Know? Matthew 2 continues the story of Jesus' birth, but Matthew chose to include a unique detail of the wise men's visit. The wise men's search, discovery, and subsequent worship of Jesus further confirmed His identity as the Messiah.

Herod's reaction to the wise men's questions was an early indicator of the effect Jesus' presence would have on political and religious leaders of His day. Herod felt threatened enough by the birth of this child that he plotted to have Him killed. This reaction highlighted Jesus' profound impact on the world around Him, even from His infancy.

Even the family's escape to Egypt, eventual return to Israel, and settling in the city of Nazareth were prophetic fulfillments. Reading the birth and infancy narratives in Matthew, we're reminded that God keeps His promises. Jesus was God's unique Son. He alone was positioned to change the world.

 PRAY: From Jesus' birth, He was threatened, misunderstood, and people plotted to kill Him. The Christian life is not a life of ease and comfort. Take some time today to pray about what you need to surrender.

DAY 235 | MATTHEW 3

BEFORE JESUS EVER PERFORMED, THE FATHER WAS PLEASED. HE IS NOT LOOKING FOR YOUR BEST PERFORMANCE, BUT YOUR SURRENDERED HEART.

H

E

A

R

What Else Should I Know? Before Jesus began His public ministry, John the Baptist prepared the way for Him by proclaiming a message of repentance and calling people to baptism as a symbol of their heart transformation. Matthew pointed out that John also fulfilled Old Testament prophecy, quoting Isaiah 40:3:

"A voice of one crying out:
Prepare the way of the LORD in the wilderness;
make a straight highway for our God in the desert."

John's baptism of Jesus marked the beginning of Jesus' earthly ministry in Matthew's Gospel. By being baptized, Jesus identified Himself with John's message and with the people He came to save. It's interesting to recognize that all three Persons of the Trinity were present at this important moment in Jesus' ministry, affirming that Jesus was the Son of God and that His mission was anointed by the Holy Spirit.

MEMORY VERSE OPTIONS: Psalm 119:105; Proverbs 29:18; Matthew 7:19-20

DAY 236 | MATTHEW 4

HIGHLIGHT the verses that speak to you.

Write out the name of the book:

Which chapter and verse numbers stand out to you?

EXPLAIN what this passage means.

To whom was it originally written? Why?

How does it fit with the verses before and after it?

What is the Holy Spirit intending to communicate through this text?

APPLY what God is saying in these verses to your life.

What does this mean today?

What is God saying to you personally?

How can you apply this message to your life?

RESPOND to what you've read.

In what ways does this passage call you to action?

How will you be different because of what you've learned?

Write out a prayer to God in response to what you read today:

What Else Should I Know? After His baptism, Matthew stated that the Holy Spirit led Jesus into the wilderness for a time of temptation. Satan tempted Jesus in three specific ways. First, Satan tempted Jesus to make bread, appealing to Jesus' hunger from His time of fasting. Next, the devil tempted Jesus to throw Himself off the temple to learn whether God would rescue Him. Finally, by trying to appeal to a desire for power and glory, Satan tempted Jesus to turn away from God and to worship him instead.

But Satan's efforts to tempt Jesus away from God's plan were futile. To each temptation Jesus responded by quoting Scripture. This exchange provides for us a concrete example of how God equips us to withstand temptation. When we face temptation, we, like Jesus, can trust in the character of God and the promises of Scripture, no matter how appealing the temptation might be.

? **QUESTION:** Jesus understands being tempted, yet He did not sin. How does His example teach us how to fight against temptation?

DAY 237 | MATTHEW 5

H

E

A

R

What Else Should I Know? The Sermon on the Mount is one of Jesus' most powerful messages. It begins with the Beatitudes, blessings God gives to people who exhibit certain spiritual attributes. These words resonate beautifully with our lives today. Blessed are the poor in spirit, Jesus said— the humble, the merciful, the pure in heart. He never said blessed are the smart, the pretty, or the strongest on the team. He didn't bless those who pray the loudest or attend church most often. Instead, God focuses on the heart—what's inside us.

One of the most powerful parts of the sermon comes at the end of the chapter, however, when Jesus called on listeners to do something radical: love their enemies. Praying for those who persecute us might seem impossible, but Christ commands it. It's easy to pray for people we love; it's much harder to pray for people we don't. But Jesus makes it clear.

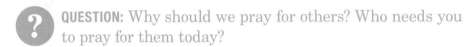

QUESTION: Why should we pray for others? Who needs you to pray for them today?

DAY 238 | MATTHEW 6

H

E

A

R

What Else Should I Know? As Jesus continued His Sermon on the Mount, He taught that religious behaviors—specifically, giving, praying, and fasting—can be carried out with healthy or unhealthy motives. Inappropriate motives focus on recognition and attention, while appropriate motives focus on sacrifice and worship. Included in this teaching is Jesus' well-known Model Prayer, which highlights prayer as a means of worshiping God, aligning ourselves with His will, and depending on Him to meet our daily physical and spiritual needs.

The end of Matthew 6 is a nice message for us today, with Jesus emphasizing how anxiety and worry can prevent us from receiving the full benefit of God's blessing. The things we give the most attention to reveal where our hearts are. When we worry, we show God that we don't trust Him. But time and time again in the New Testament, we've seen how God delivers on His promises. He is always faithful. Why would we ever worry?

PRAY: Consider your motives today. Jesus, would You give me a pure heart? Help me to seek Your will over my own desires. Let my motives be pleasing to You.

DAY 239 | MATTHEW 7

H

E

A

R

What Else Should I Know? The next section of the Sermon on the Mount focuses on relationships. God's people aren't to be judgmental and condemning, Jesus taught. Rather, the loving relationship we enjoy with God sets the standard for our relationships with others.

Jesus also taught that prayer is the primary way we function in relationship with God, who wants us to continually approach Him with our requests. He delights to give us what we need. Our prayers are powerful when we're persistent, when we believe God's promise, and when we trust God's heart.

Jesus' sermon built to a climactic conclusion in which He challenged His listeners to make a choice. Would they follow Him through the narrow gate into the kingdom, or would they choose the wide gate that many people enter, which leads to ultimate destruction? The wide gate is easy; the narrow gate is hard. But only one brings the ultimate reward.

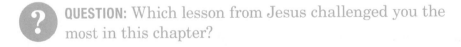

QUESTION: Which lesson from Jesus challenged you the most in this chapter?

DAY 240 | MATTHEW 8

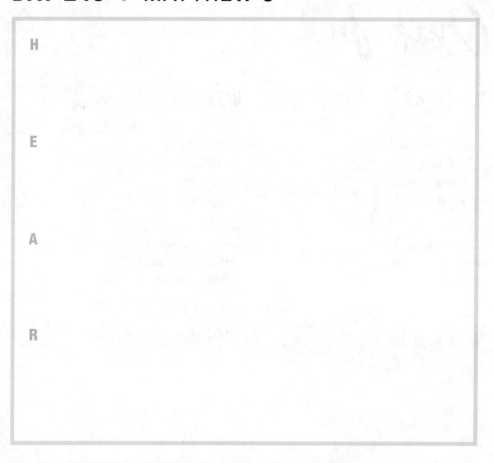

H

E

A

R

What Else Should I Know? After the Sermon on the Mount, Matthew's Gospel returns to Jesus' ministry, which was marked by miraculous healings and wonders. Matthew 8 records three miracles of healing that demonstrated slightly different aspects of Jesus' power. The cleansing of the leper demonstrated Jesus' power over one of the worst maladies of the day. The healing of the centurion's servant showed that Jesus didn't need to be physically present to heal. And at Capernaum Jesus cast out demons, demonstrating His sovereign power over evil.

The next two miracles, the calming of the storm and the two men possessed by multiple demons, revealed Jesus' power over nature itself and over evil. The complete picture of Jesus' power is on display in Matthew 8. It's a powerful chapter that shows that, through Christ, the God of the universe transforms individual lives.

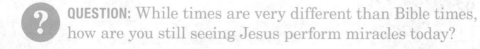

QUESTION: While times are very different than Bible times, how are you still seeing Jesus perform miracles today?

Check In

WEEK 49

- ☐ Matthew 9
- ☐ Matthew 10
- ☐ Matthew 11
- ☐ Matthew 12
- ☐ Matthew 13

MEMORY VERSES

OPTION 1: Psalm 127:1
OPTION 2: Proverbs 29:22-23
OPTION 3: Matthew 7:21-23

WEEK 51

- ☐ Matthew 19
- ☐ Matthew 20
- ☐ Matthew 21
- ☐ Matthew 22
- ☐ Matthew 23

MEMORY VERSES

OPTION 1: Psalm 145:8
OPTION 2: Proverbs 31:8-9
OPTION 3: Matthew 7:26-27

WEEK 50

- ☐ Matthew 14
- ☐ Matthew 15
- ☐ Matthew 16
- ☐ Matthew 17
- ☐ Matthew 18

MEMORY VERSES

OPTION 1: Psalm 139:23-24
OPTION 2: Proverbs 30:5
OPTION 3: Matthew 7:24-25

WEEK 52

- ☐ Matthew 24
- ☐ Matthew 25
- ☐ Matthew 26
- ☐ Matthew 27
- ☐ Matthew 28

MEMORY VERSES

OPTION 1: Psalm 150:6
OPTION 2: Proverbs 31:29-30
OPTION 3: Matthew 7:28-29

SCAN THIS QR CODE TO ACCESS A FUN SURPRISE!

MEMORY VERSE OPTIONS: Psalm 127:1; Proverbs 29:22-23; Matthew 7:21-23

DAY 241 | MATTHEW 9

HIGHLIGHT the verses that speak to you.

Write out the name of the book:

Which chapter and verse numbers stand out to you?

EXPLAIN what this passage means.

To whom was it originally written? Why?

How does it fit with the verses before and after it?

What is the Holy Spirit intending to communicate through this text?

APPLY what God is saying in these verses to your life.

What does this mean today?

What is God saying to you personally?

How can you apply this message to your life?

RESPOND to what you've read.

In what ways does this passage call you to action?

How will you be different because of what you've learned?

Write out a prayer to God in response to what you read today:

What Else Should I Know? Chapter 9 continues to focus on Jesus' earthly ministry, specifically His miraculous works and His teachings. One story, however, caused controversy with religious leaders: Jesus' call of Matthew, a tax collector, to be a disciple and His dining with other tax collectors and sinners at Matthew's house. Tax collectors were considered some of the lowest of the low in Jesus' time because they made a living by cheating people out of money. That reputation didn't matter to Jesus. He saw in Matthew someone willing and ready to follow Him.

After additional accounts of healing and conflicts with the Pharisees, Matthew included a scene unique to his Gospel (see vv. 35-38). In a behind-the-scenes look into Jesus' heart, Christ described the world around Him as a field that needed to be harvested but which lacked the workers to do so. This analogy continues to be relevant today: People all around us are ready to hear the gospel and believe in Jesus, but they need us to share this good news with them.

 QUESTION: Don't stop working. What does it look like for you to be a laborer for Christ?

DAY 242 | MATTHEW 10

JUST LIKE THE DISCIPLES, YOUR INVESTMENT MATTERS. DON'T BE AFRAID

today.

H

E

A

R

What Else Should I Know? The harvest of Matthew 9 is also the focus of chapter 10, which recounts Jesus' sending of the twelve disciples. Up to this point they had shadowed Jesus as He traveled throughout the region preaching and performing miracles. Now, however, Jesus sent out the disciples on their own to actively participate in His mission work.

Knowing the disciples would encounter persecution for their message, Jesus prepared them. His message of repentance, as well as the authority with which He shared it, was controversial, and the people who rejected Jesus would reject His disciples as well. Jesus said they could expect to be persecuted by religious leaders and councils, by governors and kings, and even by their families. We can imagine how that last part would have been particularly hard to swallow. But though His prediction was troubling, Jesus assured the disciples that the work He sent them to do was worth whatever it cost them. Their work carried the weight of eternity.

DAY 243 | MATTHEW 11

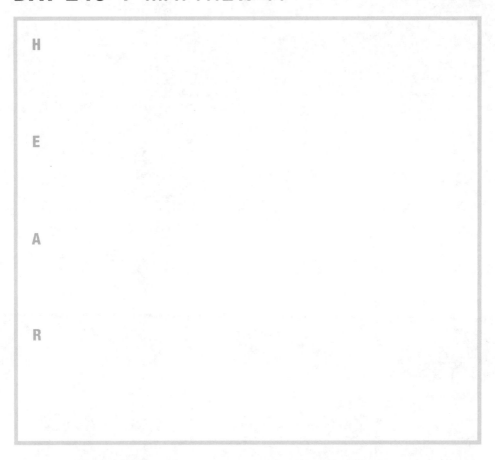

H

E

A

R

What Else Should I Know? As Jesus and His disciples traveled throughout the region, the majority of people they encountered didn't respond positively to Jesus' message and repent of their sins. Therefore, Jesus pronounced a word of judgment against these cities. Unless they turned from their sin to God, they would face a judgment worse than the judgments against some of the most sinful cities mentioned in the Old Testament. Hearing Jesus teach isn't enough; a person's heart must be truly changed in order to experience His grace.

After that word of judgment, however, Jesus invited people into the rest He offered. Jesus was referring to freedom from the law that comes with belief in Him. The Jews were bound to their religious systems and rules, which blinded them to the Messiah when He came. A relationship with Jesus frees us from our efforts to earn God's favor. It allows us to rest in Jesus' work on our behalf.

QUESTION: How can you rest in Jesus' work today?

DAY 244 | MATTHEW 12

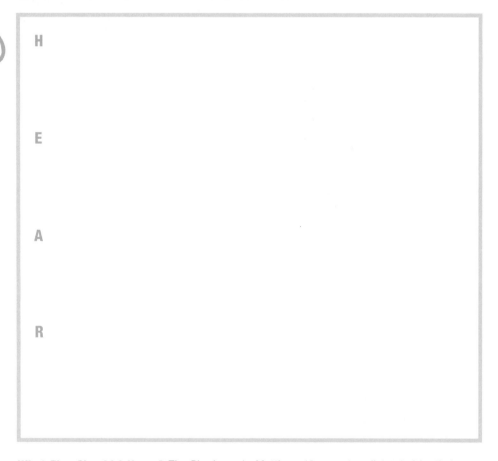

H

E

A

R

What Else Should I Know? The Pharisees in Matthew 12 were too distracted by their own priorities to see God's plan unfolding before them. Jesus used these conflicts as opportunities to confront them about their hard hearts and spiritual blindness. They thought they were holy and righteous because they rigorously obeyed the law, but Jesus described them as a "brood of vipers" (v. 34) and "an evil and adulterous generation" (v. 39).

In this chapter Matthew also included a quotation by the prophet Isaiah that gives insight into the purpose of Jesus' messianic mission. The Pharisees wanted a Messiah who would powerfully overthrow Rome and elevate the Israelites to a place of political power. But as Isaiah foretold, God's Messiah would humbly and peacefully serve as a beacon of God's hope and justice. The same humility, hope, and peace should characterize believers today as we continue to live out Jesus' redemptive mission.

QUESTION: Like the pharisees in this passage, is your heart hardened? How can you fight against a hard heart?

DAY 245 | MATTHEW 13

H

E

A

R

What Else Should I Know? After His conflict with the Pharisees, Jesus gave His disciples and the crowds insight into what God's kingdom looks like and how a person enters it. To present these truths, Jesus used His favorite teaching method, the parable.

Matthew included seven parables in this chapter. The parable of the weeds in verses 24-30 holds particularly relevant truths for us today. For now God's kingdom is present on earth, where God's people (the wheat) intermingle with unbelievers (the weeds). But a time is coming when God will separate the weeds from the wheat—unbelievers from believers—and will judge both according to their relationships with Jesus. While we wait for that day of judgment, it's critical for us to reach as many people as we can with the good news of the gospel.

PRAY: Jesus, would You deepen my passion to share the gospel? Keep me aware of what You did on the cross.

MEMORY VERSE OPTIONS: Psalm 139:23-24; Proverbs 30:5; Matthew 7:24-25

W E E K

50

DAY 246 | MATTHEW 14

HIGHLIGHT the verses that speak to you.

Write out the name of the book:

Which chapter and verse numbers stand out to you?

EXPLAIN what this passage means.

To whom was it originally written? Why?

How does it fit with the verses before and after it?

What is the Holy Spirit intending to communicate through this text?

APPLY what God is saying in these verses to your life.

What does this mean today?

What is God saying to you personally?

How can you apply this message to your life?

RESPOND to what you've read.

In what ways does this passage call you to action?

How will you be different because of what you've learned?

Write out a prayer to God in response to what you read today:

What Else Should I Know? This chapter begins with Herod's killing of John the Baptist. This news saddened Jesus, so He withdrew to a boat in order to grieve in private. After he returned to shore, the crowds had grown larger, and even in the midst of His grief, their needs moved His heart. He performed miracles of healing and fed thousands.

Jesus' miracles gave His disciples further insight into His' authority as the Messiah, the Son of God. They also revealed the disciples' insufficient faith. The disciples had been traveling with Jesus for a while, had witnessed all of His miraculous works and teachings, and had even been sent out with His authority in their lives. However, sometimes they still questioned the limits of His power. As the cross drew near, it was critically important for the disciples to understand who Jesus was so they would understand what He had to do.

CHALLENGE: Write down all the things you learned about Jesus in this passage. The Bible is not a book about us, but about Jesus. May we spend the rest of our lives learning how to be more like Him.

DAY 247 | MATTHEW 15

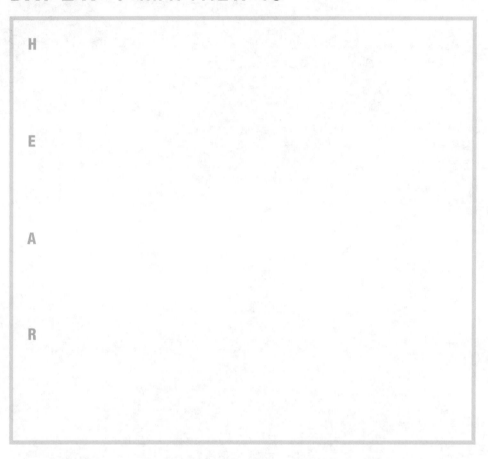

H

E

A

R

What Else Should I Know? In chapter 15 the religious leaders questioned Jesus about why the disciples didn't participate in ritual cleansing. In response, Jesus pointed out the hypocrisy of the Pharisees, who used their own laws to skirt obedience to God's commands. They were guilty of the same sin they accused the disciples of committing. This incident gave Jesus another opportunity to emphasize the heart change brought about by genuine obedience to God. Before Jesus came, faith was attributed to people who lived in obedience to God's laws. But now faith is attributed to those who believe in Him. Our words and actions overflow from our hearts, which Jesus has cleansed and changed.

Although opposition to Jesus increased, so did belief in Him. The remaining verses in this chapter show Jesus performing more miracles and illustrate the growing belief of the crowds who followed Him: "The crowd was amazed when they saw those unable to speak talking, the crippled restored, the lame walking, and the blind seeing, and they gave glory to the God of Israel" (v. 31).

QUESTION: What is the difference between worshiping God with our mouths versus worshiping God with our hearts?

DAY 248 | MATTHEW 16

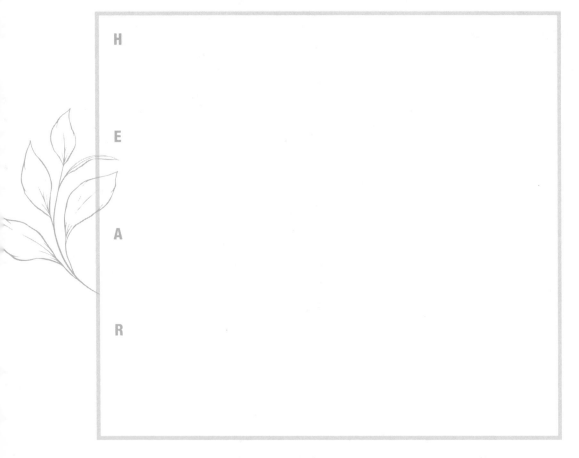

H

E

A

R

What Else Should I Know? In another attempt to trap Jesus, the religious leaders again asked Him for a sign that would prove He was the Messiah. Everything Jesus had already done, however, proved just that. He had fulfilled Old Testament prophecies, healed the sick, raised the dead, calmed the seas, and forgave sins. Because the Jews refused to believe Jesus was the Messiah, He knew no additional signs would convince them otherwise.

"The sign of Jonah" Jesus mentioned in verse 4 was a hint about His death and resurrection. As Jonah was in the belly of the fish for three days before being spat out onto land, Jesus would be dead in the tomb for three days before rising from the dead.

Jesus warned His disciples not to be led astray. He wanted them to trust in Him and not be influenced by the loud, critical voices around them. Their firm belief would become even more important once Jesus was no longer with them, a time He alluded to at the close of this chapter.

? **QUESTION:** Just like in this passage, when voices around you are loud, how do you discern the voice of the Father?

DAY 249 | MATTHEW 17

H

E

A

R

What Else Should I Know? In chapter 17 Jesus continued to prepare His disciples for His death and their responsibility after He was gone. Jesus had taught the disciples about the realities of His kingdom, both in the present and the future. What they witnessed during the transfiguration in this chapter confirmed those truths. Jesus was the Messiah, the Son of God, and although His birth initiated His kingdom on earth, the full reality of that kingdom wasn't yet visible. When the disciples got a glimpse of its glory, they didn't want to leave.

Jesus wanted his disciples to be ready to carry on His ministry after He was gone, and He knew they would need bold faith in Him to do it. Their faith needed to be strong enough to see them through the persecution and suffering that awaited them. The same is true for us. Our job as believers is to carry on Jesus' work and share His message of salvation. It's a high calling with a high price, and it demands a faith that can move mountains.

 QUESTION: What holds you back from boldly carrying out Jesus' mission?

H

E

A

R

What Else Should I Know? Jesus' teaching in Matthew 18 focused on behaviors of kingdom citizens rather than on characteristics of the kingdom itself. Jesus' teaching was prompted by a dispute among the disciples about who would be greatest in the kingdom; in other words, who was the best disciple? The disciples still didn't get it. The greatest disciples, Jesus reminded them, were humble, depended on God, and had childlike faith.

It's also important for disciples to know how Jesus wants us to respond to fellow Christians when they sin against us. Rather than react selfishly to being sinned against, we're to respond in a way that pushes the offender toward Jesus through repentance. We see this in the parable of the unforgiving debtor in verses 21-35. God has shown us unfathomable forgiveness by sacrificing Jesus for our sin. We must always pursue forgiveness with anyone who offends or wrongs us, because it's one of the clearest ways we can reflect Jesus' love and grace in that relationship.

QUESTION: Just like the parable of the lost sheep, who do you need to seek after?

W
E
E
K

51

DAY 251 | MATTHEW 19

HIGHLIGHT the verses that speak to you.

Write out the name of the book:

Which chapter and verse numbers stand out to you?

EXPLAIN what this passage means.

To whom was it originally written? Why?

How does it fit with the verses before and after it?

What is the Holy Spirit intending to communicate through this text?

APPLY what God is saying in these verses to your life.

What does this mean today?

What is God saying to you personally?

How can you apply this message to your life?

RESPOND to what you've read.

In what ways does this passage call you to action?

How will you be different because of what you've learned?

Write out a prayer to God in response to what you read today:

What Else Should I Know? By the time Jesus for Jerusalem and the cross, that conflict had reached a boiling point. In chapter 19, Jesus' conversations with the religious leaders focused on two contentious points: grounds for divorce and the way people gain eternal life. Verses 16-30 recount Jesus' conversation with the rich young ruler. When the man asked Jesus how to gain eternal life, Jesus told him to sell all his possessions and give the money to the poor. Although the man was faithful to obey the law, he refused to give up everything to follow Jesus, and he remained outside the kingdom of God.

Jesus' instruction to this man highlighted the idols in his life: his money and possessions. They were his whole identity. In contrast, Jesus taught time and again that nothing should have a greater priority in our lives than following Him. Our faith in God should be the source of our identity.

 QUESTION: Like the rich young ruler, what idols have become your identity?

H

E

A

R

What Else Should I Know? One reason the religious leaders hated Jesus is that He undermined their feelings of religious superiority. They thought they would have a place of prominence in God's kingdom because of their obedience to the law. But in Matthew 19:30, Jesus declared, "Many who are first will be last, and the last first." Unless they recognized Jesus as the Messiah, they would have no place in the kingdom at all.

The parable in Matthew 20 makes the same point. As the landowner was generous in his pay, God is generous in His grace to sinners. That grace is the same for everyone. It's available to all people, no matter how righteous or sinful, through belief in Jesus Christ. He is the only way to salvation—the way, the truth, and the life. Jesus could have given in to the religious leaders and compromised His message. But He loves us so much that He stood firm, even when He had to pay the ultimate cost.

QUESTION: In the face of controversy, how will you stand firm in your faith?

DAY 253 | MATTHEW 21

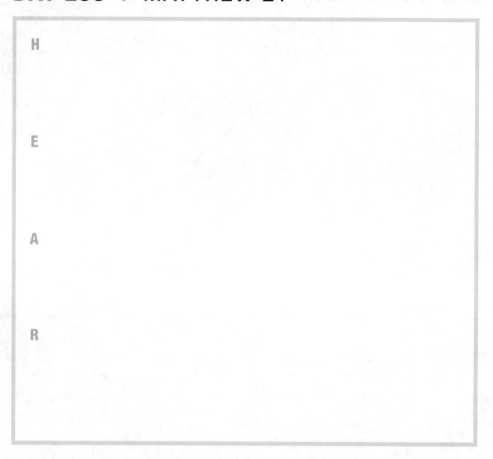

H

E

A

R

What Else Should I Know? Matthew 21 begins with Jesus' triumphal entry into Jerusalem and the cleansing of the temple, a scene Matthew focuses on to show Jesus' fulfillment of Old Testament prophecy and His identity as the King of the Jews. The Jewish religious leaders, however, failed to recognize Jesus as the Messiah. Clearly seeing their unbelief, Jesus directly rebuked them in the parable of the two sons (vv. 28-32). The religious leaders knew God's Word, but they refused to repent of their sins and believe in Him as the Messiah.

Their rejection of Jesus meant that God's kingdom was being given to the Gentiles. Matthew made it clear to his Jewish readers that their religious leaders were no longer the voice of authority for God's people. That role now belonged to Jesus. Soon it would shift to His apostles and to the leaders of the church.

PRAY: Jesus, would you help my unbelief? I want to know Your truth and walk in Your power to share hope with a lost world.

DAY 254 | MATTHEW 22

H

E

A

R

What Else Should I Know? Throughout Israel's history, God had sent many prophets who foretold the coming of the Messiah, but Israel didn't listen. We see this reflected in the parable of the wedding feast in Matthew 22: They were like the invited guests who didn't attend the wedding banquet. Consequently, God invited everyone into His kingdom. However, He stipulated one condition, highlighted in the parable by the man who wasn't wearing wedding clothes: believing in Jesus and accepting His grace. Regardless of where you come from or what religion you were brought up in, anyone who believes in Jesus will be saved.

IT'S ABOUT
relationship
NOT RELIGION.

What a beautiful promise for us today. Nothing in your past can keep you from Jesus—there's nothing you have done that's too bad for God or that makes you too unworthy. But you also can't save yourself, Jesus said, by following the law. Religion won't save you: only He can. That's the message we should carry to a world that desperately needs to hear it.

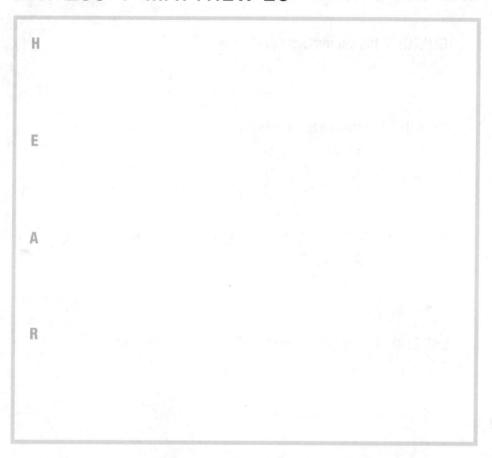

H

E

A

R

What Else Should I Know? After warning the crowd about their leaders, Jesus proclaimed seven woes against the leaders. At the heart of Jesus' denunciation was the fact that these leaders bore the responsibility to shepherd God's people and point them to His truth, but they were actually leading people away from God. Their job was to teach the Scriptures, but they manipulated and distorted God's Word.

God takes the shepherding of His people very seriously. He won't allow His people to be led astray by false teachings or misinterpretations of His Word. But that responsibility isn't just on pastors and church leaders—it's also on us. The Bible tells us everything we need to become a part of God's kingdom. Whether or not we're in roles of spiritual leadership, we must value Scripture highly, interpret it accurately, and use it to help people find Jesus.

? **QUESTION:** Are you pointing people towards Jesus or away from Him? Explain.

WEEK 52

DAY 256 | MATTHEW 24

HIGHLIGHT the verses that speak to you.

Write out the name of the book:

Which chapter and verse numbers stand out to you?

EXPLAIN what this passage means.

To whom was it originally written? Why?

How does it fit with the verses before and after it?

What is the Holy Spirit intending to communicate through this text?

APPLY what God is saying in these verses to your life.

What does this mean today?

What is God saying to you personally?

How can you apply this message to your life?

RESPOND to what you've read.

In what ways does this passage call you to action?

How will you be different because of what you've learned?

Write out a prayer to God in response to what you read today:

What Else Should I Know? As His death drew closer, Jesus knew the disciples needed to be prepared for the persecution that would come. He also knew they needed a reason to maintain hope when it did. When the disciples asked about signs of the end times, Jesus replied that we shouldn't misinterpret them. Persecutions of various types are to be expected. False messiahs will arise. People will be deceived. All of these events are preludes to the end of the age, when Jesus Himself will return and make all things right once and for all.

Scripture repeatedly teaches us that the end times will be a time of judgment. This is good news for people who know Jesus as their Savior, but it's bad news for people who don't. In Matthew 24 Jesus illustrated the certainty of judgment with the parable of the fig tree and warned against trying to predict the time of His return. Understanding and applying teachings about the end times can be difficult, but the most important lesson is that Jesus will return again. We must serve Him faithfully until He comes.

 CHALLENGE: Look for ways you can serve others faithfully this week.

DAY 257 | MATTHEW 25

H

E

A

R

What Else Should I Know? Matthew 25 continues Jesus' teachings on His second coming and the way His followers should live in the meantime. The parable of the ten virgins stresses the importance of being watchful and ready for Jesus to return, while the parable of the talents highlights the gifts and responsibilities God has given each of us and our need to steward them wisely. The final parable in this chapter, the parable of the sheep and the goats, provides a picture of Jesus' judgment in the last days, when He will separate His faithful followers from those who don't know Him. Jesus made it clear from His description of the sheep that people who love Him will love and serve others.

These teachings remind us that life isn't about interpreting signs of the times, but persevering and remaining faithful to the mission of drawing more people to Christ. While we wait for Jesus to return, we must diligently spread the gospel so that as many people as possible can have the hope and promise of eternal life with Him.

 PRAY: Spend time praying for those around you that you want to reach with the gospel.

DAY 258 | MATTHEW 26

H

E

A

R

What Else Should I Know? During the Passover meal with his disciples, Jesus connected the symbolism of their meal with the sacrifice He was about to make. The breaking of the bread, he said, was the breaking of His body; the drinking of the cup was the pouring out of His blood for the forgiveness of sins. This meal, the first Lord's Supper, quickly became an integral part of church practice we still use today to commemorate and reflect on the sacrifice Jesus made on behalf of humankind.

Matthew's portrayal of Jesus' last days shows how the Son of man surrendered to the will of His Heavenly Father in order to bring the hope of redemption to all people.

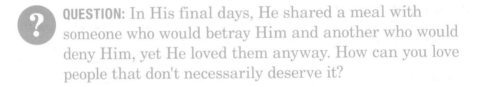

QUESTION: In His final days, He shared a meal with someone who would betray Him and another who would deny Him, yet He loved them anyway. How can you love people that don't necessarily deserve it?

DAY 259 | MATTHEW 27

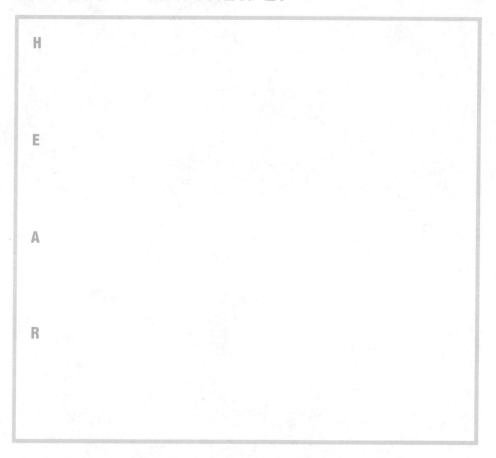

H

E

A

R

What Else Should I Know? Matthew 27 primarily concentrates on Jesus' trial and death, showing how even through injustice and persecution Jesus remained humble and steadfast in His obedience to the will of the Father. When Pilate granted the religious leaders' request to crucify Jesus and release Barabbas, Jesus, though innocent, was delivered over to death, as had been prophesied.

Jesus' sacrificial death had always been God's plan. Yet, His crucifixion produced different responses from the people who saw it. The religious leaders and soldiers mocked Him. A Roman centurion professed His identity as the Son of God. Others mourned. Regardless of people's responses, Jesus' crucifixion finished the work of His ministry on earth and covered the sins of all who place their faith in His name.

PRAY: God allowed Jesus to suffer so that we didn't have to. Take a few moments today and thank the Lord for His unending love.

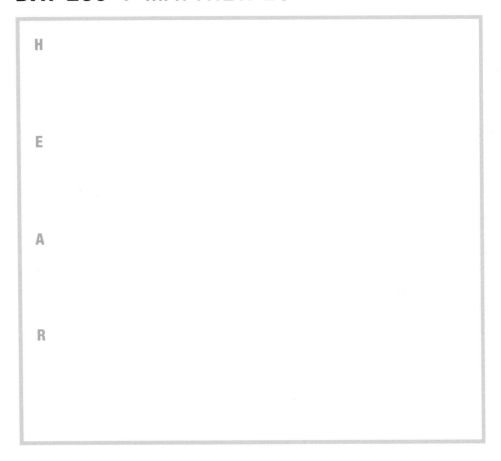

H

E

A

R

What Else Should I Know? The record of the resurrection is short in all the Gospels, yet the post-resurrection events Matthew recorded are significant for the assignment Jesus was about to give all His disciples throughout history—including us today. After Jesus appeared to the women who found the empty tomb and then to the eleven remaining disciples, He issued the Great Commission, commanding the disciples to replicate His gospel ministry by going to the world and making disciples.

Sharing Christ and bringing people into the kingdom isn't optional. It's a lifestyle. We should live it with the same sense of urgency that cost the first disciples their lives. But we should also remember we aren't working in our own strength. Our task isn't to be clever, motivational, or exciting. It isn't to show how pious we are. Jesus calls us to be obedient. Whatever the path that lies ahead of you, the New Testament beautifully lays out a promise you can carry the rest of your life: Jesus is with you always.

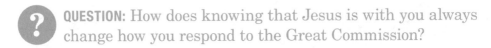

QUESTION: How does knowing that Jesus is with you always change how you respond to the Great Commission?

Wow! You did it! If you are reading this, you have read a Bible reading plan for a year and have finished it! I am so proud of you for committing to this plan and growing spiritually in your relationship with the Lord. I know He has worked mightily in and through you over this past year. I wish I could sit down with you and hear all the testimonies of what has happened in your life. If you continue this discipline each and every year, imagine what the Lord will continue to do.

If I can leave you with one thing it would be this: "Guard your heart above all else, for it is the source of life" (Prov. 4:23). This is my life verse. Guarding your heart is the same thing as guarding your mind. In life we tend to make decisions based on how we feel, often it is an emotion that we base our actions on. The emotion could be love, anger, sadness or even happiness that determines our life choices. When making decisions based on our feelings instead our faith and facts of the Bible, we will tend to make the wrong choices. I want to encourage you to guard that part of your life. Your heart and mind will want to make choices all throughout your life that will not necessarily be good for you. However, if you guard your heart and mind, you can make wise choices.

You are probably asking, "How do I guard my heart and mind?" I said this at the beginning of your journey and I want to say it again: Reading the Word and staying active in this discipline is one of the greatest ways to continue growth in the Lord and will be especially helpful in guarding your heart. This practice will prove most helpful to you through the years.

Another discipline that will be helpful is prayer. When you are journaling a particular verse, turn it into a prayer. Pray it for yourself and for others. Pray before you make a decision in life and allow the Lord to guide you.

I would love to pray for you before you go.

Lord,
You are so good and your Word is so powerful! I know you have worked in ways only you can in all the precious girls who read your Word this past year. As each one of the them finish this plan, I pray that their passion for your Word has increased beyond measure. I ask that you protect and guide them in these coming years and give them wisdom in their life choices. Lord, guard their hearts and minds like only You can. May they grow into women of the Word as they navigate this world. Let them be powerful voices for You. Give them boldness and courage to stand up for what is holy and pure. Bless them and keep them and make Your face to shine upon them now and forever. In Your sweet and strong name. Amen

I love you and blessings to you as you go,

Kandi

Quick Scripture Reference Guide

ANXIETY
- Psalm 94:19
- Proverbs 12:25
- Matthew 6:34
- Philippians 4:6-7
- 1 Peter 5:7

DEPRESSION
- Deuteronomy 31:8
- Psalm 34:17-18
- Psalm 23:4
- Philippians 4:8
- 2 Corinthians 1:3-4

DOUBT
- James 1:6
- James 1:5-8
- Mark 9:24
- Jeremiah 29:11-13
- Hebrews 11:1-40

FEAR
- Proverbs 3:5-6
- 2 Timothy 1:7
- Joshua 1:9
- Psalm 56:3
- John 14:27

GOSSIP
- Ephesians 4:29
- James 1:26
- Proverbs 10:19
- Proverbs 18:8
- Proverbs 18:21

JOY
- Romans 15:13
- Philippians 4:4
- Psalm 16:11
- Psalm 30:5
- Galatians 5:22-23

PEACE
- Isaiah 26:3
- Matthew 11:28
- John 14:27
- Psalm 119:165
- Romans 16:20

SELF-IMAGE
- Psalm 139:13-14
- Philippians 4:13
- Psalm 46:5
- Proverbs 31:25
- Psalm 28:76
- 1 Corinthians 25:10

SEX
- Hebrews 13:4
- 1 Corinthians 6:18
- 1 Corinthians 7:2
- Genesis 2:24
- 1 Thessalonians 4:3-5

TEMPTATION
- James 1:13-18
- James 4:7
- Ephesians 6:10-18
- Hebrews 4:15
- Hebrews 4:15

TRUST
- Jeremiah 17:7-8
- Psalm 56:3
- Isaiah 43:2
- Psalm 143:8
- Hebrews 13:6

What do you think discipleship is?

Discipleship is: Intentionally equipping believers with the Word of God through accountable relationships empowered by the Holy Spirit in order to replicate faithful followers of Christ.

- How many of you would say you had someone personally disciple you?
- Why do we not disciple? Often times we think we aren't equipped or we think we don't know enough.

The only absolute requirement for leading a Discipleship Group (D-Group) is for you to be intentionally pursuing Christ in your personal life. You do not need to be a master teacher or have all of the answers; you do not need to be able to say, "Listen to me." If you can say, "Follow me; I'm pursuing Christ," you have the tools you need to lead a D-Group.

If we are to lead others intentionally, we must first learn to lead ourselves.

Here are six tips on how to lead a D-Group:

1. JESUS IS OUR MODEL AND THE HOLY SPIRIT IS OUR HELPER.
Jesus poured himself into the lives of His disciples and taught them how to love, pray, trust, minister, and serve. These practices would be needed for times when He would no longer be standing beside them. Jesus also sent the Holy Spirit as a Helper to dwell within believers as they follow him (John 14:25-26; 16:13-14).

Jesus dedicated so much of His time to investing into 12 men. He had thousands that followed him, yet pulled aside to this small group. He even had His inner three—Peter, James, John and Andrew.

2. ACCOUNTABILITY IS ESSENTIAL
Effective discipleship takes place when a small group of 5-7 gather for the purpose of helping one another "grow in the grace and knowledge of our Lord and Savior Jesus Christ" (2 Pet. 3:18).

Discipleship is not only about studying God's word but doing life together. Sharing our joys and struggles and having others come alongside us on this journey called life.

3. TEACHING GIRLS GOD'S WORD
Hebrews 4:12 says, "For the word of God is living and effective and sharper than any double-edged sword, penetrating as far as the separation of soul and spirit, joints and marrow. It is able to

judge the thoughts and intentions of the heart." Since this Word is living, it is more crucial than ever to make sure we are getting into it until it gets into us. The goal is to make the girls self-feeders from the Word. To become self-feeders, the girls must learn how to study and apply God's Word for themselves.

4. GUIDING GIRLS TO DEVELOP SPIRITUAL DISCIPLINES LIKE PRAYER AND MEMORIZING SCRIPTURE
Discipline is a word we love to hate, but with the accountability that comes from a D-Group, spiritual disciplines become easier to practice. Prayer and Scripture are the most powerful tools we have in our fight against the enemy (Eph. 6:10-18). In a discipleship relationship, the girls should learn to use these tools effectively.

5. HELPING GIRLS DISCOVER AND USE THEIR SPIRITUAL GIFTS
The Holy Spirit imparts spiritual gifts to believers for the building up of the body of Christ (1 Cor. 12:6-7). When girls discover and begin using the gifts God has given them, they are more apt to engage in their churches and communities.

6. LEADING GIRLS TO SERVE LOCALLY AND GLOBALLY
Jesus said, "You will be my witnesses in Jerusalem, in all Judea and Samaria, and to the ends of the earth" (Acts 1:8). A witness is someone who tells what they know to be true. As girls study God's Word, they discover who God is and who they are in Christ. Prepared to share the Christ-Life with others, we begin the process all over again as we make disciples who will make disciples (2 Tim. 2:2).

Check-in Tips

- We know you have a busy life and you don't always have time to hang out with each girl individually all the time. Make time once a month to hang out with at least one girl in your group apart from your weekly D-Group time!

- Check in every week (if you can) over text! Simply ask how their week has been and use this time to follow up on prayer requests mentioned in the group.

- Write down important things going on in their lives so you can check in on your girls. They will feel so important that you remembered.

- Find random times to surprise each girl by coming to their school or work and dropping off their favorite snack or drink.

- Ask for their extracurricular sports or performance schedules so you can show up and cheer them on. A big part of discipleship is simply being present and showing up for things that are important to them.

- Have they shared a sin struggle with you? Try setting a reminder to pray for them on a specific day each week and text them to check in.

- Go out as a group once a month or every other month (if you have time) and just have fun together! Go out for dinner or a movie, etc.

Keep Going, Leader

You are investing your life into these teenage girls and it is SO worth it. We know there are many hard and frustrating days where it seems hard to lead or girls seem ungrateful. It's easy to get frustrated when we don't see growth or it feels like they should have learned this lesson by now.

Don't stop praying or preparing. Don't quit showing up and speaking the truth. Your faithfulness to invest in ONE could change the world. You are doing kingdom work. God sees you and knows your heart. You do not have to be perfect to lead, nor do you always have to have it "all together." God wants to use the "real," authentic you. Not the version you "wish" you were or who you feel like you "should" be. He wants to use you with all of your hurts, hang-ups, and wounds to point to His sustaining and powerful grace.

You have influence. Your voice matters.

Thank you for your faithfulness to pour out your life. It will never go unnoticed by Jesus.

Get the most from your study.

Customize your Bible study time with a guided experience and additional resources.

ADDITIONAL RESOURCES

FOUNDATIONS: NEW TESTAMENT DEVOTIONAL FOR TEENS
A 260-Day New Testament Bible Reading Plan for Teens

FOUNDATIONS: OLD TESTAMENT DEVOTIONAL FOR TEEN GIRLS
A 260-Day Old Testament Bible Reading Plan for Teen Girls

FOUNDATIONS: TEEN DEVOTIONAL
A 260-Day Bible Reading Plan for Busy Believers

Foundations: New Testament for Teen Girls is a 260-day Bible reading plan that helps you read the entire New Testament in a year—just a chapter a day, five days a week. You will learn all about the HEAR journaling method that will help you read the Bible in a way that can change your life. No longer will you focus on checking off boxes on your daily reading schedule; instead, you'll be reading in order to understand and respond to God's Word.

Features:

- 260-day Bible reading plan, one chapter a day for five days

- Using the HEAR journaling method, students will be guided through Highlighting, Explaining, Applying, and Responding to passages.

- Devotional material will connect daily reading and real-life application

Foundations: New Testament for Teen Girls is a practical devotional for new or inexperienced Bible study students, as well as those who are well-versed in the Scriptures. Using the HEAR journaling method, students will be prompted to sit and reflect on the truth of Scripture. Students will expand their understanding of the Bible by just being in the Word of God five days per week.

Lifeway designs trustworthy experiences that fuel ministry. Today, the ministries of Lifeway reach more than 160 countries around the globe. For specific information on Lifeway Students, visit lifeway.com/students.